# Social Inclusion: Canadian Perspectives

edited by Ted Richmond and Anver Saloojee

D1319576

Fernwood Publishing • Halifax

Copyediting: Amanda Hickman, Amal Madibbo

The cover design for this book is based on the colours of the
Aboriginal Medicine Wheel. Like the teachings of the Medicine Wheel,
social inclusion can be understood in a variety of ways — one of which
is the equality and unity of all races.

Printed and bound in Canada by Hignell Printing Limited

A publication of
Fernwood Publishing
Site 2A, Box 5, 32 Oceanvista Lane
Black Point, Nova Scotia, B0J 1B0
and 324 Clare Avenue
Winnipeg, Manitoba, R3L 1S3
www.fernwoodbooks.ca

Fernwood Publishing Company Limited gratefully acknowledges
the financial support of the Department of Canadian Heritage,
the Nova Scotia Department of Tourism and Culture
and the Canada Council for the Arts for our publishing program.

Library and Archives Canada Cataloguing in Publication

Social inclusion: Canadian perspectives / Ted Richmond,
Anver Saloojee, editors.

Includes index.
ISBN 1-55266-175-X

1. Social integration—Canada. 2. Marginality, Social—Canada.
I. Richmond, Ted II. Saloojee, Anver

HM683.S63 2005     305.5'6'0971     C2005-904236-2

# Contents

# Acknowledgements

The Laidlaw Foundation is a public interest foundation that uses its human and financial resources in innovative ways to strengthen civic engagement and social cohesion. The Foundation uses its capital to better the environments and fulfill the capacities of children and youth, to enhance the opportunities for human development and creativity and to sustain healthy communities and ecosystems.

The Foundation supports a diverse portfolio of innovative and often unconventional projects in a number of program areas related to creation in the performing arts, environmental contaminants and their impact on child and youth health, youth leadership and civic engagement with special attention to vulnerable and less advantaged youth, and healthy social policy for children, youth and families. Working for social inclusion is a theme that underlies much of the Foundation's activities.

The Laidlaw Foundation has never been interested in promoting a purely definitional approach to social inclusion. Our interest has been and continues to be in the potential contribution of the social inclusion discourse to better social policy, in both theory and practice. Judging this potential requires an honest examination of contrasting viewpoints and diverse experiences with respect to different forms of social exclusion and different paths to inclusion. We hope this book will be a useful contribution to this process.

The production of this book would not have been possible without the contributions of many of our colleagues. We must recognize the leadership and vision of our Board of Directors and the expertise of our many volunteers, especially the members of the Inclusive Communities for Children, Youth and Families Pilot Program (formerly the Laidlaw Children's Agenda). Of course we have to thank the authors of this collection on social inclusion for their knowledgeable and thoughtful contributions. And finally we must also recognize the guidance provided by our editors, Ted Richmond and Anver Saloojee, and our supportive publisher Errol Sharpe from Fernwood Publishing.

Most important perhaps we must recognize the contributions of all those at the grassroots level who continue to build a practice of social inclusion in the struggle against multiple forms of exclusion. A few of these projects are funded by Laidlaw Foundation; most are not; many are likely not yet even known to us. We hope the reading and discussion of the ideas in this book will play some small role in advancing our common cause.

Nathan Gilbert, Executive Director, Laidlaw Foundation

# Contributors

## Michael Bach

is Executive Vice-president of the Canadian Association for Community Living. Michael is known throughout Canada for his contributions to disability rights.

## Catherine Frazee

is Co-director of the Ryerson RBC Institute for Disability Studies Research and Education. Catherine has been involved in the equality rights movement for many years, most notably during her term as Chief Commissioner of the Ontario Human Rights Commission from 1989 to 1992.

## Martha Friendly

founded and is currently Coordinator of the Childcare Resource and Research Unit at the University of Toronto. She is also a Senior Research Associate at the university. Martha has been active for many years in research, publishing and advocacy devoted to better childcare.

## Donna Lero

is the Co-director of Research of the Centre for Families, Work and Well-Being at the University of Guelph, and an Associate Professor in the Department of Family Relations and Applied Nutrition. Donna has been involved for many years in Canadian research related to quality childcare and early childhood services.

## Meg Luxton

is a Professor of Sociology at York University. Meg has contributed to and published widely in understanding work and family issues with a feminist analysis of structural barriers to equality.

## Andrew Mitchell

is the Research Coordinator for the Social Assistance in the New Economy Project (SANE) at the Faculty of Social Work, University of Toronto. Andrew has conducted research on poverty, the declining economic status of younger families and income security programs such as social assistance.

## The National Association of Friendship Centres (NAFC)

provides a national service infrastructure and networking capacity for 117 Friendship Centres situated in every region of Canada. The NAFC chapter was written by their Researcher Alfred Gay.

## Ratna Omidvar

is Executive Director of the Maytree Foundation. Ratna is known throughout Canada for her leadership in immigrant settlement, particularly training and labour market access issues.

## Ted Richmond

works with the Laidlaw Foundation as Program Coordinator, Inclusive Communities for Children, Youth and Families Pilot Program. Ted has extensive experience in social and settlement services, community research and equity issues in Toronto.

## Anver Saloojee

is a Professor in Politics and Public Administration at Ryerson University in Toronto. Anver is currently on secondment as Special Advisor, the Presidency, Republic of South Africa.

## Uzma Shakir

is Executive Director of the Council of Agencies Serving South Asians (CASSA) and President of the Board of Directors of the Ontario Council of Agencies Serving Immigrants (OCASI). Uzma, who also serves as a volunteer at Laidlaw Foundation, is a well-known voice for anti-racism and equity.

## Richard Shillington

has been engaged in the quantitative analysis of health, social and economic policy for the past thirty years. He has worked variously for governments, the private sector and NGOs; and comments for television, radio and newspapers on issues of taxation, human rights and social policy.

# Introduction and Overview

*Ted Richmond and Anver Saloojee*

## Introduction

How is the concept of social inclusion evolving in policy terms? Are we moving towards a common understanding or "definition" of the notion? What does social inclusion mean for issues like poverty and the growing racialization of poverty? What can we learn about social inclusion in theory and practice from the perspectives of the needs of children and their parents? What are the contributions of feminism and of the disability rights movement? What does social inclusion mean for Canada's newcomers, for anti-racism and for the social citizenship of visible minority communities? What does it mean for Canada's First Nations peoples? Are we moving in some way towards a coherent and policy relevant version of social inclusion that is "made in Canada"? These are the issues explored in this volume of selected essays on social inclusion, produced by the Laidlaw Foundation with the assistance of Fernwood Publishing.

It is only a few years since the Laidlaw Board took the courageous step of endorsing funding for what was basically an idea — the idea of social inclusion. Since that time our social inclusion work has not only developed and expanded, it has also won a significant amount of attention and support. Laidlaw-sponsored activities have included a variety of seminars and conferences as well as the production of a series of working papers exploring different areas and aspects of social inclusion as both theory and applied policy. Funding was also provided for partner organizations involved in projects such as the development of inclusive indicators, as well as research and public education on the welfare of Canada's children and pilot projects demonstrating new approaches to inclusion at the grassroots level of community organizing.

This volume contains a representative selection of the working papers previously commissioned and published by Laidlaw, as well as contributions solicited for the book. An overview of the contents and key issues is provided in this introductory chapter, and an index at the end of the book provides reference to key issues and authors for all the contributions. A single book like this of course cannot be fully representative of the complexity and diversity of views in the growing range of writings on social inclusion in Canada.

Other significant contributions worthy of attention include the complete set of Working Papers on Social Inclusion produced by the Laidlaw Foundation, the publications from Health Canada Atlantic

Region and the work of the Roeher Institute on the principles and philosophy of social inclusion and on inclusive indicators. The Policy Research Initiative in Ottawa continues to work in areas like social exclusion
and poverty, and the use and measurement of social capital to build
inclusion. The Inclusive Cities Project is working with social planning
councils and the Federation of Canadian Municipalities across Canada to
develop social inclusion as urban policy. Community-based organizations
like the Ontario Prevention Clearinghouse, the Alternative Planning Group
and the Community Social Planning Council of Toronto have focused on
developing grassroots participation in establishing inclusive indicators.[1]

The support of the active and committed volunteers past and present
at the Laidlaw Foundation and the leadership of our Executive Director
Nathan Gilbert have also played a vital role in launching and promoting this Canadian dialogue on social inclusion.

## Overview of the Contributions

### Poverty, Inequality and Social Inclusion
### by Andrew Mitchell and Richard Shillington

The chapter by Mitchell and Shillington emphasizes that both social
inclusion and poverty are contested concepts. Depending on the intentions
of policymakers, inclusion can be reduced to employability and be used to
justify coercive welfare-to-work policies to undo dependence on social
assistance. The outcomes of such policies are often lower levels of well-
being for individuals and families living in earned poverty on the margins
of the market economy. For these authors, however, the concept of
inclusion can also be used to expand understanding of the conditions
for well-being, which go beyond income, poverty and employment.
This chapter presents a framework for operationalizing our understanding of exclusion for children, one which begins to explore and track the
processes and societal institutions that create unequal outcomes —
needy children in the midst of a wealthy society.

*Rethinking the Poverty Debate*
Mitchell and Shillington note that society has an interest in monitoring
the well-being of its citizens and that high on the list of indicators of
disadvantage and well-being is how many people are "poor." But in
Canada, poverty, they point out, is an intensely contested term. For
some, poverty has meaning only in absolute terms — the minimum
necessary for physical survival. For others, it can only be understood in
relative terms, compared to the living standards of the society in which
the person lives.

In Canada, the authors explain, we have tended to operationalize the
idea of relative poverty by drawing an income line that is some fraction of

the average income. But whether the poverty line is drawn higher or lower, there is mounting evidence that inequality itself has effects on outcomes of well-being. The relative gap accepted by a society (apart from those officially defined as poor) can in itself generate negative consequences.

Mitchell and Shillington contend that all concepts of poverty are inescapably relative and that the choice of measure is really a choice among policy objectives. To begin with what we should measure before knowing what outcomes we are seeking, they argue, is to put the cart before the horse. What is the public policy objective to which poverty statistics are addressed — enough resources to meet physical needs for health? Or equality of opportunity? Or equality of outcomes?

While Canadian society increases in wealth, the living standards of the poorest among us fall farther away from the norm. Should we not be concerned about the widening social distance between those who are worst-off and the rest of society and the inequality of opportunity and civic participation that characterizes life at the bottom? Does this not require a policy response? Canada might set a goal of eliminating poverty that implied providing only enough funds to meet basic needs. A broader social goal would be equality of opportunity, which would be tracked on the basis of income inequality or relative poverty. Even more ambitious would be a policy goal that included social inclusion, which has implications for citizen participation, capacity and agency.

Poverty, inequality and social inclusion are not interchangeable concepts for Mitchell and Shillington; rather they are interdependent. To be included across the different dimensions of well-being (physical, economic, human, social, political) requires sufficient resources and rights and capacity to participate within the environments and structures of the society in which one lives. Their contribution continues with explorations of the concepts of relative deprivation and capabilities in relation to our understanding of poverty and social inclusion.

*Perspectives on Inclusion, Exclusion and Poverty*
Should policies change the structures and conditions that create exclusion or should the marginalized be integrated into the existing mainstream? Perspectives on social inclusion reflect differing assumptions about its root causes and solutions, argue Mitchell and Shillington, and are based on differing ideological views.

One common view sees unemployment as the main cause of social exclusion. The main concern is typically social cohesion, built on the norm of employment. The goal of policy tends to be reduced to employability. The excluded or marginalized are to be lifted over the minimal threshold of exclusion through paid work and incorporated into existing norms. For these authors the focus on the paid labour market ignores the role and value of unpaid work and caring responsibilities; it also obscures gender, race and other inequalities in the labour market.

Another variant on social exclusion identified by Mitchell and Shillington focuses on the perceived moral and behavioural deficiencies of the excluded themselves. The central concern of this approach is the avoidance of dependence, seen as a side effect of income support, which is thought to destroy initiative and self-respect. Work is viewed as a moral necessity. The policy response is typically to increase restrictions on eligibility for and the benefits paid by income support programs.

For Mitchell and Shillington such "anti-exclusion" policies actually reinforce exclusion by recasting their subjects as somehow separate and different from the rest of the hard-working population, defective in skills or other personal attributes. Moreover, the limitations of inclusion through work are evident. In Canada as unemployment has declined significantly, poverty has remained high, many working families have remained poor, and low-wage and precarious employment is fast becoming an entrenched feature of the economy.

Policy solutions that focus on inclusion through the labour market risk simply exchanging one form of exclusion for another: exclusion from employment versus exclusion through marginal forms of employment. A better approach to social inclusion, argue Mitchell and Shillington, is to focus on poverty and inequality and the impacts of exclusion on people's lives. This view of the concept of inclusion puts greater emphasis on the responsibility of the larger society to create inclusive conditions.

## Operationalizing Inclusion/Exclusion for Children

While Mitchell and Shillington are critical of narrow definitions of social exclusion and inclusion used to serve ideological ends, they also see potential in exploring these concepts from a comprehensive perspective. For these authors the concept of social exclusion directs attention not just to the fact of exclusion or to its consequences, but also to the institutions and processes that create exclusion. It begins with what we really care about — individual well-being — and asks who is affected and how. Losing one's job, for example, does not necessarily have to lead to poverty and marginalization. Policies affecting employment, income support, education and health can turn disadvantage into exclusion; they can sustain individual capabilities or undermine them. The chapter continues with an exploration of an appropriate framework of dimensions of inclusion and exclusion for children in Canada.

Mitchell and Shillington in this chapter remind us that institutions, agents and processes can be used for inclusion or exclusion, depending on policy intent. For example, housing policies can create marginalized ghettos or economically and socially diverse neighbourhoods. Employment and income support policies can be used to create a low-wage labour pool or foster a high-wage, high-skill economy that values equality and recognizes the need for work-family balance. The process of policy-making itself can promote exclusion if citizens experience a lack of voice in issues that directly affect them, or it can foster civic participation.

These authors call for policies that promote people's capacities to act as citizens with equal freedom to conduct a life they have reason to value. An agenda of inclusion, they argue, will require supports that not only provide the income necessary to purchase necessities, but also facilitate the conditions to create equality of outcomes in employment, education and health and span the full dimensions of well-being.

## Social Inclusion Through Early Childhood Education and Care by Martha Friendly and Donna Lero

This chapter makes the case that, under the right conditions, early childhood education and care (ECEC) can make a significant contribution to social inclusion by supporting children's development, family well-being, community cohesion and equity. However, Canada has made little progress in creating the right conditions that would enable ECEC to strengthen social inclusion. Key structural changes needed to create an integrated, high-quality, accessible system for all preschool children, including those with special needs, are outlined.

Can ECEC contribute to social inclusion? The authors' understanding of social inclusion draws on Amartya Sen's conception that an inclusive society is one in which members participate meaningfully and actively, enjoy equality, share social experiences and attain fundamental well-being. They see inclusion as an active, transformative process that goes beyond remediation of deficits and reduction of risk. Social inclusion promotes human development and ensures that opportunities are not missed — not just for some, but for all children.

The authors note that there is a growing consensus internationally that care and education for young children are inseparable concepts. ECEC services can fulfill a wide range of objectives, including care, learning and social support. At a practical level, ECEC services include childcare centres, other care services like family day care, kindergarten, nursery/preschools and some elements of family resource programs. These activities are intended to enhance child development and well-being, and to support parents, both in and out of the paid workforce. The authors identify four overall goals for ECEC that are associated with social inclusion.

## Enhancing Children's Well-being, Development and Prospects for Lifelong Learning

If social inclusion over the life span is enhanced by full development in early childhood of one's talents, skills and capabilities, ECEC programs that support development can play a significant role. There are many inter-related factors that combine in complicated ways to produce children in good health who are confident, content, competent, resilient and socially responsible — or not. ECEC outside the home can have a profound effect. Indeed, it can be a determining factor.

A high-quality program provides intellectual and social stimulation that promotes cognitive development and social competence and forms a foundation for the child's future success. A high-quality program also improves life quality for the child in the here-and-now. High quality is short-hand for characteristics of ECEC that go beyond basic health and safety requirements to support children's development and learning.

## Supporting Parents in Education, Training, Employment and Social Life

ECEC services can support parents by helping reduce social exclusion linked to poverty, unemployment, marginal employment, disempowerment and social isolation. Dependable care for children is essential if mothers are to participate in the labour force. Poor accessibility to adequate childcare contributes to gender exclusion from the workforce and to marginalization of women across social classes. Without ECEC services, parents living in poverty do not have access to opportunities for education, training or paid work.

## Fostering Social Solidarity and Social Cohesion

Early childhood institutions are forums located in civil society. They can build social cohesion by becoming community focal points for parents, childcare providers, health and social services, and community volunteers. They can bring people together across class, ethnic and racial boundaries. As well they can help children learn tolerance and acceptance of difference in an environment that values diversity.

## Providing Equity for Diverse Groups in Society

An inclusive society is one that provides equality of life chances. ECEC has a role in promoting equity through development of capabilities and access to society's resources for all children. Children with disabilities, special learning needs and chronic health problems require programs that welcome them and supports that enable them to participate with other children. For women, childcare is the ramp that provides equal access to the workforce. Without fully accessible services, equality for women cannot be a reality.

What are the conditions that enable ECEC to contribute to social inclusion? Does Canada have them? The authors maintain that ECEC can only play a fully effective role in enhancing social inclusion if certain characteristics of public policy and service delivery are in place. A major contribution in this chapter is a summary of eight policy lessons based on the results of a twelve-nation Thematic Review of ECEC in 1998–2001 by the Organisation for Economic Co-operation and Development (OECD).

How do we move from aspirations to reality? The authors argue that closing the inclusion gap requires vision, commitment and the political will to turn aspirations into reality through transformative processes of policy and program development. Written prior to the current (2005) negotiations over a new and major federal childcare initiative in Canada, the chapter identifies key steps that can be taken immediately to strengthen ECEC policy as a form of inclusion. They suggest that considerable knowledge exists to move forward in four good areas of departure:

- systematic planning for quality improvement in both policy and practice;
- including children with special needs effectively;
- policy and service coherence (a good example is ECEC for Aboriginal communities, where recent initiatives have not been integrated); and
- serving the needs of a diverse population more effectively through improved training and centre practices.

## Feminist Perspectives on Social Inclusion and Children's Well-Being
### by Meg Luxton

Meg Luxton starts this chapter with the observation that the current debates on social inclusion and exclusion have had little to say about children. This limitation, she believes, is explained in part by the underlying concepts about families and markets that are central to prevailing liberal political and economic theory. Children are assumed to be the private responsibility of parents, and the only work that counts is market-based.

Luxton argues that the feminist concept of social reproduction offers a corrective. Social reproduction recognizes the bearing and rearing of children as a social responsibility. It views children as citizens and as part of networks of family, community, cultural groups and societal institutions that affect their well-being. It provides a different framework for social inclusion that invites debate about how we maintain and reproduce our society and make children a priority.

## Dominant Assumptions

The difficulties involved in generating a child-centred concept of social inclusion, according to Luxton, arise not simply because analysts have not paid attention to children. Rather, they are rooted in the assumptions of classical liberal theory, which understands society as constituted by individuals who interact competitively in markets. These assumptions dominate current thinking. The focus is on the individual relating to the market. Children are understood as the private responsibility of their families and families are assumed to be responsible for making private decisions about whether, when and how many children to have and for generating a livelihood sufficient to support them. Outside intervention is considered acceptable only when parents have put their children at risk.

Luxton explores the fundamental assumptions behind this narrow thinking about children and their rights. As the private responsibility of their parents, for example, children are vulnerable to the circumstances of their caregivers. They are unable to act as independent decision-making agents and are ineligible to make citizenship claims in their own right. Furthermore, the assumption of classical liberal theory that activities are only economically productive if they are market-based limits our notion of "work" to either paid employment or production for exchange in the market. Therefore most childcare and all the unpaid, non-market activities that are involved in raising children are not recognized as work. Caring for children is not seen as making a contribution to the economy and is not considered socially necessary or valuable.

This narrow framework has enormous practical and ideological power. It renders invisible all the activities involved in bearing and rearing children and obscures the political debate about the extent to which children's well-being and care is a private family matter or a social responsibility. It produces policies that take for granted that the nuclear family is responsible for caring for children and that, within the family, women should carry the major load. When policies do not solve the problems, nothing in their articulation invites an assessment of why the policies fail.

An example explored in this chapter is the tendency to blame the breakdown of the nuclear family and the rise in single-parent, mother-led families for an increase in child poverty. As Luxton stresses, however, family separations and lone parenthood do not cause child poverty, and policies developed on that assumption will fail. In reality, child poverty is caused by division of labour by gender, labour market segregation and segmentation, pay inequalities, lack of public support for caregiving and men's widespread reluctance to pay child support. It is these social practices that result in women's poverty and, by extension, impoverish their children. What is required therefore is a rethinking of current assumptions about paid and unpaid work, societal and family responsibilities and our willingness to invest in Canada's children and their well-being.

## A Social Reproduction Analysis

The feminist concept of social reproduction challenges the common assumptions about families and markets in liberal theory. Luxton suggests that it offers a compelling argument for the development of socially inclusive policies that will benefit all children in Canada.

Social reproduction puts children, as both dependents and as active members of their society, at the heart of social relations. It recognizes that the conditions under which children are conceived, born and raised produce not just individual adults, but the next generation. Children are not a private hobby of their parents, but a social responsibility of all. They are social actors in their own right, involved in making decisions that affect their lives. Luxton in this chapter explores the implications of the notion of social reproduction with respect to the role of "domestic labour," or unpaid labour in the home, and the responsibilities associated with child bearing and rearing. This perspective understands children as individuals who have rights to make citizenship claims on the world community and on the states, local communities and families in which they live. It recognizes gender, race, ethnicity and class relations as central to the organization of daily life. It rejects the assumption that the culturally normative family is white, western European, heterosexual and two-parent.

## Social Inclusion and Children

The concept of social inclusion has been limited, for Luxton, by its use mainly in connection with rights to employment and welfare. These rights do not apply directly to children. But social inclusion has potential strength as a policy approach for children's well-being, especially if it brings to the surface fundamental issues identified through social reproduction analysis.

The issue of work and family is one that can be explored profitably with a social inclusion perspective. Children's well-being depends on the resources of time, energy and money that their parents have to give them. Many families are struggling to balance the competing demands of paid work/household income and unpaid domestic labour/childcare. Regarding this as a conflict for individual families to resolve misses the depth of the issue. At a deeper level, this conflict involves the allocation of costs between producing and sustaining people and the process of private profit maximization. Pivotal is how societies divide costs across gender and age and the degree to which working people bear the costs themselves or have access to services and policies that share the burden. What is at stake is the standard of living available to people in different social locations.

For Luxton, families and states are both key sites of the struggle over the extent to which women must absorb the costs of social reproduction or can demand they be redistributed to men, employers and society as a whole. In Canada, governments have been unable to decide whether to support women as mothers, workers or both, resulting in policy paralysis and an undeveloped system of support to families and children. The chapter continues with a further exploration of several vital and complex policy issues within this perspective of social inclusion and a social reproduction framework.

A social inclusion focus reveals a contradiction between current neoliberal economic policies, which inevitably exacerbate inequalities, and expressions of political intent to reduce social exclusion, especially that of children. A commitment to social inclusion confronts the way social power is situated. It shows that unequal access to economic resources, political power and social status all affect personal behaviour, regardless of individual intentions. The more individuals and families have to bear the costs of social reproduction, and the more children are the individual responsibility of their mothers in a context that assumes women's primary role is as mothers, the more likely children are to risk poverty and other forms of social exclusion.

Social inclusion as outlined in this chapter assumes that existing social relations, institutions and cultural practices must be transformed in order to accommodate everyone. It implies that the centre must be reconfigured to encompass the practices of those from the margins. This aspect of social inclusion is particularly important when it comes to eliminating inequality while ensuring and supporting diversity. Great care must be taken to ensure that policies aimed at integration do not result in assimilation.

For Luxton therefore a social inclusion approach would represent a major departure from the policies that governments in Canada have pursued since the 1980s, which have reduced public services and left families to cope. Social inclusion policies would be based on a different assumption — that while children have the right to expect support, care and love from their parents, they also have the right to expect other sources of support and care from their society.

## Thumbs Up! Inclusion, Rights and Equality
## As Experienced by Youth with Disabilities
## by Catherine Frazee

In this chapter Catherine Frazee shows that, perceived through the lens of disability and examined through the eyes of young people, social inclusion is about more than access to participation. It is also about access to respect, selfhood and human community. Inclusion and equality are considered complementary principles, both serving just social outcomes. The chapter highlights how rights-based mechanisms may remedy restrictions on activity, but miss the being and belonging, the sense of self in relationship with others, at the heart of social inclusion.

## "To Be Who I Am... and Do What They Do"

> Inclusion is being able to be with kids my own age and do the things they do and go where they go. Inclusion is being with them. Inclusion helps people see that there is a lot more to me than autism. It helps them see that I'm just a regular teenager. Inclusion is important because it allows me to be who I am and to be with my friends and do what they do.

The meaning of inclusion, as expressed above, was provided by Aaron, age sixteen, a grade-ten high-school student, and one of six young people from Alberta, aged fifteen to eighteen, who contributed their views, through a series of e-mail dialogues with the author, to inform this contribution by Frazee. Two of them have disabilities and the others are close friends or relatives of a child or youth with disabilities. For the most part, these young people defined inclusion in terms of opportunity — to participate, to achieve, to be seen and understood, to belong. Most striking was the emphasis that most placed upon the twin values of participation and acceptance.

Inclusion demands vigilant attention to barrier removal, notes Frazee. An inclusive community, her informants told her, is one in which opportunities to act in the social world are not, as the Supreme Court of Canada noted in *Eldridge v. British Columbia* (1997), "conditional upon [the] emulation of able-bodied norms." But while much remains to be done to dismantle the multiple physical, structural and systemic barriers and restrictions that impede disabled persons' opportunities to act in the social world, the voices of these young people call our attention to a notion of inclusion that goes beyond the common understanding of access as the mechanical challenge of entry into buildings or the bureaucratic challenge of eligibility for civic opportunities.

Frazee argues that access must also be about making one's way into citizenship and human community and about feeling secure and worthy. Framed in this way, inclusion calls for access to respect; access to a sense of oneself as a whole person; and access to identity as a valued contributor, a bearer of rights, knowledge and power. This access involves relationships and engagement with others. Her chapter explores these notions in vivid terms based on the learnings from the young persons that were interviewed.

Almost without exception, these young people described inclusion primarily as an experience — an experience of growth and discovery, regarded as personally emancipatory and socially rewarding. For each individual, inclusion confers the valued prize of friendship, and with that prize, the coming into being of a self connected to others, known, honoured and cared for. For Kyle and others, the question of "how we feel and think about ourselves" is inextricably linked to feelings of being included:

"It feels Thumbs Up to be included and it feels really bad when you are not." The relationships they describe are untainted by the charitable impulse that society tends to adopt towards disability. Instead, there is mutuality and respect, cooperation and trust.

## Rights and Relationships

Frazee acknowledges that Canadian equality law, expressed in Section 15 of the *Charter of Rights and Freedoms*, and in federal and provincial human rights legislation, has taken us a good distance toward exposing prejudice and uprooting deeply embedded patterns of discrimination and disadvantage. Equality rights jurisprudence has provided important legal and analytical tools for remediation and redress from discrimination.

But Frazee also emphasizes that there are inherent limitations to the rights/equality paradigm. Rights, it seems, are oriented to doing and acting. Being and belonging may be less readily justiciable, particularly given a social, legal and policy context characterized by an unconscious but pervasive bias — a climate that requires the "emulation of able-bodied norms" to enter the social mainstream. Again her chapter provides dramatic examples from the experiences of the young persons interviewed.

Instead of focusing on the kinds of relationships that need to be cultivated to ensure a young person's well-being, leading to a critical exploration of resources and methods most likely to yield this result, Frazee believes that conventional rights discourse may sideline children whose differences confound the imaginations of those who should protect their being and belonging.

The prevailing attitude of adults and their institutions is one of low expectations and limited understanding of children and youth with disabilities. As Kyle puts it, we lack creativity in finding appropriate routes to inclusion:

> Sometimes inclusion is difficult at school because sometimes people do not believe that I can do things and don't even give me a chance. When people's expectations are set, it gets in the way of inclusion happening because they don't use their imaginations to find ways to make it happen.

## Inclusion and Equality

Frazee concludes with important reflections on the relation between social inclusion and equality. She maintains that as a process, social inclusion invokes us to cultivate in all children an appetite for involvement, self-expression and self-discovery, along with a well-founded expectation that their participation will be welcomed, their choices supported, their contributions valued and their integrity safeguarded. As an outcome, for Frazee, social inclusion shows itself in communities that afford a range of meaningful and respectful opportunities for children's involvement, expression and discovery, consistently and concurrently promoting children's being and becoming, as well as their doing and acting.

Inclusion and equality can be seen, through the lens of disability, as complementary principles, both serving just social outcomes. Equality is expressed in the currency of rights, while inclusion is expressed in the currency of relationships. Each is weakened in the absence of the other; each reinforces the other. They command us to equal attention and regard.

## Social Inclusion as Solidarity: Rethinking the Child Rights Agenda by Michael Bach

Michael Bach's chapter defines social inclusion as the process of bringing valued recognition to the marginalized, with a particular focus on children with disabilities. It argues that while a human rights agenda is essential, it is not sufficient to ensure that children with disabilities and other groups can participate fully in social, cultural and economic life. A social solidarity agenda is proposed to promote change that will enable those who are now devalued to speak their voices, exercise their rights and secure their own path to well-being. Bach's vision of citizenship goes beyond the exercise of political rights and social and economic claims on the state. It demands social, cultural and economic participation in civil society — a life well-lived in community.

Many groups have been struggling for years to be included among those granted benefit and advantage by the state and major institutions of society. A call for inclusion is particularly resonant within the disability movement, according to Bach, because it speaks directly to the issue of recognition and mis-recognition of others.

How do we mis-recognize others? The author suggests we do so by knowing them so incompletely or impersonally that we see them as something less than fully human, less deserving of the same moral and legal status as others. What we come to know of one another, how we come to know it and the institutionalized distinctions on which our views of one another rest — these are things that matter fundamentally. The process of social inclusion is one of constructing forms of knowledge and institutional rules and boundaries that confer recognition and respect on individuals and groups as valued members of society and that do not systematically undermine that respect.

A child with disabilities is denied education in a regular classroom, for example, because her competencies are deemed to justify segregation. Inclusion requires an understanding of the child as a child first, beyond a bio-medical account of disability. It means providing the necessary physical, curricular and other accommodation to enable the child to participate in the regular activities and personal relationships by which children come to be known personally by teachers and peers. Social inclusion is not an agenda for homogenization, but rather one that seeks to close the distances between us in ways that bring respect and value to the differences that define us.

Calls for social inclusion are becoming louder as the limitations of an exclusive reliance on human rights law to secure equal recognition and dignity in society become clear. An impressive framework of constitutional and statutory rights has been established in Canada. Yet evidence abounds that exclusions persist for many groups.

The extension of human rights is a condition of valued recognition, argues Bach in this chapter, but it does not mean that valued recognition necessarily follows. The rights-based approach to citizenship has given children and adults with disabilities and their families a claim to press on the state to challenge the abuse, poverty and exclusion from education faced by so many. But although there have been many successes in developing instruments of human rights, people are still excluded. Bach sees three primary reasons for this state of affairs.

First of all, while statutory and case law define and grant rights, they also define conditions for exercising those rights and for being known and recognized as a person or group able to exercise those rights. This is where the formula that equates the granting of rights with securing equal and valued recognition breaks down. The "exit" systems that the law establishes can result in the devaluing of certain groups. For example, exit systems allow governments, employers and service providers to avoid their responsibilities when the financial costs seem too high.

Second, the application of human rights law in Canada tends to result in individual compensation for discrimination rather than systemic change.

Third, human rights laws are fragile structures. They often do not inform policies — for example, children with disabilities have no entitlement to the supports they need to live at home with their families. And the application of human rights laws is subject to political agendas — for example, an employment equity law that simply required large employers to report on plans to address barriers was repealed in Ontario in the mid-1990s.

Where do we turn if a human rights strategy cannot, on its own, address exclusion? Bach proposes an agenda to build social solidarity, which would aim to bring value and recognition across differences, including those of language, communication, culture, age and ability. This solidarity agenda would supplement, not replace, the rights agenda.

Solidarity for Bach is not simply about coalition-building or forging alliances for a particular political struggle. It is much more about bringing to critical light the extent of recognition granted to different forms of human life, the breadth of diversity allowed by cultural and institutional arrangements and the forms of knowledge that fortify exclusionary divides.

This chapter outlines three priorities for a solidarity agenda for children with disabilities. When the issues go beyond education or the need for disability supports or child poverty *per se*, says Bach, when the debate is about forms of recognition that exclude some children, then new and deeper issues arise. One of these issues is *stereotyping in public policy* — challenging the prevailing notions of "whose knowledge counts."

Another issue is *public policy and genetic value*. As the Human Genome Project draws the boundary around what it means to be genetically human, the status of those with genotypes outside the norm comes into question and human value tends to be reduced to genetic makeup.

A third issue is the *measurement of child development in public policy*. Theories of healthy "normal" development emphasize that infants, toddlers, young children and adolescent youth reach and pass through certain developmental stages or benchmarks. Failure to reach certain stages is usually regarded as a sign of "abnormal" development. When viewed from the perspective of a child with disability, the cultural bias of these benchmarks is clear. A more inclusive set of outcomes and indicators, argues Bach, needs to be developed and made the basis for public investment and monitoring. These crucial issues of public policy are explored in detail in this chapter.

Michael Bach's contribution to this book emphasizes social inclusion as a process of rewriting the rules, recasting our cultural images and resources, and instituting practices to accord equal value and status to those who have been assigned a place of lesser value and status in Canadian society — its education systems, workplaces and communities. Valued recognition of others entails respecting their differences and identities in ways that enable them to speak their voices, exercise their rights and secure their own path to well-being.

## Immigrant Settlement and Social Inclusion in Canada
### by Ratna Omidvar and Ted Richmond

This chapter describes how Canada's immigrant settlement policies are failing recent immigrants and refugees, most of whom are visible minorities, and calls for a new vision of immigrant settlement focused on true social inclusion.

The role of Canada's newcomers is central to any meaningful development of the notion of social inclusion. Canada has one of the highest proportions of immigrants to total resident population of any country in the world. For immigrants and refugees, according to Omidvar and Richmond, social inclusion requires the realization of full and equal participation in the economic, social, cultural and political dimensions of life in their new country.

The authors note that Canada has what is considered to be one of the most open and welcoming immigration policies in the world. It is an officially multicultural and anti-racist society, with one of the world's most inclusive policies of citizenship acquisition, encouraging newcomers to become citizens after three years. Canada has a history of about forty years of successful integration of immigrants into the social and economic mainstream after the Second World War. Yet currently, as outlined in this chapter, we are witness to a glaring contradiction between official inclusion policies and the reality of growing social exclusion for Canada's newcomers in both the economic sphere and in public life in general. There are warnings of looming social instability and political tension created by the gap between promise and practice. Recent studies document increasing barriers to labour market integration for recently arrived newcomers, and disturbing trends towards the "racialization of poverty" for the immigrant communities (made up mainly of visible minorities) in Canada's major cities. This chapter examines both the causes for this waste of human potential and some elements of solutions.

Omidvar and Richmond note as well that there are other groups of newcomers who are even worse off than the highly educated immigrants, whose skills and experience are ill-recognized and unfairly compensated. Temporary immigrants, for example, work in Canadian agriculture under harsh conditions with minimal legal rights.

For people claiming refugee status after arrival in Canada and channelled into the refugee determination process, there are usually years of legal limbo, with significant barriers to employment and social services. They are excluded from most government-sponsored employment and training programs because of their immigration status, and they have difficulty getting housing. They have access only to "essential" health services, not to routine services. They cannot get a bank or a student loan or vote or work in certain professions, such as education and health care. This situation is creating a new underclass of persons without status who are most in need of help.

Also vulnerable to social exclusion, for different reasons, are immigrant and refugee children and youth. The settlement process has a major effect on the next generation, and many newcomer youth feel torn between apparently irreconcilable values or cultures and a desire to fit in. When these conflicts are combined with a life lived in poverty, there is a real danger of fostering a culture of alienation among youth who do not feel connected to their parents, their country of origin or the host society.

The authors of this chapter argue that immigrant settlement policy in Canada is currently in a state of crisis mainly because it lacks an integrated, long-term perspective that recognizes that immigration to a new country involves a lifetime of adjustment, with effects that extend at least into the next generation. Canadian settlement policies focus mainly on immediate needs, such as language training. In the medium term, newcomers may need assistance with such issues as employment, housing and legal assistance. In a later phase of adjustment, immigrants and refugees strive to become equal participants in all aspects of life in their new home.

The delivery system for immigrant settlement services has been weakened by changes in government funding. Delivery of these services is provided mainly by non-governmental, community-based immigrant service agencies. The funds for services come from the federal, provincial and municipal governments, community charities and private foundations. These service agencies, which welcome and support newcomers and advocate for them, have been hit with government funding cutbacks and imposed restructuring. Most government funders no longer provide core funding for organizations and instead contract with them for program delivery. Many smaller agencies do not have the administrative resources to manage these contractual arrangements and have had to curtail their services or shut their doors. Moreover, the new contractual terms of service require much closer administrative control, which jeopardizes the autonomy of these independent community agencies.

The potential consequences of an immigrant settlement system that cannot meet the needs of newcomers are grave, according to Omidvar and Richmond. In this context the notion of social inclusion provides a powerful metaphor and an important starting point for change. Applying an inclusive perspective to the challenges of immigrant settlement provides an alternative to focusing immigration policy on recruiting "the best and the brightest," continually raising the bar for admissions to Canada while sidelining the needs of family reunification and refugee resettlement and ignoring the barriers of social exclusion experienced by those who have already begun the settlement journey here. The chapter explores examples of solutions to current settlement-related policy challenges within this perspective.

The policy alternatives presented could be implemented incrementally, building public support during the process of reform. But the overarching recommendation of the authors is for the development of an integrated, pan-Canadian, adequately resourced, multi-facetted, multi-agency and publicly accountable immigrant settlement system based on a new vision. Essential elements of this vision of inclusive settlement include:

- the restoration of government responsibilities for universal social programs as a pre-condition for inclusion of both newcomers and the Canadian-born;
- the targeting of social programs to the most disadvantaged, including immigrants and refugees excluded from equitable participation in the labour market and other aspects of civic life; and
- a rights-based approach to deal with the reality of differential legal and practical rights for newcomers based on immigration status (whether one is a citizen, immigrant or refugee, in selected or family class, a sponsored refugee or refugee claimant).

The new vision must redefine immigrant settlement, recognizing it is a journey of a lifetime that extends into the next generation. It must identify mutual obligations and benefits for newcomers and society. All levels and departments of government must tackle the challenges and be held accountable for the results of newcomer settlement. All stakeholders must be included in the development of new policies. Funding must be restored for settlement services, and the autonomy of community-based agencies must be protected.

For Omidvar and Richmond, however, it is not just the settlement system that requires an overhaul. Their vision of inclusion is based on a framework of anti-exclusion, anti-discrimination and anti-racism, taking into account the limits of official multiculturalism and the realities of systemic racism in contemporary Canada. True inclusion requires the creation of new common ground for civic engagement in an inclusive and diverse society.

# Social Inclusion, Anti-Racism and Democratic Citizenship by Anver Saloojee

This chapter identifies racism as a form of social exclusion. It discusses the potential of social inclusion to move beyond the limitations of a public policy of multiculturalism by "democratizing democracy" and developing active and meaningful forms of social citizenship. From an anti-racist perspective, Saloojee describes the building blocks necessary for creating an inclusive society and outlines some policy implications involved in getting there.

## Racism as Social Exclusion

Saloojee outlines the nature of racism as an ideology and a set of practices based on distinguishing between the various groups that comprise the human species by such physical features as skin colour. As ideology, it proclaims the superiority of the group that constitutes the status quo and works to ensure socio-political domination over the others. In practice, racism works to constantly exclude, marginalize and disadvantage the subordinated, racialized groups. Racialization involves attaching meaning and significance to differences like skin colour.

For Saloojee racism is a form of social exclusion. Racial discrimination in all its manifestations is the process by which that exclusion occurs. Exclusion for racialized groups means unequal access to rights, to the valued goods and services in society, to the labour market and to all fields of public life. Because of their skin colour, members of racialized minority communities encounter barriers that result in incomplete citizenship, undervalued rights, undervalued recognition and undervalued participation.

Saloojee argues that racial inequality and discrimination are both the product and the confirmation of power imbalances in society. Structural constraints that are woven into the fabric of society ensure that race, ethnic and gender inequalities persist in spite of the widely held assumption that market forces are blind to these differences among humans.

This chapter outlines some of the ways that equality in the workplace and in society have proven very difficult to achieve. Recent reports show that members of racialized minority groups experience lower rates of employment, higher rates of unemployment and are overrepresented in low-end jobs with less favourable rates of pay, types of work and working conditions. There are significant income disparities between members of these minority groups and other Canadians — the gap in median before-tax income in 1998 was 28 percent. The education, professional training and experience obtained by immigrants before coming to Canada are underutilized in this country.

Another significant phenomenon addressed in the chapter is the racialization of poverty. The poverty rate in Canada, according to 1996 Census data, was 21 percent, compared to 38 percent for racialized groups, 70 percent of whom were foreign-born. For children, the rate was 45 percent for racialized groups, compared to 26 percent for all children in Canada. Poverty among recent immigrants is particularly high. The Canadian Council on Social Development found that despite the economic recovery in the 1990s, poverty among recent immigrants, three-quarters of whom are members of racialized minorities, was 27 percent, compared to 13 percent among the rest of the Canadian population.

## Democratic Citizenship and Multiculturalism

Saloojee views social inclusion as beginning from the premise that it is democratic citizenship that is at risk when a society fails to develop the talents and capacities of its members. Democratic citizenship is about valued participation, valued recognition and belonging. It involves not only all the political rights associated with formal equality, but also a relationship with one's community and the resources necessary to exercise one's citizenship.

Canada has used multiculturalism policy to try to deal with racial discrimination and determine the nature of state-minority relations. In its early phase, this policy encouraged group social cohesion through preservation of culture and language. But this approach, suggests Saloojee, still left minority communities on the margins, outside the mainstream culture and far from the centres of decision-making. As a result, ethno-racial communities shifted their focus to an assessment of their rightful place in a democratic society that espoused the ideals of equality. Power, access, equity and participation were among their core issues.

Under federal law, multiculturalism was redefined from a celebration of diversity to a fundamental characteristic of Canadian society, at the heart of nation-building. Its importance was recognized when it was constitutionally entrenched in the *Charter of Rights and Freedoms*. While some critics of multiculturalism suggest that it has encouraged fragmentation and hyphenated Canadians, Saloojee argues that it is the pervasiveness of prejudice directed at disadvantaged groups and widespread discrimination that have contributed to growing fault lines in Canadian society. He also notes the views of those who fear that multiculturalism is simply another version of assimilation in disguise and proposes social inclusion as way to overcome the limits of multiculturalism policy, which, despite its ideals, has not led to valued recognition and participation for minority communities.

For Saloojee therefore, social inclusion is about developing a proactive stance towards the democratization of democracy. It will democratize by developing a new way of approaching old problems, by positing a radically different concept of citizenship and community, by arguing for new measures of accountability, by providing the impetus for the emergence of new modes of evaluation of public policies, by arguing for increased representation and participation by marginalized groups, and by encouraging the development of the skills, talents and capacities of all.

## Making Social Inclusion Real

Saloojee sees social inclusion as a new way of thinking about the problems of injustice, inequalities and exclusion. He believes it is capable of meeting the greatest challenges posed by diversity — to build on the traditions of equality espoused in liberalism and to move to the incorporation of the ideals of antiracism and anti-discrimination as core ideals exemplifying national values.

Social inclusion is capable of this, Saloojee proposes, because it is about respect for differences and the removal of barriers to effective and equitable participation in all spheres of public life. It is also about engaging in inclusive practices and about continuous evaluations of institutions, laws, policies and practices to ensure that they are genuinely inclusive. Finally, it is also about public accountability.

Social inclusion in this chapter therefore becomes an agenda for an inclusive democracy that places issues of social justice at the heart of the urban question. Democracy is the locus of citizenship, and it is essential to recognize that the very definition of the public sphere and citizenship in the urban environment is contested by racialized minority groups. There is no single public sphere, no single acceptable notion of citizenship and no single notion of social cohesion. There are instead multiple spheres and spaces in which historically marginalized groups develop their own sense of cohesion to contest oppression, discrimination and exclusion. In this process they posit a different understanding of space, citizenship and social cohesion, seeking an alternative that is about inclusion as valued participants in a society that is committed to the eradication of discrimination and disadvantage in all its forms and manifestations.

Saloojee continues in this chapter by outlining essential characteristics, from an anti-racist perspective, of an inclusive society. Next he examines several contemporary and key policy challenges from the same perspective. He emphasizes as well that strengthening the bonds of civic engagement and democratic citizenship requires that society invest in children, especially in their education.

From Saloojee's perspective, for social inclusion to matter, for the concept to resonate, it must provide space for a discussion of oppression and discrimination. Social inclusion must promote a transformative agenda that links the often disparate struggles against oppression, inequality and injustice. The glue that would bind these social movements together is a kind of inclusion that would lead to the creation of a more just and equitable society.

## Dangers of a New Dogma: Inclusion or Else...! by Uzma Shakir

This contribution by Uzma Shakir is an attempt to explore her unease with the concept — or dogma, as she argues it has indeed become — of "social inclusion." The author notes that people stare at her in disbelief when she says that she has problems with social inclusion. How could anyone possibly deny either the discourse or the opportunity to be included in something as desirable as society? The potency and indeed the orthodoxy of this policy lingo is one of the reasons she is sceptical about it.

The chapter begins with some elements of the history of the concepts of inclusion, noting that the term social exclusion pre-dates the concept of social inclusion. However, both these concepts have a history and a location in terms of time, geography and indeed the material conditions in which they emerged. Discourse of "social exclusion" dates to the 1970s and '80s in Europe at a time when rapid changes in society on many fronts were causing considerable economic, political and social tensions across various European nations: the erosion of the welfare state through the retreat of the government; recognition that increasingly large numbers of people were slipping through the social welfare net; slow economic growth and "stagflation"; globalization and European integration leading to the intensive restructuring of European economies; greater numbers of immigrants and refugees coming from developing countries (many from former colonies); and the commensurate growth in racial and social tensions. The discourse was soon adopted by the European Union (EU) as a broad label for describing and developing policy solutions to address the internal inequities among member countries.

Thus conceptually both the terms "exclusion" and "inclusion" have a distinct history of emergence at a time when racial, social and economic changes in Western society were all seen to pose unmistakable threats.

However, for Shakir this way of understanding inclusion is not neutral. It has a history and materiality that gives rise to the need for the social exclusion/inclusion discourse to emerge in the first place. It has values attached to it — for example, it is good to be "within it" and, correspondingly, bad to be "outside it." Thus, while exclusion/inclusion discourse has a history grounded in particular material conditions of different societies, the proponents of the discourse offer the concepts as universally neutral solutions — an important contradiction.

Shakir continues with a focus on the "Canadian version" of social inclusion discourse. In Canada, she maintains, the concept has followed the logic of social accommodation that views inclusion as a continuum on which exclusion is the problem and inclusion is the solution. Thus, in this formulation of the concept there is more emphasis on moral self-righteousness than critical thinking.

As a consequence major questions arise: how and why do people become "excluded" in the first place? Is exclusion a quantitative problem? When excluded you have "a lack of...," whereas if included you have "more of..." There is also an assumption that social inclusion is something you do "for" people — since those who are excluded presumably cannot change their circumstances (otherwise they would not be excluded in the first place) — others now must make them feel wanted and help them to participate. Since there is no structural analysis of marginality or exclusion and the concept is, once again, familiarly linear, social inclusion becomes a paternalistic policy option rather than one that challenges historical and existing power imbalances in our society in order to create real change. The proponents of social inclusion according to Shakir fail to investigate a crucial question: whether inclusion ought to be a goal of public policy or whether material conditions of contemporary exclusion of some groups in society may in fact be a product of existing public policy, all of which would at least appropriately place the spotlight on public policy as a contested space.

The prevailing discourse of inclusion, for Shakir, implies either that "someone" outside the lived reality of privilege and marginality in society exists and could benevolently create this middle, or that those within could deliberately move in order to create it. But just who is this benevolent but neutral outsider? As for the insiders, if the excluded could "move," why didn't they? Might there be an element of movement as well as self-control in marginalization? If so, why move to the middle unless everyone shares the same ideas about where they want to be? Yet surely the whole point of "diversity" is accepting the lack of a universal point of reference? How does this logic lead towards a state of "inclusion"? At best, this thought process is paternalistic and hegemonic, while at worst, it blames the victims for their exclusion.

Another question that remains unanswered in Canadian discourse for Shakir is who is defining inclusion? Who is to include whom? Furthermore, if we accept diversity as a given, then how might we be expected to construct shared aspirations and values? The concept of social inclusion is presented in such a way that only commonality is permitted with inclusion. Differences are seen as manifestations of exclusion. Yet surely, the "norm" in Canada cannot be universal. It has a history and is very much defined by cultural, linguistic and racial specificity. However, it remains in a relationship of dominant power *vis-à-vis* the other two. Thus, the "norm" is defining the degree of "difference from..." This is a nearly pure relationship of power. So to create an inclusionary space without unmasking this culturally, linguistically and racially dominant relationship, according to Shakir, is to risk perpetuating marginality in the guise of inclusion.

For Shakir social reality cannot be neutral and ahistorical; yet that is what social inclusion appears to demand. By definition, society is a construct and as such it must have a history. Therefore, the lived realities of inclusion/exclusion of an individual or a group within a society must also have a history. Yet the Canadian discourse has tended to ignore the historical aspects of minoritizing and racializing diversity and thus the very construction of marginality in our society. Shakir therefore sees as dangerous the Canadian social inclusion discourse that insists on a range of normative assumptions that inevitably lead to the creeping emergence of a "meta-definition" of social inclusion. Furthermore, power structures define the level of exclusion for some and inclusion for others. Therefore, it becomes logical to assume that social inclusion must be, at the very least, a dialectical concept.

Shakir's chapter examines some of the more critical versions of social inclusion in Canada, which describe the nature of marginalization and seek to unearth the conditions of exclusion in order to create inclusion. She cites the work of Galabuzi, along with others, in identifying the concrete forms of exclusion based on economic inequities and discrimination for racialized and newcomer communities, and the contributions of Saloojee with respect to social inclusion as a contestation of racism and a movement towards equitable social citizenship. Shakir also outlines the contributions of forums like the Alternative Planning Group (APG) in Toronto, which she sees as contributing to more genuinely inclusive social planning without overtly embracing the social inclusion discourse.

Shakir concludes that even in its most critical form, social inclusion/exclusion can only become a strategic means of continuing negotiation between isolated groups. In an ethnically, culturally, racially and linguistically diverse and heterogeneous society like Canada, any static notion of inclusion will inevitably be hegemonic and oppressive. To be meaningful, social inclusion can only be strategic and focused on possible points of common interest. For Shakir, claiming to be inclusionary is not the same as creating and living inclusion! Inclusion is an enactment, a process that marginalized groups, communities and individuals need to traverse —

and power structures need to be susceptible to — rather than an end itself. Possessing and exercising the right and, more importantly, the ability to contest, to re-structure relations of power and ultimately re-imagine Canada is social inclusion.

## Urban Aboriginal Peoples: A Challenge to the National by the National Association of Friendship Centres (NAFC)

This chapter is a contribution of the National Association of Friendship Centres (NAFC) and was written by their researcher Alfred Gay. As outlined in the chapter, the Friendship Centre Movement (FCM) originated fifty years ago in response to the needs of Aboriginal peoples who were migrating to urban areas in search of a better life — a migration rooted in the unjust and culturally destructive historical policies and practices of the Government of Canada. Today, the FCM has in place a national service infrastructure and networking capacity that includes 117 Friendship Centres at the local community level, situated in every region of Canada. Friendship Centres are represented at the provincial level by seven provincial/territorial associations (PTAs) and at the national level by the National Association of Friendship Centres (NAFC).

This contribution emphasizes that the FCM has continually demonstrated measurable results, through the delivery of its programs and services in a transparent, accountable and efficient manner. Its members are committed to a "people first" approach to community and economic development initiatives, as opposed to participating in programs for the sake of accepting funding. Programs have developed from expressed community needs, rather than government or corporate agendas. Services are delivered in a culturally appropriate manner and, above all, through a process that is accountable to their constituency. For fifty years, the FCM has strived to be at the forefront of urban Aboriginal community development and tireless in its efforts to restore the dignity of Aboriginal peoples.

The chapter focuses on the situation of urban Aboriginals, communities which constitute a major and growing demographic factor in Canadian social policy, but which do not receive sufficient attention in policy decisions. This contribution also provides important factual and analytical insights into the needs of urban Aboriginal children and youth. The evidence presented shows that there can be no doubt that the quality of life of urban Aboriginal children is "shameful." In many urban areas, Aboriginal peoples make up a large and rising proportion of residents of low-income neighborhoods. More and more Aboriginal children face life in Canada's racialized ghettos.

Above all, the NAFC contribution emphasizes the current reality of social exclusion for urban Aboriginals as the starting point in addressing the issues of social inclusion.

## Investing in Healthy Communities

The NAFC contribution emphasizes the substantive evidence linking health status with the social determinants of health. There is growing recognition of the need for all sectors to adapt program and policy changes that address the social determinants of health: food security, early learning, housing and human capital.

The importance of this perspective is emphasized by the fact that Aboriginal people who live off-reserve in cities and towns are generally in poorer health than the non-Aboriginal population. This chapter calls for the Government of Canada to exercise leadership in the area of public health for urban Aboriginal peoples. It also speaks to the need for a renewed vision of an Aboriginal health system that strives to ensure equitable access to quality health services, seamless service from community to hospital and a greater focus on preventing illness and promoting good health.

## Securing Safe and Affordable Housing

Friendship Centres serve numerous Aboriginal peoples living in large urban centres where housing problems persist. Shocking disparities exist between the housing conditions of Aboriginal and non-Aboriginal peoples living in census metropolitan areas. The NAFC contribution reminds us that crowded housing conditions can lead to a host of difficulties, including increased risk for injuries, mental health problems, family tensions and violence.

Although the Universal Declaration of Human Rights, Article 25(1) and the International Covenant on Economic, Social and Cultural Rights provide for the right to housing, in Canada, this right has not been recognized or implemented. An affordable housing strategy, as outlined in this chapter, would be part of a federal government initiative towards a New Deal for Communities.

## Education and Early Childhood Development

The NAFC contribution provides concrete recommendations on early childhood development for urban Aboriginal children, within the context of the Government of Canada's commitment to the development of a new national system of early learning and childcare with the engagement of Aboriginal leaders. It also supports the ongoing work of Friendship Centres in securing funding for programming aimed at children six to twelve years of age in providing culturally appropriate guidance and development services, noting that the 2001 Aboriginal Peoples Survey demonstrated a correlation between participation in extra-curricular activities and school achievement. Opportunities to participate in organized extra-curricular activities, this chapter stresses, should not be denied to children due to their socio-economic situation.

In 2001, almost half (48 percent) of the off-reserve Aboriginal population age 20–24 had incomplete high school as their highest level of schooling, compared to one in four Canadian youth of the same age with incomplete high school. This chapter emphasizes the importance of the specific factors behind these statistics. "Being bored with school" topped the reasons given by young off-reserve Aboriginal people (age 15–19) for leaving elementary or high school prior to completion. However, nearly one in five young Aboriginal men (age 15–19) who had left school said they did so because they wanted to work. As well, one in four of young Aboriginal women (age 15–19) who had left school reported that they did so because of pregnancy or the need to care for children.

The NAFC contribution stresses the importance of post-secondary education for Aboriginal peoples in Canada. They are more likely than others to return to school later in life, meaning that they are pursuing post-secondary education as mature students. The challenges facing older adults who return to school are different than those facing young adults; for example, a large number of Aboriginal people who are attending school are also raising children. Programs which facilitate the achievement of post-secondary qualifications for First Nations and Inuit students are a means by which Aboriginal peoples can begin to reverse the trend of their historic social and economic exclusion from influential centres of decision-making.

## Creating Opportunities in Employment

This chapter reminds us that there has been considerable attention and focus on the emerging skills and labour shortages throughout every jurisdiction in Canada. The demographic and geographic realities are putting many jurisdictions in competition with one another for a scarce, skilled and capable workforce. The western provinces in particular have invested heavily in understanding the policy challenges as the challenges are more acute there. There is an abundance of evidence and reports addressing the employment and training needs of Aboriginal peoples.

As well it is clear that the circumstances of urban and off-reserve Aboriginal peoples with respect to human capital development are quite different than of those living on reserves. The NAFC chapter outlines some of the legal disputes and precedents with respect to the recognition of urban Aboriginal communities as organized, self determined and distinct. By examining social, economic and demographic realities of urban Aboriginal communities, it becomes apparent that the priorities and needs of urban Aboriginal communities differ from reserve communities. Different needs and priorities, including the needs of the urban North American Aboriginal population who do not have registered Indian status, require that the locus of control for the delivery and design of employment and training programs be found within the community that is being served.

## Government Fiscal Policy and the
## Challenges of Canadian Federalism

This contribution by NAFC also examines the current reality of the federal "fiscal toolkit" and the implications of the Canada Social Transfer (CST) announced by the Government of Canada to be effective in April 1, 2004, in support of post-secondary education, social assistance and social services, including early childhood development. The chapter notes the challenges faced by all levels of government in their efforts to ensure social, political and economic justice for all Canadians, in particular those of the western provinces, with an increasing proportion of Aboriginal peoples.

The Government of Canada has taken the position that provinces are responsible for providing services and supports for Aboriginal peoples within their legislative sphere, while the provinces maintain the federal government is wholly responsible for all Aboriginal peoples. Municipal governments have expressed their desire to work with Aboriginal governments and institutions given the financial means. As a fourth option, Aboriginal service delivery providers, including the Friendship Centres, are a viable mechanism worthy of closer scrutiny.

Nevertheless, Canadians are no longer willing to allow large fiscal resources to be channelled to provincial coffers without a legitimate expectation of results. While fiscal federalism is a reality, there is also an increased public expectation to know that we are getting the best return on investment. In reaching consensus on redesigned funding mechanisms, according to this NAFC contribution, the Government of Canada is left with the difficult task of enforcing proposed national standards, accountability provisions and measured outcomes.

## Urban Aboriginals and Social Inclusion

This contribution by NAFC provides a wealth of useful evidence and argument concerning the situation of Aboriginal peoples in contemporary Canada. Furthermore, by examining the social, economic and demographic realities of urban Aboriginal communities, the NAFC contribution makes apparent that the priorities and needs of urban Aboriginal communities differ from those of reserve communities and that the needs of urban Aboriginal children and youth are of the highest priority with respect to social policy. For urban Aboriginals, the struggle for meaningful social inclusion must start from the documented realities of multiple and dramatic forms of contemporary social exclusion.

## Looking Forward: Research and Policy Perspectives

Given the variety of critical insights and the diversity of viewpoints expressed in the contributions to this book, what can we say at this point about the significance of social inclusion as an approach to social policy in Canada? First and foremost we should recognize that in privileging the discourse of social inclusion as the entry point into social analysis, we are placing at the centre of our research concerns a proactive human development approach that calls for more than the removal of barriers and risks. In this sense we are dealing both with a normative concept and an evaluative tool. Theoretical frameworks and the research based on them are very much about normative social science. Social inclusion is about a kind of social science that is rationally motivated to engage in social transformation. It is not about change for the sake of change; it is about research and social policy and social practice that would make for a better society, a better state of affairs than exclusion. Hence, in social inclusion we have a concept that has tremendous political potential — building bridges of solidarity that transcend the potential fragmenting and siloing effects of "identity politics." In this sense we can make a very compelling case for a social inclusion analytical framework as a preferred entry point to social enquiry. It may not be the only useful point of entry but it is the most illuminating and the most compelling analytically, conceptually as well as politically.

The utility of the concept of social inclusion will depend however, on the extent and degree to which it successfully deals with social exclusion in a society that is fractured along numerous fault lines. It is important to distinguish between weak and strong versions of the social inclusion discourse. The former focus simply on integration of the excluded — primarily into the labour market. The latter take a structural approach that focuses on historical processes that continually reproduce oppression, discrimination and exclusion. Strong approaches to the social inclusion discourse therefore are intimately concerned with rights, citizenship and restructured relations between marginalized and excluded communities and the institutions of the dominant society. They focus on valued recognition and valued participation by those excluded from full participation in society and from the benefits of society.

For some the attraction of the social inclusion discourse may be that it focuses attention on social exclusion as a failure to integrate into the paid labour market. But this approach may be too narrowly focused on the economic dimensions of poverty and labour market integration. Potentially this approach obscures a bigger debate about exploitation, and the extent to which various forms of oppression and marginalization increase the social distance between and among groups of people in society. Broadening out the analysis of social exclusion to include the discourse on discrimination and conversely broadening out the concept of social inclusion to embrace an anti-discrimination discourse then requires an analysis of rights and responsibilities in society. This broader definition of social inclusion is also about political mobilization and solidarity, social and political participation and respect, rights, entitlements, responsibilities and obligations.

We are suggesting therefore that the theoretical and practical meanings of social inclusion need to be developed in particular national, sub-national and supra-national contexts. In Canada some of these essential factors include demographic changes, particularly the growing proportion of recent immigrants and visible minorities within our population. They also include the movement towards the politicization of human rights issues, and the need to construct an active version of social citizenship or substantive political representation and engagement that goes beyond the limits of formal rights to legal citizenship and voting in parliamentary elections. As well they must include the First Nations' claims to sovereignty and the right to self determination.

Social inclusion therefore must be understood in the context of the equity and social justice claims advanced by excluded groups in Canada — racialized minority communities, newcomer communities, women, persons with disabilities, gays, lesbians and transgendered persons and the First Nations Aboriginal communities. These groups are demanding their rightful place in Canadian society. The claims they are making are not merely for formal representation; they are substantive claims involving issues of equity and social justice. Democratic citizenship, from a social inclusion perspective, is about valued participation, valued recognition and belonging. At a minimum, it is characterized by:

- all the political rights associated with formal equality;
- a right to equality and a right to be free from discrimination;
- an intimate relationship between the individual and the community;
- reciprocal relationship of rights and obligations;
- barrier free access, a sense of belonging and not being "othered" and marginalized;
- a commitment on the part of the state to ensure that all members of society have equal access to developing their talents and capacities; and
- providing all members of society with the resources to exercise democratic citizenship.

Can we conclude therefore that we are moving towards a uniquely Canadian definition of social inclusion? The contributions in this volume certainly demonstrate the richness and sophistication with which the debate has developed in our country within a relatively short period of time. However they reveal as well that attempts to understand social inclusion in purely definitional terms are certainly premature and likely counter-productive. The inherently political nature of the social inclusion discourse, as well as the diversity of responses to exclusion represented in the debates, reveals that the meaning of social inclusion will continue to be contested. In our view this is a strength, rather than a weakness, in the current discussions. Without further extensive and meaningful debate, there are serious risks that the social inclusion discourse will be co-opted as a form of government rhetoric masking inaction on major issues of exclusion or a new form of assimilation discourse masquerading as liberal social policy.

Within this perspective of continuing debate however, we remain committed to the fundamental importance of social inclusion as a tool of social analysis for the following essential reasons:

- Social inclusion is the political response to exclusion. It is about more than the removal of barriers; it concerns a comprehensive vision that includes all. It is about valued recognition, and valued participation, in the struggle for an inclusive society.
- Social inclusion is proactive. It is about anti-discrimination. It is not about the passive protection of rights; it is about the active intervention to promote rights; and it confers responsibility on the state to adopt and enforce policies that will ensure social inclusion of all members of society (not just formal citizens, or consumers or taxpayers or clients).
- Social inclusion, by virtue of the fact that it is both process and outcome can hold governments and institutions accountable for their policies. The yardstick by which to measure good government therefore becomes the extent to which it advances the well-being of the most vulnerable and the excluded in society.
- Social inclusion is about advocacy and transformation. It is about the political struggle and the political will to remove barriers to full and equitable participation in society by all, and in particular by members of racialized communities. Furthermore, the vision of social inclusion is a positive vision that binds its proponents and adherents to action.
- Social inclusion is embracing. It posits a notion of democratic citizenship as opposed to formal citizenship. Democratic citizens possess rights and entitlements by virtue of their being a part of the polity, not by virtue of their formal status (for example as immigrants, refugees or citizens).

Within this broad perspective the development of a social inclusion research and policy agenda requires further attention to the variety of fundamental issues addressed in this volume, as well as a number of emerging issues.[2] One of these issues is the continuing restructuring of the Canadian labour market, with a general deterioration of opportunities for vulnerable groups such as newcomers, the disabled, young families, single parents and urban Aboriginals.

The world of work in Canada is becoming more precarious; the low-paid segment of the labour force is growing as a portion of the total employed, and long-term poverty is becoming more associated with paid employment. From a social inclusion perspective, we need to ask why certain groups identified more by social or cultural characteristics rather than economic features are at such risk of long-term poverty. We must also question why the "bottom end" of the labour market continues to grow in a restructured, knowledge-intensive and globalized economy. The answers should lead us away from neo-liberal economic policies towards an emphasis on the universal benefits of general economic growth and into a deeper understanding of the social supports and policy reforms that are needed by specific excluded communities.

Another issue of great concern is the role of non-governmental service and umbrella organizations in public education and advocacy, which is increasingly threatened by the restructuring of funding for community organizations. The transition to narrowly defined service contract funding as the dominant form of government support to the community sector cannot be allowed to destroy the social capital represented by these organizations. Community organizations play vital roles in both "bonding" and "bridging" networks and linkages that are vital for combating exclusion with vulnerable groups; and while government cannot create social capital, government policies can facilitate its development. Exploration of this issue requires further attention to the links between social capital, social citizenship and social inclusion and may lead us to a more "asset-based" approach to community development in areas like newcomer settlement.

The development of inclusive indicators is another area of applied research that is essential to bridging social inclusion theory with social inclusion practice. We know that what is not measured does not "count" as a problem and therefore does not receive attention or resources. While considerable work has been done in this field in the past years, it generally remains divided between process-oriented projects, which have not yet produced usable indicators, and more data-focused projects, which are little known in excluded communities.

The movement towards social inclusion in Canada therefore is one in development; it is not fixed as a concept or theory. As well as recognizing and respecting differences of interpretation, social inclusion must be tested in practice through local initiatives of excluded communities. These projects by necessity will have an experimental nature; new practices will give rise to new debates and to further strengthening of our understanding of social inclusion as applied social policy.

The social inclusion work we want to develop therefore must combine theory and practice and must exhibit four essential features. It must deal with the structural roots of exclusion. It must be rooted in community (self-) organization and mobilization. It must be transformative — leading to real, applied policy changes transforming the structures that promote exclusion and limit inclusion. Above all the movement for social inclusion must itself be inclusive, recognizing the voices of those who do not use the same language but are grappling with the same fundamental issues of discrimination, injustice and exploitation. This volume of selected Canadian writings on social inclusion is offered as one contribution to this important process.

# Notes

1. For access to these and other references on social inclusion, see the links on the Laidlaw Foundation website at <www.laidlawfdn.org>.
2. For a variety of references on these topics refer to the Laidlaw Foundation website at <www.laidlawfdn.org>.

# Poverty, Inequality and Social Inclusion

*Andrew Mitchell and Richard Shillington*

## Introduction

Canada may set a limited social goal of poverty elimination that might narrowly imply providing sufficient funds to meet basic needs. A broader social goal would be "equality of opportunity," which would be tracked based on income inequality or relative poverty. Even more ambitious would be a policy objective that advanced social inclusion. This goal has implications for citizen participation, capacity and agency, because it encourages the tools (economic, social, health, educational and legal) that make autonomy possible.

The opportunity provided by the concepts of exclusion and inclusion comes with some risks. Social inclusion, like poverty, is a contested concept. The meanings of social inclusion span the range from narrow labour market insertion policies, policies which have questionable impact on broad notions of inclusion, to broader notions of capability and participation. However, it may be riskier still to ignore a discourse that is encroaching on the social policy domain in North America, after coming to dominate discussions in Europe.

This chapter explores the relationship among the related concepts of poverty, inequality and social exclusion/inclusion. Although there are similarities and overlaps among them, and they are occasionally used interchangeably, they are distinct. Each has an impact on welfare, and indeed, they are interdependent. Poverty reduction is necessary for survival. Inequality affects self-esteem but also autonomy, freedom and social inclusion, which are prerequisites for well-being. Our choice of definition rests in part on the purposes for which we seek social inclusion — individual well-being versus broader social cohesion as the focus of our concerns.

This chapter is based on a number of contentions that are key to an understanding of social inclusion and exclusion and to their application to public policies and practices:

1.  Income sufficient first for basic needs and second for decency is but a stepping stone to well-being. This is demonstrated by the notion of poverty as "capability deprivation," as developed by Amartya Sen (1992). His broader conception, focusing on capacity instead of poverty, has strong parallels with the notions of exclusion/inclusion.[1] Social inclusion encourages a focus on capabilities broader than income.[2] These can include limited access to basic health and basic education.

As well, the impediments to capacity include the denial of human rights (UN covenants include basic income, shelter, health and education as a human right).

2. Social inclusion and exclusion are multidimensional since there are many different domains of potential deprivation that come into play singly or in combination to create exclusion, and many different ways to promote inclusion. They begin with the thing we really care about — individual well-being — and then ask who is affected, and how. The concepts of income poverty and inequality are central, but inclusion is broader than these, encompassing physical and economic dimensions, human assets, social assets and political abilities.

3. Social and political actors and institutions create exclusion, and the focus on these actors and processes is one of the advantages of examining social exclusion. Policy and practice can reinforce disadvantages emanating from other sources, transforming original disadvantage into exclusion. The recognition of disadvantage, however defined, does not automatically lead to a strategy for its elimination.

4. Social inclusion provides a comprehensive perspective that tests the limitations of prevalent forms of anti-exclusion policy. In particular, social inclusion highlights the deficiencies of anti-exclusion policies that seek to promote inclusion solely by integrating the marginalized through labour market attachment. Such limited perspectives ignore gender and other inequalities in the labour market, the value of caring responsibilities and the limits to inclusion through work implied by wage polarization and the flexibility of the labour market.

Opposing social exclusion and advancing inclusion are not necessarily synonymous. The term social inclusion carries policy tensions that social exclusion may not. The former suggests the existence of a marginalized group, in need of rehabilitation to return to the mainstream. The latter suggests that it is society that must adapt to ensure that all are included.

## Poverty, Inequality, Capacity and Social Inclusion

Society has an interest in monitoring the well-being of its citizens. We employ a variety of indicators that capture our conception of disadvantage and well-being for this purpose. High on this list of indicators is our interest in knowing how many people are "poor." Such indicators can range from a narrow focus on the income needed to meet physical needs, to a broader focus on the individual's position in relation to his or her community.

This section reviews the contemporary debate over the meaning of poverty in Canada. We argue that all concepts of poverty are inescapably relative and that the choice of measure is really a choice among policy objectives. Particularly when we take an intergenerational perspective, it is difficult if not impossible to distinguish between equality of *opportunity* and equality of *outcome*. The outcomes of one generation shape the opportunities of the next.

## Poverty in Canada

Poverty is an intensely contested term in Canada. For some commentators poverty has meaning only in terms of the minimum necessary for physical survival — "the capacity to buy food and all the goods necessary for the fulfillment of basic physical needs" (Bourgignon 1999: 2), although it can relate to something more than mere subsistence. Others, following Townsend, argue that poverty can only be understood as a relative concept, and therefore closely related to, if not synonymous with, too much income inequality.

These varying approaches have yielded an assortment of definitions. In Canada, operationalizing the idea of relative poverty has usually meant drawing an income line that is some fraction of the average income in the society as a whole. At the other end of the spectrum, the standard that comes closest to the absolutist ideal of poverty as mere physical survival are the poverty lines established by the Fraser Institute. In the view of the Fraser Institute, what we consider poverty should not be affected by the living standards that exist in the rest of society or by changes in those living standards. In between are a variety of hybrid definitions incorporating elements of both.

Although space does not allow for a full exploration of the concepts of absolute versus relative poverty, it may at least be stated that the distinction between absolute and relative poverty is perhaps more tenuous than is currently acknowledged. There is accumulating evidence that inequality itself has effects on outcomes and basic capabilities such as health and education, quite apart from the absolute level of income (Raphael 2000).

Moreover, when children are the subjects, we are explicitly taking an intergenerational perspective. Equality of opportunity is difficult to disentangle from equality of outcome when an intergenerational perspective is taken, and the outcomes of one generation shape the opportunities of the next.

### Poverty and policy objectives

The choice of poverty measure implies a choice among policy objectives. What is the outcome we seek? To begin with what we should measure before knowing what outcomes we are seeking is to put the cart before the horse. What is the public policy objective to which poverty statistics are addressed? Is it sufficient resources to meet the physical needs for health?

Is it equality of opportunity or equality of outcome?

It is worthwhile to consider the implications, particularly regarding social inclusion, of an absolute approach to poverty. In a scenario in which the living standards of low-income Canadians remain constant, but are falling behind the norm, absolute rates of poverty will be constant but relative rates will increase. The policy implication is that the living standards set for low-income Canadians need not be related to the "norm"— that of middle-income families — and in turn, that increasing societal wealth need not be shared with those who are worst-off. The prospect would be an ever-widening "social distance" in society, even as our indicators of poverty signal that there is no issue requiring a policy response.

Thus, for those whose policy objective is simply to meet people's basic physical needs, an absolute measure of poverty will suffice. For those more interested in equality of opportunity and the civic participation of otherwise excluded populations, income inequality will also be of interest. The debate about social inclusion further broadens our sphere of interest.

## Sen's Critique — Capabilities, functionings and well-being

Regardless of their other disagreements, virtually all commentators have defined poverty as a concept focused on income inadequacy. A more fundamental re-thinking of the meaning of poverty is provided by Amartya Sen, who argues that deprivation is not determined by what people possess, but by what it enables them to do. In other words, Sen distinguishes between the mere possession of certain goods, or the income that can command them and that which is truly significant — individual capabilities to meet social conventions, participate in social activities and maintain self-respect. Sen's capability approach concentrates on the tools and capacities available to people that allow them to shape their own lives.

These capabilities include having the resources necessary to make one's life something one has reason to value. They go beyond income to include health and the capacity and freedom (economic and political) to influence one's environment. This, in turn, draws our attention to the rights to those goods and the command families have over them, using various economic, political and social opportunities (de Haan 1998a: 14–15).

Sen sees life as consisting of a set of interrelated "functionings." These functionings vary from such basic ones such as being adequately nourished, being in good health and avoiding escapable morbidity and premature mortality, to more complex achievements such as being happy, having self-respect, taking part in the life of the community and so on. "The claim is that functionings are constitutive of a person's being, and an evaluation of well-being has to take the form of an assessment of these constituent elements" (Sen 1992: 39).

"Capabilities" consist of sets of possible functionings and reflect a person's freedom to lead one type of life or another. The "capability set" reflects the person's freedom to choose from possible livings (Sen 1992: 40).

Sen argues that achieved functionings constitute a person's well-being and that the capability to achieve functionings constitutes the person's real freedom — the real opportunities — to have well-being. It is equal freedom in this sense that Sen is arguing for — the equality of capability to achieve valuable functionings that make up our lives. This freedom is good for *instrumental* reasons (judging how good a "deal" an individual has), but also for *intrinsic* reasons — a society of freedom is also a good society. Choosing is itself a valuable part of living.

Sen therefore understands poverty as

> the failure of basic capabilities to reach certain minimally acceptable levels. The functionings relevant to this analysis can vary from elementary physical ones such as being well-nourished, being adequately clothed and sheltered, avoiding preventable morbidity, etc., to more complex social achievements such as taking part in the life of the community, being able to appear in public without shame, and so on. (Sen 1992: 110)

The social exclusion consequences of income inequality can be mitigated with broad-based basic health care and education services. Income, health and education inequalities are all basic since these are not only building blocks for capacities for basic survival, but also for capacities to live in good health and provide for oneself and one's family. Sen argues that income is not irrelevant, but insufficient to a proper understanding of deprivation:

> If we want to identify poverty in terms of income, it cannot be adequate to look only at incomes ... independently of the capability to function derivable from those incomes. Income adequacy to escape poverty varies with personal characteristics and circumstances. (Sen 1992: 110–11)

Sen reminds us that

> resources are important for freedom, and income is crucial for avoiding poverty. But if our concern is ultimately with freedom, we cannot — given human diversity — treat resources as the same thing as freedom. Similarly, if our concern is with the failure of certain minimal capabilities because of a lack of economic means, we cannot identify poverty simply as low income, dissociated from the interpersonally variable connection between income and capability.
> The idea of "income inadequacy"... goes well beyond that of

"low income" as such, since the former is sensitive to the conversion of income into capability in a way that the size of income cannot be. (Sen 1992: 112)

This notion of poverty is inescapably relative. Relative poverty "arises any time an individual cannot afford doing, or 'functioning' in the words of Sen, as 'most' people do in the society he/she is living in" (Bourgignon 1999: 2). In a market-based society, income and the command over resources it provides, is central to key capabilities: "Relative deprivation in terms of income, e.g., the inability to buy certain commodities, can become absolute deprivation in terms of capabilities. It can lead to the impossibility of certain social functions, for example, appearing in public without shame" (Sen 1992: 115; see also Abbey 1999: 2).

This also provides a critique of the idea of "equality of opportunity," which is particularly relevant for children. Because the outcomes of one generation shape the opportunities of the next, it is meaningless to try to separate equality of opportunity from substantive equality of outcomes.

Sen's work has been influential in shaping the United Nations' approach to poverty. To gauge human development, that is, realized capacities, the UN utilizes a set of indicators intended to assess foundation conditions, as well as achieved functionings. The widely quoted Human Development Index (HDI) includes four indicators: life expectancy, adult literacy, gross enrolment ratio and per capita income — indicators that represent foundation conditions such as achieved standard of living and achieved functionings in health and education. Since no single indicator, or even group of indicators, can satisfactorily describe national achievements in human development, the UN also publishes a Human Poverty Index for developing and developed countries (HPI-1 and HPI-2), and a Gender Development Index (GDI).

While the HDI measures average national achievements in the various dimensions, the Human Poverty Index looks at specific deprivations in those categories, measuring the probability of not surviving to age sixty, the adult illiteracy rate, the incidence of poverty and the long-term unemployment rate. The Gender Development Index looks at the same dimension of well-being as the HDI, but focuses on gender inequality by taking into account the differential achievements between men and women. A Gender Empowerment Measure further supplements this with measures of gender differences in economic and political opportunities.

As we shall argue in subsequent sections, relative deprivation in the sense of capabilities as defined by Sen is closely related to the concept of social exclusion.

# Exploring Social Inclusion and Exclusion

## Multi-dimensionality

A common element in many of the definitions of exclusion and inclusion is that they are multi-dimensional. That is, there are many different domains of potential deprivation that come into play singly or in combination to create exclusion. This is not entirely unique to the social inclusion literature. Many authors have pointed out that disadvantage and marginalization can take place in a variety of domains apart from the economic (Jenson 2000; Chambers 1983).

> While an absence of economic resources may, to be sure, characterize a marginalized group, lack of knowledge, political rights and capacity, recognition and power are also factors of marginalization. (Jenson 2000: 1)

One example of an attempt to operationalize the concept of exclusion is provided by de Haan (1998a), who provides a framework of dimensions of inclusion and exclusion that includes the physical, economic, human capital, social capital and political. An adapted version of de Haan's framework is presented in Table 1 and has been modified in two ways: first, we focused on Canada rather than on India, and second, we attempted to adapt it to focus on children. In some cases this involves changing the focus of traditional indicators to make the child the unit of analysis; in others it involves the development of new indicators and data sources. At this point it is important not to be limited by existing data.

The number of possible indicators is almost unlimited. Good indicators should satisfy a range of criteria (Bradshaw 2000: 20). These criteria might include the following:

- The indicators should cover the different dimensions of well-being.
- Indicators should focus on outcomes — the actual results of exclusion.
- Indicators should not be subject to administrative manipulation. For example, the number of households receiving social assistance is certainly an indicator of households seriously marginalized and distanced from the mainstream, but since eligibility rules and administrative procedures can have as large an impact on the size of the caseload as economic conditions or initiative in other policy areas, it is inadequate as an indicator.
- Data should be national, but also capture major distinctions relevant to the Canadian context — regional, urban/rural, age and immigration periods and racial divisions.
- Indicators should be comparable cross-nationally.

- As we are concerned with exclusion and inclusion among children, indicators should capture both current conditions of exclusion, as well as factors that are future and opportunity oriented — that affect the risk of exclusion in the future. Indicators should also reflect major life-cycle transitions among children (Endean 2001: 51).

## The dimensions of exclusion

Table 1 attempts to concretize the notion of exclusion along the major dimensions of well-being for children. In it, exclusion can take place in a number of dimensions: physical, economic, human assets, social assets (these last two terms are used in preference to the more commonly used "human capital" and "social capital" which imply a reduction of human life to economic purposes) and lastly political.

*Physical and economic dimensions* are foundation conditions for the inclusion of children, that is, they are necessary, if not sufficient conditions for maximizing the capabilities of children. Economic aspects include an indicator of inequality based on the argument that inequality itself matters in key areas of well-being and Sen's argument that relative deprivation in terms of incomes can lead to absolute deprivation in capabilities. The physical dimensions will include spatial aspects of inclusion, such as the housing and transportation infrastructure that are critical to both social and physical distance among people.

*Human assets* consist of outcome indicators such as the health indicators, which are also instrumental in enabling future capabilities. The education indicators are a mix of outcomes (attainment) and indicators of the quality of the environment in which we expect children to thrive.

*Social assets* also reflect individual characteristics (race and gender) that will play a role in shaping a child's opportunities as well as measures that reflect the degree of engagement with the rest of the community (opportunities for participation in organized groups).

*Political* — Children are traditionally excluded from politics in the limited sense of voting. But this is only a limited understanding of political inclusion in any event. In the case of children, political inclusion might be understood in a broader sense, where inclusion implies "an opportunity to participate in the public decision-making procedure which circumscribes his/her life chance" (Suzumara 1999, quoted in Freiler 2001b). This dimension of inclusion reflects the value placed on the capacity to choose as an element of well-being in Sen's capability framework.

At least some definitions suggest that exclusion implies multiple and overlapping sources of deprivation. Empirically, apart from a small and severely disadvantaged minority, most people do not appear to suffer from multiple disadvantages (Phipps 2000; Brandolini 2000). However, while many forms of deprivation do not necessarily overlap, poverty and inequality are intimately linked with many, if not most dimensions of exclusion — health, discrimination, housing and neighbourhoods, political participation and voice.

The framework presented in Table 1 makes clear that exclusion is not simply co-extensive with poverty, at least in the conventional sense of income and assets (Atkinson 1998; Klasen 1998). Atkinson, for example, has argued that poverty, unemployment and exclusion are related, but distinct concepts. They often coincide, but need not. "People may be poor without being socially excluded ... People may be socially excluded without being poor" (Atkinson 1998: 9). In the former case, in a society where poverty is widespread one wouldn't necessarily be socially excluded. Similarly, if poverty is a temporary phenomenon it needn't lead to exclusion. In this case, policy will have much to do with the risks of short-term poverty leading to exclusion. In the latter case, people can be the victims of discrimination without necessarily being poor, although, again, the two often go together.

UN reports make it clear that the link between affluence and human development is not automatic. Income is important, but only part of what is required; a means, with human development the end (UNDP 1997:14). Countries with comparable levels of income per capita can, and often do, have very different levels of human development — that is, very different achievements in converting income into capabilities (UNDP 2000: 148). Similarly, employment can increase capacity and autonomy, but may not if it is low-wage, contingent, incompatible with parenting or saps employees of their self-respect. With these thoughts in mind, one can examine government policies to assess whether they enhance or inhibit the capacity and autonomy of marginalized Canadians.

However, at least in market-based societies income and well-being are inextricably tied, as a means of acquiring the goods and services that are necessary, as part of "the good life," and as a measure of status in and of itself. "People may be excluded if they are unable to participate in the customary consumption activities of the society in which they live" (Atkinson 1998: 10).

Employment is an important source of well-being, quite apart from the income it generates. Unemployment may lead to poverty and social exclusion, but importantly it need not, depending on the duration of the experience, the social security system, family arrangements and culture (Saraceno 2001: 6). The rate of poverty among the unemployed varies dramatically from country to county (Saraceno 2001: 12). The increase in unemployment in Europe has not been accompanied by an increase in poverty like that experienced by North Americans because of stronger income protection. Similarly, labour market policy can seek high employment, and therefore high likelihood of the unemployed being reabsorbed. This is a reflection of Klasen's point that exclusion can be the result of direct sources of disadvantage, but may also be the result of policy responses to those original sources of disadvantage (Klasen 1998: 9).

Atkinson (1998) points out that exclusion is necessarily relative, that

## Table 1 – Operationalizing Exclusion for Children

| Dimension | Aspect | Indicators |
|---|---|---|
| Physical | Location | Geographic isolation |
| | | Access to public parks (clean, safe) |
| | Infrastructure | Access to public transit |
| | | Availability of public library |
| | Housing | Children in "core housing need' |
| | | Children in shelters or temporary accommodation |
| | | Tenure |
| | | Shelter costs |
| Economic | Income | Child and family poverty |
| | | Duration of poverty |
| | | Intra-family distribution of income |
| | | Gini index of income inequality |
| | Labour market | Parental employment |
| | | Job quality |
| | | Youth unemployment |
| | Assets | Non-pension financial assets per family member |
| Human assets | Health | Low-birth weight |
| | | Infant mortality |
| | | Child mortality |
| | | Disability |
| | | Access to health services — coverage by supplementary health care insurance |
| | Education | Quality of school environment (including teaching resources, extra-curricular activities) |
| | | Educational attainment |
| Social assets | Social background | Gender |
| | | Race |
| | Civic engagement | Opportunities for participation in organized sports |
| | Psychological | Self-esteem |
| | | Teen suicide |
| Political | Power | Formal legal rights |
| | | Procedural access |
| | Participation | Consultation versus power |
| | Agency | Effective political participation |
| | Citizenship | Immigrants, non-citizens |

Source: Adapted from de Haan (1998b: 15); Freiler (2001b)

people can only be excluded in relation to something else. Atkinson also adds a dynamic, future-oriented element to the analysis, arguing that people are excluded not just because they are currently without a job or income, but because they have few prospects for the future.

To make a point that will be taken up in greater detail later, low unemployment, like adequate income, is probably a necessary, but not a sufficient condition for inclusion. Although unemployment can lead to social exclusion, employment is not a guarantee of inclusion. Marginal forms of work and "flexibility" of the labour market are potential routes to exclusion through employment.

## Process and agency

A second advantage of the concept of exclusion/inclusion is that it focuses on exclusionary forces. Exclusion and inclusion are active terms and suggest that they are the result of processes and acts by identifiable institutions and individual actors. They directly address who and what is responsible for impoverishment and marginalization — the institutions and individuals responsible for excluding or including. Although it is common in traditional poverty analysis to go beyond simply presenting the numbers of people who fall below a poverty threshold, to focus on the structures and policies that have created that deprivation, a focus on inclusion makes these central questions.

The concept goes beyond the description of deprivation to focus on the social relations and the processes and institutions that underlie it. This can represent a shift away from looking at deprivation in terms of individual attributes and towards a focus on mechanisms, institutions and actors that are responsible for deprivation. It explicitly makes possible a discussion of power and inequality.

Social and political actors and institutions create exclusion, and the focus on these actors and processes is one of the advantages of examining social exclusion. Klasen and others have made the point that government policy plays a role in exclusion. Policy can create exclusion, and it can reinforce disadvantages emanating from other sources, transforming original disadvantage into exclusion. Job loss or marital breakdown can create instability and result in a loss of income and status. How policy responds to these conditions can further entrench people in poverty and/ or compound these disadvantages and misfortunes to create exclusion. As Saraceno (2001: 25) puts it: "... many rules concerning entitlement to social and political rights act effectively to exclude groups who cannot fulfill the set requirements: e.g., time rules concerning residence, or definitions of what counts as work...."

Again adapting from de Haan (1998b), Table 2 attempts to operationalize the institutions and processes responsible for exclusion. Note that the examples are hypothetical only to illustrate how these ideas

## Table 2 — The Institutions and Processes of Exclusion

| Aspect | Indicator | Institutions/agents | Processes |
|---|---|---|---|
| Location | Geographic isolation Access to public parks and spaces | Local government planners. Neighbourhood and ratepayer associations. | Municipal zoning practices and planning process. NUMBYism |
| Infrastructure | Access to public transit Availability of public library | Transportation planners/government officials | Local and senior government budget processes |
| Housing | Children in "core housing need' Children in shelters or temporary accommodation Tenure Shelter costs | Landlords Politicians Administrative restrictions; by-laws, lease, restrictions associated with social housing | Discrimination Evasion of tenancy laws Budget priority-setting process |
| Income | Child and family poverty Duration of poverty Gini index of income inequality Intra-family distribution of income | Labour market Government authorities Culture and custom Men | Macro-economic policy Income security policy Local economic policy (i.e., labour matching, training policy) Gender discrimination |
| Labour Market | Parental unemployment Youth unemployment Wealth, home ownership | Labour market Government authorities Employers | Macro-economic policy. Local economic policy (i.e., labour matching, training policy) |
| Assets | Low-birth weight Infant mortality | | Discrimination Security against financial mishaps |
| Health | Child mortality Disability Access to health services — coverage by supplementary health care insurance | Public health system Private/public health insurance | Access to needed health care services, devices, drugs etc. |
| Education | Educational attainment Drop-out Educational streaming Integration of children with special needs | Public educational system | Tuition, user fees for education, access to student loans and childcare |
| Social Background | Gender Race | Systemic sexism and racism | Sexism and racism |
| Civic Engagement | Participation — sports groups, clubs, other organized groups. | Community and school based sports, volunteer and community groups | |
| Psychological | Self-esteem | | |
| Agency | Economic, civic and personal autonomy | Multitude of public and private institutions | Capacity (including legal protections, voting, economic and social autonomy) |

Adapted from de Haan 1998b: 21.

might be put into practice. However, it is apparent from Table 2 that the identification of institutions and actors, and the processes through which exclusion or inclusion occur, are not fixed or predetermined, but reflect the ideological preferences and social, political context.

The weakening of a strong primary tier of income support such as unemployment insurance, as has been the case in Canada repeatedly in the 1990s, can mean that the unemployed are forced to rely more on their individual resources or social assistance as a means of support. The former implies exhausting assets intended for other purposes. The latter implies subjecting oneself to the highly stigmatizing social assistance system in which recipients have been demonized to the public as "dependants," drug addicts or illiterates (Mitchell 2001). The stigma of social assistance is so great that the recipients frequently hide their status from friends, neighbours, family and even their own children. Typically benefits are so low that recipients are not merely impoverished but precluded from participating in many of the typical activities of the wider society. This can result in a profound social isolation that can prevent people from interacting with the rest of the community, even in activities that do not require money.

Also housing policies can create marginalized ghettos, or ensure economically and socially diverse neighbourhoods — tackling the potential for exclusion in the "location" and "housing" areas identified in Table 2. Lack of a housing program — effectively rationing housing according to market outcomes — means that for low-income families this original source of market disadvantage is compounded when they are forced into poorer housing, concentrated in low-income neighbourhoods where they are physically and socially distanced from other members of the community. This result clearly exacerbates economic and social differences, undermining the work that institutions such as public education can achieve in bridging social distance. There is evidence of this process of "economic spatial segregation" in major cities across Canada (Myles et al. 2000).

In a similar fashion, policies in the fields of health, education and housing often accentuate social exclusion. For instance, while health and education programs targeted at marginalized populations do provide assistance, they also exaggerate the sense of separateness experienced by members of these populations.

With reference to Table 2, we can also talk about how policy is formed as an aspect of creating inclusion. The process of creating policy has characteristics that can create exclusion or promote inclusion. Citizens can experience a lack of "voice" — i.e., the absence of excluded individuals from policy debates that directly affect them. This exclusion and lack of effective voice is not experienced similarly across the population — low-income Canadians are more profoundly excluded from policy debates that affect them than high-income Canadians, who have greater access to the political and policy process. This is a form of social exclusion — low-income Canadians are disenfranchised to the extent that they have no effective impact on the design of programs that are significant for their well-being.

Public officials under political direction design programs, that is, government programs that support low-income Canadians are designed and administered by individuals who are not low-income. The interests of the low-income beneficiaries are presented only through benevolence. Politicians and public officials will respond to a perceived issue of concern, while recognizing that their political masters can succeed without the support of low-income Canadians. This leaves the way open for poor design, arbitrary exclusions and contradictory and capricious regulations.

The professional scrutiny that protects the interests of the affluent is largely absent. There is little analysis or study of low-income support programs. In contrast, consider the scrutiny that the income tax system is subject to. A highly educated and well-endowed analytical community — referred to as "Bay Street" — studies the legislation in detail and can articulate and promote the changes needed from their perspective. Using the press and political connections, they can advocate for changes to legislation to correct features that do not serve their clients' interests.

Contrast this with programs such as welfare, subsidized housing and subsidized child-care. No organization analyzes the combined effect of the various programs that benefit low-income Canadians. So, there is little well informed and documented research of the impact of the programs. There is no source of information that low-income people can access that will indicate how they can organize their finances to maximize their benefits. The financial community that provides this service for middle- and high-income Canadians does not have the information or motivation to provide this service for low-income Canadians. There is no political interest or broader social interest in improving program design for low-income Canadians.

## Policy Implications: Promoting Inclusion or Preventing Exclusion?

### Perspectives on social inclusion and exclusion

Multi-dimensionality, the importance of actors and processes and the centrality of inequality are all important aspects of inclusion. However, this recognition does not take us very far in terms of policy.

According to Novick (2001), the central question confronting an agenda of social inclusion is the same question confronting social policy throughout its history: Should policy address failures in existing social and economic structures that fail to create inclusive conditions for all citizens, or is it the task of policy to integrate the marginalized into fundamentally just and sound structures? The distinction between the two is the difference between creating inclusion and preventing exclusion — that is, who is required to adjust.

The different answers to that question illustrate the different ideological preferences and perspectives on what constitutes exclusion and therefore form the backdrop to policies intended to promote inclusion. Perspectives on social inclusion reflect differing assumptions about its root causes, and therefore its solutions. Silver (1994) and Levitas (1998) have attempted to identify distinguishable threads among varying uses of the term. Both identify three distinct approaches to social exclusion, and both are clear that the different uses of the term "are embedded in conflicting social science paradigms and political ideologies" (Silver 1994: 6).

Silver labels her categories the solidarity, specialization and monopoly paradigms, which correspond to the French, British and Nordic traditions respectively and are grounded in the different political philosophies that have shaped each tradition's understanding of disadvantage. In a similar way, Levitas labels her "three discourses" of exclusion: social integrationist, redistributionist and moral underclass. The three approaches differ in how they identify the boundary between insiders and outsiders, and therefore how to achieve inclusion (Levitas 1998: 7).

Under the social integration view of social exclusion, which Levitas labels SID (for Social Integration Discourse), unemployment is seen as the main cause of exclusion. Paid employment is seen as a critical component of identity and self-esteem, and therefore necessarily the principal means of inclusion.

Typically, for those following this approach the principal concern is *social cohesion* built on the norm of employment. The problem of exclusion is seen in terms of its effect on the wider society — exclusion undermines cohesion and in doing so, imposes costs on society.

Indicators of success in fighting exclusion from this perspective would be an increase in the participation rate, particularly among target groups such as youth, or long-term unemployed. Inclusion through work is not addressed through employment, but instead is reduced to *employability* as the goal of policy. Reducing overall patterns of inequality is not the goal of fighting exclusion, but rather, merely to lift the excluded over the minimal threshold of inclusion through paid work. It is the marginalized whose exclusion is to be addressed by incorporating them into existing norms through employment.

The focus on the paid labour market results in ignoring the role and value of unpaid work and caring responsibilities. It also obscures gender, race and other inequalities in the labour market.

In the *moral underclass* (MUD) variant of social exclusion, the focus is on the moral and behavioural deficiencies of the excluded themselves, which defines the boundary between the included and the excluded.

The central concern of this approach is the avoidance of dependence, which is thought to be one of the side effects of income support. Income support is thought to destroy initiative, independence and self-respect. Work is a moral necessity to avoid dependence, and coercion in this regard is justified. Reducing the number of people on unemployment insurance and social assistance would be a key indicator of success in fighting exclusion. However, as Saraceno (2001: 16) points out, the reason why receipt of social assistance might lead to exclusion might have less to do with its corrupting influence than its programmatic stigmatizing design — social assistance may foster exclusion because it is designed that way.

In the *redistributionist* or RED variant of exclusion, the central concerns are poverty and inequality and the impacts of exclusion on the lives of the excluded themselves. Unemployment is thought to be a prime cause of poverty, and the realization of equal opportunity is recognized as resting on a degree of substantive equality. In this variant there is greater emphasis on the responsibility of the larger society to create inclusive conditions. Where jobs are available, compulsion is thought to be unnecessary, and possibly destructive to self-esteem and a route to further exclusion, when they are not. For RED therefore, a key indicator in the fight against exclusion would be the absolute and relative living standards of the poor — the extent and depth of poverty and a measure of income inequality like the Gini index.

For SID and MUD, and also to a lesser extent RED, paid work is seen as a key element in inclusion. The redistributionist variant would add the caveat that the quality of the work is also important and must reduce poverty. However, there is the possibility that inclusion in paid work may interfere with inclusion in other respects, due to long hours and the impact on family life and an increase in women's workload. The negatives of employment — stress, lack of parenting time and the inability to participate in a child's schooling — are not seen as contributing to exclusion. This illustrates how narrow policy responses to exclusion are, as well as their failure to address key dimensions of exclusion. In our view, these failures prevent such policy from being a sound basis for inclusion in anything other than the narrowest terms.

## The limits to inclusion through work

Many writers have emphasized the centrality of work to social inclusion and the importance of the income, self-esteem, social links and integration that are thought to occur through employment. The European Commission stated that "employment is the key route to integration and social inclusion; unemployment is the major factor of exclusion, particularly long-term unemployment and the increasing concentration of unemployment in households with no one in work" (Commission of the European Communities 2000: 6).

Of course, this is in no small way socially and policy-constructed. If employment creates inclusion, and non-work is socially unacceptable, it is in part because we have constructed social and economic arrangements this way, and fashioned policy to reinforce these preferences.

The moral crusade against dependence, which is the overriding concern of MUD, typically manifests itself in a highly restrictive approach to income support benefits and eligibility. Programs that owe their inspiration more to SID add to these strategies to quickly integrate people into the workforce through labour force attachment programs.

In brief, our contention is that the narrow focus of such policy responses ignores key dimensions of inclusion and therefore cannot serve as a credible basis for inclusive policy. Moreover, policies that purport to promote inclusion through work and employability are not even very successful on these limited terms. Poverty and inequality, not to mention the many other facets of full inclusion must be key components of a strategy of inclusion in order to be faithful to a multi-dimensional conception of inclusion.

The limits to inclusion through work are evident enough. In 1998, in the midst of a robust economic recovery when the official rate of unemployment had fallen to 8.3 percent from over 11 percent at the trough of the recession, the rate of poverty in Canada remained close to the levels experienced in the worst part of the recession. In fact, for the first time since incomes and poverty have been regularly reported in Canada, a recovery has not been accompanied by a significant decline in poverty (Figure 1).

It is a commonplace observation, but significant in this context, that work itself does not guarantee freedom from poverty. In 1998, 18 percent of two-parent families with a single earner were poor. Adding a second earner reduced the risk of poverty to 3.7 percent. Among sole-support parents, 27.2 percent of those with earnings (three-quarters of all such families) remained poor. Among unattached individuals, 20.5 percent of non-elderly male earners were poor in 1998, as were 25.9 percent of non-elderly female earners (Statistics Canada 2000b).

In fact, in 1996, 5 percent of families with a head who was a full-time, full-year worker were still poor, as were 10.4 percent of unattached individuals who were full-time, full-year workers. Put yet another way, 19.6 percent of poor families were headed by a full-time, full-year worker, and 9.5 percent of poor individuals also worked full-time, full-year (Statistics Canada 1997).

Moreover, low-wage and precarious employment is becoming an entrenched feature of the economy. Not only is the incidence of low-wage employment increasing, but it is also becoming more difficult to move up and out of bad jobs (Finnie 1997). While there is significant mobility upwards and out of poverty, those who leave poverty tend not to rise very far (Finnie 2000). The number of families whose market income fell below

## Figure 1 — Unemployment rate versus poverty/Canada 1980–2000

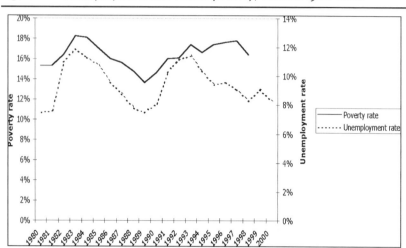

## Figure 2 — Distribution by market income groups, all families and unattached individuals, Canada, 1980–1998

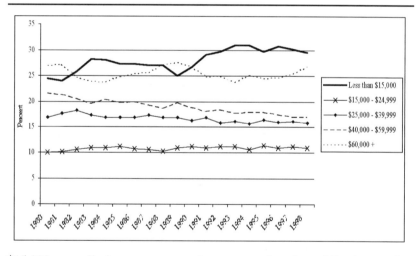

$15,000 annually has grown over the past two decades, while the number with middle-level incomes has shrunk (Figure 2). A growing proportion of jobs are either part-time or contingent/temporary.

Of course there is another side to the polarization of the labour market. The number of people working long hours is increasing and there is evidence that this too can be harmful to health and linked to other forms of exclusion, what Jackson and Scott (2001) have termed "hyper-inclusion" in the labour market:

An increasing number of workers report they experience more fatigue, time pressure, speedup and inability to achieve a desired balance in their lives between paid work and their family, personal and civic time. (Golden and Figart 2000)

Discrimination will also limit the inclusion of many people through the labour market. Ornstein (2000) finds evidence of substantial occupational segregation (to low-skill jobs) and higher rates of part-time work among racially identified groups in the City of Toronto. What are termed "ethnic economies" exist to some extent in cities with high levels of immigration, in which immigrant groups find employment in certain segments and niches, but which can limit their access to the broader labour market. Mere inclusion in the labour market will do nothing to address the exclusionary forces of discrimination.

### Policies to combat exclusion internationally

Space does not permit anything other than a few observations regarding policy agendas implemented internationally to combat exclusion. However, a review of three significant strands of policy, in Great Britain, France and North America, highlights some of the major points of departure for policy.

# Great Britain

British usage of the term has its origins in liberal individualism and is highly influenced by social policy developments imported from the United States, redefining citizenship in terms of duties and obligations rather than the Marshallian notion of political, civil and social rights (Abbey 1999: 2).

The Social Exclusion Unit of the Cabinet Office has a wide-ranging research agenda on a variety of topics related to social exclusion, focused particularly on severely and multiply deprived populations: truants, rough sleepers (homeless), poor neighbourhoods; teenagers not in education employment or training; and pregnant teenagers. However, these are mostly for rhetorical show. The centrepiece is clearly New Labour's New Deal welfare-to-work program. It is the only one to date that has actually been translated into policy with substantial budgetary backing. Table 3 outlines the major elements of the New Deal.

New Labour's New Deal has a clear emphasis on employability and promoting labour market attachment, reducing the problem of exclusion to exclusion from the paid labour market, and then to individual at-tributes and attitudes. "There will be no fifth option — to stay at home on full benefit" according to the oft-repeated refrain of the chancellor, employing North American anti-welfare dependency rhetoric and redolent of Levitas' moral underclass discourse of exclusion.

**Table 3 — Great Britain's "New Deal'**

| Target group | Programming |
| --- | --- |
| 1. Aged 18–25 and unemployed more than six months | Subsidized job with an employer (£60 per week subsidy for six months; also £750 per person training allowance);<br>Full-time education and training;<br>Voluntary sector job;<br>Environmental Task Force. |
| 2. Unemployed for two years or more | Wage subsidy of £75 pounds for 6 months |
| 3. Lone parents whose youngest child is in the 2nd term of full-time schooling | Lone-parents on income support will be "invited"to a Job Centre to develop an action plan. Participation is voluntary<br>Participants are fast-tracked for Family Credit and child maintenance. |
| 4. Disabled in receipt of disability and incapacity benefits | |

Source: Peck 2001: 304–305.

No consideration is given to the quality of employment or to other aspects of exclusion that may in fact be exacerbated through promoting labour market attachment among some groups, such as lone parents, and attention to barriers such as the need for additional education and training and other supports is limited.

If SID- and MUD-inspired anti-exclusion policies in fact reinforce exclusion by re-casting their subjects as somehow separate and different from the rest of the "hard-working population"; defective, in skills or other personal attributes, even the financing of the New Deal program reinforces this exclusionary message. Money for the program came from a special one-time tax on privatized utilities, which communicated the message that financing the New Deal would not require a contribution from other taxpayers, now or in the future (Peck 2001: 301).

## France

In contrast to the narrowness of the New Deal there is the breadth of policy that is wielded to combat exclusion in France.[4] The 1998 *Loi de prévention et de lutte contre les exclusions* of the Jospin government contained policies in a number of areas: employment and training, on both the supply and demand side, income support, housing and homelessness, health care, education, social services, citizenship and political rights, culture and citizenship. "Just as exclusion is conceived as having many economic and social dimensions, so the anti-exclusion law has a number of parts." (Silver 1998: 46)

## Table 4 — Act to Combat and Prevent Exclusion, Jospin Government 1998

| | |
|---|---|
| Employment and Training | Capacity building for insertion of young and adult job-seekers and prevention of long-term unemployment; Training policies; Business programs; Labour market regulation. |
| Hiring and other incentives for business | For example, short-term exemptions from social charges to create business. |
| Third sector | Double number of businesses supporting integration; PLIE (local partnerships for employment); Solidarity subsidies for vacations, especially in public interest grouping of charitable and unemployment associations. |
| Changes to social minima | Work incentives for RMI, ASS and API allowing a declining portion of part-time, minimum-wage earnings to be kept over the first year of employment; ASS (targetted solidarity allocations), API (support to isolated parents) benefits raised and indexed to prices; Minimum income at RMI level guaranteed in other programs; Program to allow over-indebted and bankrupt people to extend re-payments and so earn income and keep homes; Reduced gap between CES (solidarity employment contracts) and social minima. |
| Housing and homelessness policies (subsequently ruled unconstitutional) | Housing solidarity funds; Tax on vacant property; Protection from eviction; Policy to encourage geographic and social mixing. |
| Health | Universal coverage; Regional access to hospitals and general medicine. |
| Education | Re-launch ZEP (priority education zones). |
| Social services | Mobile emergency units to prevent family breakups and utility cut-offs. |
| Citizenship | Help homeless to vote, to get legal assistance, a bank account and national identification. |
| Culture | Access to artistic and cultural practices; cultural establishments combat exclusion; mediator jobs. |

Source: Silver 1998: 38–73.

The employment aspect of the French law is especially noteworthy for going well beyond the narrow supply-side focus of British policy. It includes not just the expected supply and matching policies, but also policies to enhance the demand side of the labour market, to promote equality in the labour market and policies for helping to balance family and work.

In this breadth one can recognize an attempt to address both of Saraceno's levels of exclusion: the macro issues that create exclusion, as well as the micro experiences which create a lack of belonging for individuals.

## Welfare-to-What in North America?

Social inclusion, or exclusion, as a focus of policy, is still in its infancy in North America so it is in some ways premature to characterize it. While policy exists to address some dimensions of inclusion, others are ignored, and none are part of a coordinated inclusion agenda. Of course, Canada does enjoy universal public health care and education. However, it has been noted above how the benefits of one policy — public education — can be undermined by a failure to address the exclusion created by another policy — housing. In the absence of any comprehensive view of inclusion it appears that policy in Canada is drifting towards an understanding of exclusion and inclusion firmly rooted in the moral underclass (MUD) and social integration approaches (SID).[5] Federal and provincial housing programs have been terminated or gutted, child benefits have been revamped to encourage paid work and social assistance programs have become ever more fixated on promoting work, to the exclusion of protecting the well-being of recipients.

If there is a policy direction that most clearly reflects the underlying social exclusion philosophy of SID and MUD it would have to be the welfare-to-work programs that are epidemic in North America, and have now migrated to Europe. Such programs are the very manifestation of attempts to integrate the excluded through employment. It is important to understand, review and critique welfare-to-work programs from an inclusion perspective because this is the policy mechanism through which the promotion of inclusion through work is most likely to manifest itself in Canada.

Such programs are typically narrowly focused on immediate employability and involve only minimal investments in skills. Their goal is rapid employment at low cost. It is here that the limitations of promoting inclusion for disadvantaged groups through labour market attachment are most evident.

The outcomes of such programs are at best modest, even by their own narrow employment and earnings objectives, never mind any broader standard such as those implied by social inclusion. Jobs held by former welfare recipients tend to be low-skill, low-paid and unstable. Upward mobility is limited. Few provide any benefits. Unemployment and welfare recidivism are high. This has been shown to be the case in such divergent jurisdictions as the United States (Friedlander and Burtless 1995; Loprest 2001; Boushey and Gundersen 2001), Ontario (Mitchell 1998; Ontario 1998), Alberta (Shillington 1998; Elton et al. 1997), New Brunswick and British Columbia (Card and Robbins 1996) and Quebec (Reynolds 1995).

Research in both Canada and the U.S. has shown that a large proportion of those leaving assistance experience critical hardships, even when employed after leaving welfare (Loprest 2001; Boushey and Gundersen 2001; Elton et al. 1997). Large numbers of former recipients *who were working* report critical hardships such as going without food, being unable to pay housing or utility bills or losing their housing altogether (Loprest 2001). Large numbers also report serious hardships such as worries about basic needs and inadequate supports and services such as health care and child-care (Boushey and Gundersen 2001).

What is less well-documented is the impact of welfare reform on dimensions of child and family well-being other than the narrowly economic. There is, in policy circles, a presumption of the virtuous impact of parental employment for the family, regardless of its quality, elevating paid work above all other functions, if not completely ignoring any possible valued role that a parent might play. However, there is a growing number of anecdotal and journalistic accounts of the increased stress of combining low-paid work and parenting as a result of welfare reform. The few studies that included measures of child and family well-being have found that, as with the economic outcomes, improvements in child and family well-being were mixed, with some indicators showing improvements on average, with others showing negative or no change.[6] The outcomes were also mixed in terms of relationships with children and friends (Knox et al. 2000; Bancroft and Currie 1995: 14; Morris and Michalopoulos 2000).

What of the broader inclusive effects of such policies? Clearly these limited investments address few of the potential dimensions of child well-being, or the processes of exclusion and inclusion outlined earlier, apart from that which flows from parental employment.

If concerns about social cohesion have emerged in the wake of widespread economic dislocation, then one way of understanding such policies is as a partial attempt to restore cohesion, in a context where the traditional tools of governments are being undermined or removed. Such policies may allow the marginalized at least some contact with the wider society and the social norm of employment, if intermittently and in the lower tier of the labour market. From a policy-maker's perspective this may prevent complete exclusion, with wider social consequences that may accompany a breakdown in social cohesion. If such policies do not promote full inclusion they may at least prevent total exclusion and the perceived threat to cohesion that may accompany it.

Policy agendas that focus simply on inclusion through the labour market and employability fail to address issues of poverty and inequality that are necessary, if not sufficient, to promote social inclusion. They fail to address the quality of employment and the possible role that low-wage employment may have in *reinforcing* economic exclusion, not to mention the many other dimensions of possible exclusion. Perhaps still worse, it is possible, if not indeed likely, that a policy-created low-wage labour supply will help to reshape the contingent labour market, expanding the supply of such jobs as employers readjust their employment to take advantage of the labour supply (Peck 1998).

Such policies may well reduce the numbers on assistance, but in-work poverty and inequality may increase, as the social distance between social assistance recipients, the working poor and the rest of society widens. As such one would have to conclude that they promote one narrow and incomplete dimension of inclusion while sacrificing many others.

## Conclusions and Implications for Practice

The concept of social inclusion, particularly as described using Sen's concept of capacity is a more complete model for tracking social well-being than simple income or employment. While these are important foundation conditions for family and child well-being, they are insufficient mechanisms for full inclusion on their own. The difference being spoken of is the difference between being a consumer and being a citizen. What is needed are policies that promote people's capacities to act as citizens with equal freedom to conduct a life they have reason to value.

For those who wish to promote an agenda of inclusion this implies further changes in focus that are subtle, but important. It implies a focus on capabilities and achieved outcomes rather than simply foundation conditions such as income. This also implies that supports should provide not only the income necessary to purchase necessities, but also should facilitate employment (effective access to child-care), education (including secondary and post-secondary) and regulations that do not punish economic behaviour such as saving.

Second, as a frame for social policy this concept requires that we take a more holistic view of child and family well-being. This in turn requires that we recognize the interrelationship of various forms of exclusion.

Third, it suggests a greater priority be given to looking at the potential, and limitations, of local governments, for promoting inclusion. While senior levels of government can have greater influence over foundation conditions, cities can do much to lessen other aspects of social and physical distance among people (Andrew 2001). And citizens have great confidence in their ability to understand and respond to the social needs of communities (Community Social Planning Council of Toronto 2001).

Fourth, the focus on the actors and processes through which inclusion can be created suggests that we need to look beyond the *content* of policy, to also scrutinize the *way* in which policy is made. This would offer some check against poor design, arbitrary exclusions, contradictory and capricious regulations.

One subtle form of social exclusion comes from the political process. This leads to exclusion from policy development. As a consequence, income and social support programs are developed by upper- and middle-income professionals "on behalf of" lower-income populations. This not only undermines the effectiveness of the programs, but also underlines the social exclusion of vulnerable populations as they are alienated from the development of policies and programs that affect their lives.

The growing number of national governments that identify social exclusion as a priority problem to be addressed, as well as a focus for policy provides an opportunity. Although there is a wide difference in understanding of what promoting inclusion might mean, it is no broader than the different points of view on what it means to fight poverty. The challenge is to do this without losing the significance of poverty and inequality, violations of the foundation conditions necessary to pursue valued lives.

However, if social inclusion doesn't come equipped with all of the answers, it may encourage us to better ask the right questions and provide an opportunity for additional points of discussion and debate.

## Notes

1. Indeed it appears that the major distinction Sen draws between the two concepts is based upon the difference between "active" versus "passive" exclusion and the consequent policy implications (Das Gupta 1999: 2).
2. The concentration on income is understandable. It is clearly significant but it is also possible that it has been given more weight simply because income is easier to measure than health, literacy, social development and political engagement.
3. The unemployment rate has since fallen to around 7 percent (Statistics Canada 2000a).
4. One can admire the breadth of policy thinking, without necessarily supporting the underlying social integrationist and cohesion objectives of the program.
5. See for example, Michael Hatfield's presentation to the Laidlaw Foundation conference (Hatfield 2001), in which the problem of exclusion is defined as persistent low income then reduced to exclusion from paid work.
6. Impacts on family life were measured in terms of marriage rates, home ownership, quality of home environment, depression, domestic violence, child behaviour, self-perceived health, school performance and school engagement. Slightly more than half of the indicators had positive changes that were statistically significant, the others were either negative, or not significant. Marginal positive improvements on average suggest that many respondents would have experienced negative outcomes.

# Social Inclusion through Early Childhood Education and Care

*Martha Friendly and Donna Lero*

> Comprehensive early childhood care is a key to creating a world characterized by hope and change rather than by deprivation and despair and to building countries that are thriving and free. (United Nations Children's Fund 2001)

## Introduction

This chapter explores how childhood education and care services contribute to social inclusion in society. Its basic premise is that "the process of development is an expansion of human freedom" (Sen 1999: 1). It draws on Amartya Sen's conception that a society that promotes a high degree of social inclusion is one in which members participate meaningfully and actively, have varied opportunities for joining in collective experiences, enjoy equality, share social experiences and attain fundamental well-being. In this sense, an inclusive society provides equality of life chances and offers all citizens a basic level of well-being (ibid. 2000). Our definition of social inclusion features an active, transformative process of policy and program development designed to reduce barriers, promote human development, create the kind of community-based infrastructure that directly contributes to children's development and provide opportunities for children and families to participate meaningfully in their communities and to be valued. We make the case that, under the right conditions, early childhood education and care, or ECEC, can be a primary means to enhance this kind of social inclusion.

The chapter's main purpose is to examine the circumstances under which ECEC services contribute to this conception of social inclusion, and when they don't. The following section examines the key concepts upon which this is based. Then, applying a framework drawn from an international policy study, we consider the specific policy and program elements that enable ECEC services to contribute to social inclusion. Finally, we examine whether the current ECEC situation in Canada is constructed and supported in ways that contribute to social inclusion, what changes are needed to enable it to do so, some implications for practice and future policy directions.

The definition of ECEC employed here is one commonly used in Canada and internationally to describe ECEC broadly and holistically to:

reflect the growing consensus in OECD countries that "care" and "education" are inseparable concepts ... the use of the term ECEC supports an integrated and coherent approach to policy and provision, which is inclusive of all children and all parents regardless of employment or socioeconomic status. This approach recognizes that such arrangements may fulfill a wide range of objectives including care, learning and social support. (OECD 2001: 14)

At a practical level, this encompasses childcare centres and other "care" services like family daycare as well as kindergartens and nursery/preschools whose primary purpose is "early childhood education." Some elements of family resource programs (which tend to be more focused on supporting parents than on providing "care" or "early childhood education") are included as well. These are all intended to enhance child development and well-being, and to support parents in a variety of ways, in and out of the paid workforce.

## Basic Concepts

The approach to social inclusion and early childhood education and care used in this chapter is based on four concepts. The first is that the development of talents, skills and capabilities in the early years has an effect not only on childhood well-being, but also on the social, educational, financial and personal domains as children mature into adulthood. This concept of social inclusion as "the goal and the process of developing the talents, skills and capabilities of children to participate in the social and economic mainstream of community life by providing the opportunities and removing the barriers for children" (Freiler 2000) provides a key rationale for the importance of investing in ECEC. According to Sen's conception, the capabilities "that adults enjoy are deeply conditional on their experiences as children" (1999: 5) and expand the possibilities that people can "lead the kind of lives they value" (1999: 18). Thus, what happens in the early years has implications "not only for what happens in childhood but also for future life" (Sen 1999: 2). In this paradigm, political, social and economic institutions have important roles as agents that support and enhance human development and thus, freedom. That "the child is father to the man" is one important reason it is imperative that ECEC environments are designed to be truly developmental.

Second, the family and its environment — shaped by class, income and culture — have a significant impact on the developing child. The family's experience of exclusion and inclusion affects not only its adult members, but also its children during childhood and over the life cycle. Children are dependent on their families for income, care, food, shelter, health and safety and relationships. Consequently, while children's well-being and future prospects can be affected directly by developmental, enriching environments, they are also enhanced if their families are sustained economically and socially through employment, income security and community supports. In this way, social exclusion and inclusion are mediated through the family as well as directly experienced by the child. This suggests why it is important for children as well as for parents that ECEC services are sensitive to parents' employment, training and social needs as well as supportive of child development and well-being.

A third basic concept is that social inclusion is not merely the converse of social exclusion but is used to connote an assertive approach, not just amelioration of deficits. Thus, social inclusion is not only about mitigating vulnerabilities in a remedial approach to life chances, but also about developing talents, skills and capabilities in a more proactive, hopeful model (Freiler 2000). In this conception, social inclusion is not only about reducing risk, but also about ensuring that opportunities are not missed. This has significant implications for whether ECEC services are mostly offered to those presumed to be at risk or are freely available for all children in a universal model.

A final concept relates to the nature of childhood. We propose that while developing talents, skills and capabilities in early childhood is appropriate and important, children are not merely adults-in-training. Thus, children should be valued as children, not simply for what they may become later on. This relates to the extent to which developmental capabilities are valued primarily because they create human capital for the future labour force or because children are valued as citizens with entitlement to a fair share of society's resources. The United Nations Convention on the Rights of the Child fully reinforces this idea of children as citizens with at least equal, if not predominant rights. Internationally, this has become a mainstream theme in discourse about children:

> Many countries are seeking to balance views of childhood in the "here-and-now" with views of childhood as an investment with the future adult in mind. These diverse views have important implications for the organization of policy and provision in different countries. (OECD 2001: 38)

The nature and content of ECEC programs — how didactic they are or whether they are attuned to the whole child — depends in part on where the balance of these views about the nature of childhood falls.

## The Context for Early Childhood Education and Care

Key social, demographic and economic trends in Canada that are consistent with international trends — together with knowledge derived from human development research — have implications for ECEC policies and programs.

First, the demographic environment in Canada includes a shrinking child population. In the 1990s, child populations in Canada, particularly those under age six, declined, especially in regions that experienced out-migration (Childcare Resource and Research Unit 2000). Concern about low birth rate has not been as pronounced in Canada (outside of Quebec, at least) as it has been in Europe; this may be related to the fact that Canada relies heavily on immigration as a source of workers. While Canada has long been a diverse nation, immigrants and refugees now form a substantial portion of the population in some cities, with First Nations and other Aboriginal people a majority in some regions. Canada's diverse ethnic, racial, cultural and linguistic flavour together with its unique approach to multiculturalism has implications for the form and content of ECEC services.

Another trend that forms part of the context for ECEC is that in the past two decades, child and family poverty have increased; in 1998, 19 percent of Canadian children were calculated to live in poverty (Campaign 2000 2000), with poor children disproportionately living in lone-parent families. Poverty is more common among families with younger children (both two- and single-parent families) and is also more likely to be more severe and of longer duration (National Council of Welfare 2001). According to recent analyses by Statistics Canada of child poverty based on after-tax income, 29 percent of children under six years of age were poor in at least one year between 1993 and 1998 (Morrisette and Zhang 2001). Moreover, more than 15 percent of children under six years of age were poor for three or more years during that six-year period — and this does not include children living in the Yukon or Northwest Territories or on reserves, a much higher proportion of whom are very poor. The timing, severity and duration of early childhood poverty has been shown to have long-lasting effects on children's language and cognitive development and school performance, and be associated with increased stresses on parents, all of which contribute to a trajectory of compromised life chances (Duncan and Brooks-Gunn 1997).

Some countries have redistributive policies intended to raise incomes for families with young children. In Canada, a new National Child Benefit (NCB) was introduced in 1998 to provide financial support to low-income families with employed parents. Both the NCB and provincial welfare reforms are prompting (or forcing) more parents with young children into the labour force, often into low-waged, insecure jobs. This policy design requiring parental employment has very significant implications for how ECEC services are designed and distributed.

A third cross-national social and economic change in families of primary importance to ECEC is the shift from a single-breadwinner family model to one in which the norm and the expectation is that both fathers and mothers will be employed while their children are young. Canadian employment patterns among mothers with young children have changed dramatically over the last quarter century. In 1976, the labour force participation rate for women with children under age sixteen was 39 percent. In 2001, 62 percent of mothers of children younger than three years were employed, as were 67 percent of women whose youngest child was between three and five years of age (Statistics Canada 2002); the majority were employed full time.

Having two earners in the family has been critically important for maintaining economic security over the last decade when many parents experienced unemployment or had to adapt to the increased casualization of the labour force and declining or stagnating income. In 1997, the earnings of wives in dual-earner families accounted for almost one-third of family income. Where family incomes improved over the last decade, it is largely due to having two earners working longer hours. Current studies reflect the growing stress parents experience due to increased work demands, longer hours, limited flexibility and concerns about their children's well-being (Johnson, Lero and Rooney 2001).

At the same time, the increased prevalence of single-parent families with young children means that these factors are even more salient for these mothers who are more likely to be poor and, if employed, to have low-waged jobs that are more insecure with fewer benefits. An important additional point that is worth noting is the timing of parental separation and divorce. Not only are more children experiencing life in single-parent families, but they are doing so at increasingly younger ages (Marcil-Gratton and Le Bourdais 1999). This has implications for the need for high quality ECEC programs for children and parents during the very years that are most critical for child development.

Finally, maternity and parental leaves are part of the context for ECEC services as these determine when parents begin to need alternative care for very young children. Typically, in contrast to twenty-five years ago, women now have a continuous attachment to the labour force throughout the childbearing years. Almost 90 percent of Canadian women who were employed when pregnant returned to work within a year after birth, with 60 percent having returned within six months after childbirth. Most countries provide paid maternity and parental leaves that vary considerably in the extent and nature of coverage, flexibility and adequacy of income replacement. Canada has improved the length of its payment period twice in the past fifteen years so that payments of about a year are now available for eligible parents although the length of the leave period varies by province. The benefit level, however, is low at 55 percent of insurable earnings to a ceiling of $413 a week, and the eligibility criteria (under Employment Insurance) exclude many new mothers and fathers.

In addition to these demographic, social and economic elements, research on human development and conceptions about prosperity in modern societies also contribute heavily to the context for early childhood education and care. In the past decade or so, there has been a convergence of ideas about the importance of learning and skills development in creating "knowledge economies." Courchene (2001) argues that universal ECEC must be part of a strategy for human capital that some consider to be critical for modern, competitive countries. While others question whether a traditional economically driven human capital approach provides a complete rationale (for example, Keating 2001), human capital rationales form part of the international and Canadian context for ECEC. The importance of "valuing and supporting universal early childhood education, making it an integral part of the learning system so that all children develop the literacy skills they need to become lifelong learners" (Lowe 2001: 1) is well supported by research and has gained considerable currency. As the OECD points out, "The early years are increasingly viewed as the first step in lifelong learning and a key component of a successful educational, social, and family policy agenda" (OECD 2001: 6).

## Goals and Objectives of ECEC

The objectives that provide the rationale for ECEC have shifted again and again over the years as social needs, cultural attitudes and political priorities have come and gone. In Canada, since the 1980s, rationales for ECEC have included:

* fulfilling children's right to well-being and development;
* school readiness and later educational outcomes ("readiness to learn");
* women's equality;
* mothers' participation in the workforce;
* alleviating child and family poverty;
* balancing work and family responsibilities;
* supporting "at-risk" children and families;
* equity for children with disabilities;
* supporting parents in their parenting role;
* lifelong learning (for children and mothers);
* social integration of newcomers;
* sustaining social cohesion.

Some of these purposes are focused on children (well-being and development; school readiness; lifelong learning; equity for children with disabilities). Others — women's equality and labour force participation; balancing work and family; alleviating poverty and unemployment; supporting at-risk families; supporting the parenting role — are more focused on families or adults. Others are more associated with the community or the larger society (alleviating socially unacceptable behaviour presumed to be connected to "at-risk" status; social integration; social cohesion). Some of these purposes are closely connected to another; for example, healthy child development, school readiness and lifelong learning are closely associated with one another as are mother's participation in the paid workforce, women's equality, lifelong learning and alleviating poverty. While Canada has taken what can be described as a serial approach to ECEC, there is now wide agreement that these policies and programs can — if well designed — serve a number of objectives simultaneously.

# Considering Four Goals for ECEC that Contribute to Social Inclusion

The purposes for ECEC identified above embody four overall goals that are associated with social inclusion. The following section, organized by these four goals, explores the linkages between social inclusion and early childhood education and care in more detail.

## Goal 1: Enhancing children's well-being, development and prospects for lifelong learning

The child developmental dimension of social inclusion is linked to opportunities for full realization of capabilities during childhood and, in the longer term, to the adult the child will ultimately become. If social inclusion over the lifespan is enhanced by full development in early childhood of talents, skills and capabilities, ECEC programs that support this can play a significant role.

Persuasive evidence backs the idea that social determinants have significant implications for lifelong mental and physical health (Keating and Hertzman 1999). Many factors affect whether children develop into healthy adults — innate characteristics, prenatal conditions, the physical environment, nutrition, family attributes and interaction, the community, institutions of learning, civil society and the socio-economic environment. These factors affect one another, combining in complicated ways to produce children in good health who are confident, content, competent, resilient and socially responsible or, conversely, contribute to maturation of children who lack these attributes. Although ECEC outside the family is one among a number of factors that make a difference, it can have a profound effect on child development — indeed, it can be a determining factor.

The idea that high quality ECEC services play an important developmental role in early childhood is well supported by research. If an ECEC program is high quality, it provides intellectual and social simulation that promotes cognitive development and social competence with effects that can persist into elementary school to establish a foundation for later success. The findings about the benefits of ECEC programs pertain regardless of social class (although poor children may derive more benefit) and whether or not the mother is in the paid workforce (Burchanel et al. 2000; Lamb 1998).

It is important to note that the positive effects of ECEC programs only occur if the services are high quality; poor quality programs may even have a negative effect. Research shows that the quality of ECEC services is critical in determining how developmentally effective they are. Indeed, "the positive relation between childcare quality and virtually every facet of children's development that has been studied is one of the most consistent findings in developmental science" (Shonkoff and Phillips 2001: 313). While acknowledging that cultural variations shape the content and meaning of "quality" (Dahlberg, Moss and Pence 1999), it is generally agreed that "high quality" is shorthand for characteristics of ECEC services that go beyond basic health and safety requirements to those that support children's development and learning. "High quality" ECEC services employ staff who are educated for their work, have decent working conditions and wages; work with groups of children of a manageable size; provide challenging but non-didactic, creative, enjoyable activities for children; and ensure consistent adult and peer groups in stable social and physical environments. "High quality" ECEC services are also understood to be responsive to diverse populations of children and parents, include children with disabilities in a meaningful way and be adequately supported by infrastructure like regulation and funding (Doherty 1993; European Commission Network on Childcare 1996; Penn 1999). Research shows that ECEC services that have these characteristics enhance children's development of talents, skills and capabilities in childhood and that these effects persist into adulthood.

While considering these developmental aspects of ECEC associated with social inclusion, it should be noted that the child development literature is often inclined to treat "development" as normative. Healthy development is usually conceptualized and measured using developmental milestones — physical, motor, intellectual and social — linked to age. The Roeher Institute (2001) points out that "all children have a unique developmental and learning path" and that an inclusive approach to children with disabilities requires alternative ways of approaching developmental outcomes and learning. (Inclusion in ECEC for children with disabilities is considered in a later section).

Finally, it should be observed that while the ECEC research literature cited here is not explicitly about human capital, it tends to be more focused on the child's value in the future — value added by enhanced language, cognitive, social and emotional development — than on children's well-being at the present time. A complementary idea is that ECEC services can help create a good quality of life for children "here-and-now." This treats childhood as an important phase of life, not merely as a way station to adulthood, and the child as active and competent. This also presumes that ECEC programs are part of children's culture — an institution for meeting children's own interests, respecting "children's need to be children on their own premises and based on their own interests" (Norwegian

Ministry of Children and Family Affairs 1998: 42). As a Danish study described this:

> For the children, day care became an important extension of the exclusive private sphere that they shared with their mothers (and, in some cases, siblings), exposing them to a wider playful social world, expanding the circle of nurturing adults and enabling the children to form an independent peer social network. (Polakow et al. 2001: 156)

## Goal 2: Supporting parents in education, training, employment and child-rearing

ECEC services can support families by helping reduce social exclusion linked to poverty, unemployment and marginal employment, disempowerment and social isolation. This applies both to the family as a unit and to women (a group with specific needs that may or may not be the same as those of the family unit). These effects advance the interests of the family and its members and also can be mediated through the family to the child.

Canadian women are in the paid labour force for two reasons: first, financial pressures on families — especially those who are poor, working class, and lone parents — and, second, modern perceptions that paid employment is an appropriate role for women. Whatever the motivation, dependable care for children is essential if mothers who would have been expected to provide it a generation ago are to participate in the labour force, training or education. Without access to reliable ECEC, women may be compelled to remain out of the paid labour force, work at poorly paid part-time employment, or not take advancement; some are forced into dependence on public assistance and poverty. Thus, ECEC services are fundamental if mothers are employed and are essential for reducing family poverty by permitting parents — in dual- or single-parent families — to be educated, participate in training, or be employed. Indeed, without alternative childcare, poor families may never be able to escape poverty. In this way, poor accessibility to adequate childcare contributes to gender exclusion from the labour force and to marginalization for women across classes.

ECEC as a support to parental employment is connected to social inclusion for children as well as parents as social exclusion and inclusion are mediated through the family as well as directly experienced by the child. Children in poor families may experience the effects of social exclusion in childhood by not being financially able to participate in school and neighbourhood activities, being ill-housed, ill-clothed and even hungry while the intellectual, social and financial effects of poverty may persist over the lifespan. The timing, severity and duration of early childhood poverty has been shown to have long-lasting effects on children's language and cognitive development and school performance, and be associated with both increased stresses on parents and poorer neighbourhoods as the environment in which young children live (Duncan and Brooks-Gunn 1997), all of which contribute to trajectories of compromised life chances and reduced human and social capital. Thus, children's possibilities are enhanced if their families are sustained economically and socially. While paid work may not necessarily mean that family income provides an adequate living standard, without income from employment, families and their children lack even the possibility of escaping poverty.

## Goal 3: Fostering social solidarity and social cohesion

In addition to enhancing children's well-being and supporting families, ECEC programs as community institutions have the capacity to foster neighbourhood, community and interpersonal cooperation and social solidarity:

> Early childhood institutions ... are forums located in civil society. They make important contributions to other projects of social, cultural and political significance.... Further, early childhood institutions can play an important part as the primary means for constituting civil society... and for fostering the visibility, inclusion and active participation of the young child and its family in civil society. (Dahlberg, Moss and Pence 1999: 7)

Community-based ECEC services can be a focal point for parents, childcare providers, health and social service professionals and community volunteers, exemplifying and helping build social cohesion at the community level. Inclusive ECEC services can enhance social solidarity in the long-term through their impact on children as future adults since early childhood is a critical period not only for language learning but for the early stages of understanding concepts of difference and diversity, and establishing the basis for tolerance and acceptance of difference.

Community-based ECEC programs can also be community institutions that facilitate parents' participation in common activities related to the well-being of their children, strengthening solidarity within a geographic community and across class, ethnic and racial boundaries. Parents who are new to a neighbourhood or are new immigrants or refugees can develop friendships, expand their social networks, access services and supports and contribute to their communities by participating in community-based early childhood programs that are holistic and welcoming in their approach and well connected to other community supports and services.

Statistics Canada (1997) reports that more than 32 percent of the population have a mother tongue other than French or English. ECEC services provide opportunities to include and unite families from diverse origins through participation in common environments related to their children, demonstrating to adults and children alike that cooperation among social classes and ethnic groups is possible and valued. Thus, social integration across cultural, racial and linguistic communities in an environment that both informs about and values diversity can be an important contribution of ECEC programs. Canadian research shows that, while much needs to be done, ECE (training) programs are beginning to make the required changes (Bernhard et al. 1995: 77).

In these ways, high quality, inclusive ECEC services that include parents, coordinate community resources and validate cultural diversity have the capacity to promote equity among classes, levels of ability, racial and ethnic groups and generations, and to enhance social cohesion.

## Goal 4: Providing equity for diverse groups in society

The definition of an inclusive society given at the beginning of this chapter is key to this final goal for ECEC services — that of providing equity. If an inclusive society is one that provides "equality of life chances" as in Sen's definition, all of ECEC's goals and objectives can be seen as linked to the goal of equity either through development of capabilities or access to society's resources as have been discussed in previous sections. For two groups, however — women and children with disabilities — access to ECEC services is a particularly important equity and social justice issue.

The word "inclusion" has a specific meaning when it is used to refer to an environment in which children with disabilities, special learning needs and chronic health problems are welcomed into and are enabled to participate in programs alongside typically developing peers (Odom et al. 1996). The history of inclusive practice in ECEC (Irwin 1992; Irwin et al. 2001) indicates both that progress has been made to ensure that all children have the opportunity to participate in ECEC programs, and that there is still a need to ensure that such opportunities are real, not merely rhetorical.

Ensuring the rights of children with disabilities and their parents is a matter of social justice. Over the last several decades, many countries have progressed from neglect and institutionalization to the development of separate schools and facilities, more recently adopting approaches that ensure that all individuals have the right to full participation in their community and in society — in schools, workplaces and public settings, including ECEC programs. For young children and their parents, the opportunity to participate in and benefit from appropriate supports is critical for children's development, for supporting parents and for normalizing their lives.

Research demonstrates that with appropriate training and specialized support, inclusion in ECEC programs can benefit children with disabilities especially when teachers promote social integration (Jenkins et al. 1989). Effective inclusion of children with disabilities is now regarded as a characteristic of high quality programs and is becoming well accepted as a goal and standard of practice. Research conducted in Canada indicates that most ECEC directors and teaching staff believe that most children with disabilities can, and should, be accommodated (Irwin and Lero 2000).

That "childcare is the ramp that provides equal access to the workforce for mothers" (Abella 1984: 178) is not a new idea and was discussed in a different context in an earlier section. However, framing this as an equity issue goes beyond the pragmatic consideration of whether mothers of young children have access to childcare so they can be in the workforce. The argument that universal childcare is required to support women's equality as a basic citizenship right is associated with the idea that social rights constitute a key element of citizenship, and that a woman's position in the family is important in determining her relationship to the public sphere. While from a practical point of view, the burden of household and caring work has huge implications for women's economic and social status, this in turn is, as well, a matter of citizenship rights. Additionally, whether or not women are in the paid labour force, opportunities for personal development, participation in the community, development of skills and access to a range of formal and informal supports and services are fundamental to social inclusion and full citizenship. Thus, ECEC must be a cornerstone of any consideration of women's equality. Simply put, without full access to ECEC services, equality for women cannot be a reality.

## What Are the Conditions that Enable ECEC to Contribute to Social Inclusion? A Policy Framework

Thus far, this chapter has discussed how ECEC can contribute to social inclusion. But while ECEC services have the capacity to play a role — even a central role — in creating a socially inclusive society, they will be able to do this in a fully effective way only if certain characteristics of public policy and service delivery are present. The empirical research that has been cited in the previous sections of this chapter provides ample evidence for how ECEC is linked to a range of aspects of social inclusion. A recent comparative policy study provides an opportunity for a comprehensive, systematic assessment of these links.

Conducted by the Organisation for Economic Co-operation and Development[1] (OECD) between 1998 and 2001, the Thematic Review of Early Childhood Education and Care provides an evidence-based framework for examining the enabling conditions for socially inclusive ECEC and their implications for public policy. The study, in which twelve member nations of the OECD participated,[2] begins with the observation that early childhood education and care has experienced a surge of policy attention in OECD countries over the past decade. Detailed studies of ECEC policy and provision[3] in the twelve participating countries led to the study's conclusion that eight interrelated aspects of policy and program are the "key elements ... that are likely to promote equitable access to quality ECEC" (OECD 2001: 125). The research found that provision of quality, equitably accessible ECEC services is more likely if the following eight elements, or "policy lessons," are present. These form a useful framework for examining the conditions under which ECEC contributes to social inclusion.

*Policy Lesson 1*
*A systematic and integrated approach to policy development and implementation.* The Thematic Review emphasized the importance of a clear vision of children as a social group to underpin ECEC policy. A systematic and integrated approach requires a coordinated policy framework and a lead ministry that works in cooperation with other departments and sectors.

*Policy Lesson 2*
*A strong and equal partnership with the education system* suggests that the nation supports a lifelong learning approach from birth to encourage smooth transitions for children and recognize ECEC as a foundation of the education process.

*Policy Lesson 3*
*A universal approach to access, with particular attention to children in need of special support* is linked to equitable access so all children can have the equal and fair opportunities provided by high quality ECEC regardless of family income, parental employment status, special educational needs or ethnic/language background.

*Policy Lesson 4*
*Substantial public investment in services and the infrastructure.* The Thematic Review found that while a combination of sources may fund ECEC, substantial government investment is required to support a sustainable system of quality, accessible services.

*Policy Lesson 5*
*A participatory approach to quality improvement and assurance* begins with the premise that all forms of ECEC should be regulated and monitored. Defining, ensuring and monitoring quality should be a participatory and democratic process. Pedagogical frameworks focusing on children's holistic development and strategies for ongoing quality improvement are key parts of this element.

*Policy Lesson 6*
*Appropriate training and working conditions for staff in all forms of provision* is a foundation for quality ECEC services, which depend on strong staffing and fair working conditions. Strategies for recruiting and retaining a qualified, diverse, mixed-gender workforce and for ensuring that a career in ECEC is satisfying, respected and financially viable are essential.

*Policy Lesson 7*
*Systematic attention to monitoring and data collection* with coherent procedures for collecting and analyzing data on the status of young children, ECEC provision and the early childhood workforce are required.

*Policy Lesson 8*
*A stable framework and long-term agenda for research and evaluation* requires sustained investment to support research on key policy goals and is a necessary part of a process of continuous improvement.

In summary, the Thematic Review found that:

> countries that have adopted some or all of these elements of successful policy share a strong public commitment to young children and their families. In different ways, these countries have made efforts to ensure that access is inclusive of all children, and have initiated special efforts for those in need of special support. Quality is high on the agenda as a means to ensure that children not only have equal opportunities to participate in ECEC but also to benefit from these experiences in ways that promote their development and learning. (OECD 2001: 135)

# Does ECEC Contribute to Social Inclusion in Canada? If So, How? If Not, Why Not?

This chapter has examined how, and under what circumstances, ECEC contributes to social inclusion. It makes the case that, under the right circumstances, ECEC is an important vehicle for bringing about social inclusion for children, families and communities. The following eight questions, derived from the preceding "policy lessons" offer a systematic way of examining Canada's approaches to ECEC policy and service provision to assess their contribution to social inclusion.

## 1. Is a systematic and integrated approach to policy development and implementation utilized?

It has been well documented that Canada does not have a systematic, integrated approach to ECEC in either policy or service delivery (Friendly 1995; Beach and Bertrand 2000). There are childcare centres, kindergartens, nursery schools, preschools, parenting programs and an array of funding arrangements. But Canadian ECEC has developed so incoherently that although each province and territory has a tangle of programs, only a small minority of children and families has services that provide the reliable "care" parents need or the early childhood education programs that benefit development and a sense of community. Rather than a coherent policy approach, a mix of piecemeal solutions has arisen to address narrowly defined issues serially.

This absence of a systematic approach is directly linked to poor accessibility. Few Canadian children under the age of five have a chance to participate in high quality ECEC programs that benefit their development, and only a minority of parents can rely on the "care" that they need to train or work. From the perspective of child development, fragmentation of services engenders inconsistency, so are a poor fit with knowledge about the kinds of environments that enhance child development. In a more societal sense, families and children have to fit into narrow eligibility categories, segregated into class, income, racial and lifestyle "silos" to qualify for different ECEC programs. This weakens solidarity and undermines the potential that ECEC services have to serve as focal points for building community solidarity and social cohesion. Overall, Canada's fragmented approach to ECEC policy development and implementation is a major barrier to the potential these programs have to play a role in building equity or community and developing skills, talents and capabilities for children and families.

## 2. Is there a strong and equal partnership with the education system?

Although, "care" and "early childhood education" are inevitably tied together, Canadian ECEC does not blend these two functions. Generally, kindergarten (public education) is regarded as a foundation for lifelong learning and treated as a public good, while "care" services remain a poor cousin. Responsibility for "care" is primarily private rather than public; targeted rather than universal; of uneven quality, so that whether they are "educational" is questionable; in short supply; and heavily dependent on user fees and donations rather than publicly funded. While Quebec has taken a positive step with introduction of full-day public kindergarten for all five-year-old children and acknowledged the educational value of universal, publicly funded care for children from birth to age four, ECEC partnerships between social service authorities and education systems (for example, locating childcare centres in schools) have been eroded in other provinces. Overall, the partnership between childcare and the education system in Canada is limited, not "strong and equal."

## 3. Is there a universal approach to access, with particular attention to children in need of special support?

This is essential for ensuring that all children have opportunities to attend quality ECEC regardless of family income, parental employment status, special educational needs or ethnic/language background. While there are universal approaches to ECEC in public kindergarten for five-year-old children and in Quebec, generally, Canadian practice and this policy lesson diverge considerably.

To be universally accessible, ECEC services must be available, affordable and appropriate, requiring an adequate supply of services while costs to parents must be affordable (either free, very low cost, or geared to income). In addition, services must fit the needs and characteristics of the family and the child; that is, they must be age and culturally appropriate and responsive to parents' work schedules. And they must go beyond being merely available to families and children with special needs to "pay particular attention to children in need of special support" (OECD 2001: 126).

Overall, most Canadian ECEC services serve only small proportions of preschool-age children (Childcare Resource and Research Unit 2000). In addition to short supply, the current financing system for regulated childcare establishes financial barriers to access; participation in regulated childcare is primarily supported by parent user fees that are barriers to access for poor families. While systems of fee subsidies are in place in all regions, modest and middle-income families are not eligible for them and underfunding means that subsidies are not available even to families who qualify (Friendly 2001). This restricts both parents' access to employment and children's access to developmental opportunities, and ultimately contributes to the social exclusion linked to these barriers. Research with parents of children with disabilities underscores this: without access to ECEC, after-school and summer programs and respite care, parents and their disabled children are excluded from many activities and opportunities (Irwin and Lero 1997).

Further, targeting in one way or another is a barrier to equity in almost all of Canada's ECEC services (except kindergarten) (Doherty 2001). This results in segregation of families by class and circumstances and is a key factor that mitigates against ECEC's contribution to social inclusion. Reversion to emphasis on targeting in ECEC seems to be associated with a renewal of distinction between deserving and undeserving recipients of social goods, which has become prevalent in Canada in the 1990s (Mahon and Phillips 2002). The stigmatizing effects of targeting may, as Klasen (1998) describes, have the effect of furthering social exclusion. While means-tested subsidies may permit participation in childcare services, having to undergo a humiliating testing process can contribute to a low-income parent's sense of exclusion and low self-esteem. At the same time, identifying services as intended for low-income or "at-risk" children and families not only problematizes or even pathologizes the recipients, but can have the effect of making the services undesirable to modest- and middle-income families.

Generally, ECEC in Canada is not moving towards "a universal approach to access, with particular attention to children in need of special support" (OECD 2001: 126). Instead, it is best described as a situation of scarcity, eligibility based on narrow categories, children in need of special support being left unserved and a renewed trend towards targeting.

## 4. Is there substantial public investment in ECEC services and infrastructure?

As described earlier, there are multiple ECEC policy, program and funding routes. Even regulated childcare has multiple funding routes — fee subsidies, operating and wage grants, tax measures and vouchers. Overall though, regulated childcare is primarily a user pay program.

Cross-Canada data show that 49 percent of an average full-day childcare centre's revenue came from parent fees in 1998 (Goelman et al. 2000), although provinces spent more than $1 billion dollars on regulated childcare, an average expenditure of $206 per child up to age twelve (Childcare Resource and Research Unit 2000). (Figures for total spending on kindergarten are not available.)

In addition, the federal government allocated $300 million (in 2001, rising to $500 million in 2004) to the provinces for four categories of children's services, one of which is "early learning and care." An estimate based on an economic analysis by Cleveland and Krashinsky (1998) calculates universal ECEC for Canadian children aged one to six years to cost $7.4 billion net (Friendly and Rothman 2000). As a point of comparison, the European Union proposes national spending on ECEC of 1 percent of GDP (European Commission Network on Child-Care 1996). (Canada's GDP was somewhat more than $1 trillion in 2000). Canadian and American research shows that financing is directly linked to accessibility and quality (Whitebook et al. 1990; Goelman et al. 2000). The OECD Thematic Review suggests that while funds from parent fees and other sources can make a contribution to ECEC, ensuring equity by providing access to high quality ECEC requires secure, substantial and coherent government funding to services and to infrastructure.

## 5. Is there a participatory approach to quality improvement and assurance?

As described, research documents the characteristics of ECEC services that determine whether they are likely to meet not only basic health and safety requirements, but also provide environments that ensure development and learning. Two structural elements have been shown to be key in determining the likelihood that high quality will occur in an ECEC program.

The first of these — financing — was discussed in the previous section. The second — regulation — has been shown to be linked to quality through the form and content of programs, especially staffing (Gallagher et al. 1999).

In Canada, many studies and reports have identified concerns about quality in regulated childcare services (e.g., Lyon and Canning 1997; Doherty and Stuart 1997). A Canada-wide study of quality in centre-based childcare found that:

> fewer than half of the preschool rooms (44.3% and slightly more than a quarter of the infant/toddler rooms (28.7%)) are providing activities and materials that encourage children's development. Instead, the majority of the centres in Canada are providing care that is of minimal or mediocre quality. The children's physical and emotional health and safety are protected but few opportunities for learning are provided. (Goelman et al. 2000: ix)

A companion study on regulated family daycare had similar findings (Doherty et al. 2000).

Analysis of the YBIC! centre-based data confirms what other research has shown — significant provincial differences suggest that strength of regulation is one of several key factors that influence the quality of the services (Doherty and Friendly 2002).

At the same time, many Canadian preschoo- age children are in unregulated ECEC environments that provide "care" while mothers work — unregulated family or in-own-home childcare — that are outside systems of quality assurance altogether. While research on the precise details of these arrangements is sparse, enough is known to suggest that the majority of preschool-age children whose mothers work outside the home spend a good deal of time in environments that are unlikely to be developmental environments.

The OECD study suggests that while ensuring minimum standards through regulation is fundamental, it is also important to involve parents and professionals in a participatory and democratic way. The findings from the Thematic Review also advise that equal access to quality means that regulation needs to apply to all ECEC settings and that governments at national, regional and local levels play key roles in assuring quality.

To date, there has been only limited discussion in Canada about the complex pieces that make up this policy lesson. Even in regulated childcare, there is little discussion about systematic strategies for ongoing improvements in quality. The kind of approach to quality that the Thematic Review links to the high quality, equitable ECEC services that contribute to social inclusion is not yet a reality in Canada.

## 6. Are there appropriate training and working conditions for staff?

As human relationships and interaction make up the substance of a child's ECEC experiences, caregivers or teachers are the essence of ECEC programs. Research shows that adequate training and fair working conditions — wages and benefits, working environments, turnover, training and morale — are all strongly and directly associated with the quality of a child's experience, with child development and, ultimately, with social inclusion (Goelman et al. 2000; Whitebook et al. 1990).

There are few points about ECEC about which there is better agreement than the inadequacy of the working conditions and training in regulated childcare (Environics Research Group 1998). A national study of the "childcare workforce" concluded that Canadian society places little value on the work and skills of the women who care for young children. It found that Canadian caregivers receive little public support, few resources, and unacceptably low wages. Education in the field is poorly coordinated and there are many gaps in training (Beach et al. 1998).

The OECD observes that

> most staff working with 3–5 year olds in publicly funded settings are trained at a high level... those working with children under age three in the welfare sector tend to have lower levels of training, compensation and poorer working conditions than education staff. (OECD 2001: 132)

This in some ways describes Canada's situation. Where Canada diverges, however, is in the absence of publicly funded ECEC services even for three to five year olds. Wages and working conditions for staff caring for over-threes in Canada (other than public kindergarten) are more like those described in services for younger age groups elsewhere. Poor working conditions, public recognition and training for staff in ECEC programs thus present an impediment to ECEC's contribution to social inclusion.

## 7. Is there systematic attention to monitoring and data collection?

The absence of consistent data on Canadian ECEC has been frequently noted (Beach et al. 1998). An analysis of Canadian ECEC data needs concludes that Canada essentially has no reliable, consistent, comparable data on various aspects of ECEC that can inform policy or improvements to service provision, or assess changes and effects on children and families over time (Friendly et al. in preparation). The Thematic Review concluded that systematic attention to data collection requires "coherent procedures for collecting and analyzing data on the status of young children, ECEC provision, and the early childhood workforce" (OECD 2001: 126).

## 8. Is there a stable framework and long-term agenda for research and evaluation?

The OECD observes that "sustained investment to support research on key policy goals is required as part of a process of continuous improvement" (2001: 134). As we pointed out earlier, Canada does not have clear policy goals for ECEC. Over the years, there has been research and evaluation of ECEC programs, human resources, best practices and policy, mostly through a series of federal research programs. While these have yielded valuable information, there has not been the "stable framework and long-term agenda" that this policy lesson suggests is a crucial component of a process of ongoing improvement. The systematic monitoring and data collection discussed in the previous section is linked to this research agenda; basic data to provide public accountability should be a complement to a research and evaluation agenda that can help provide answers to more complex questions. A Canadian long-term and stable research agenda utilizing a variety of disciplines, methodologies and paradigms is essential as a tool to "inform effective policy-making and raise the overall quality of ECEC" (OECD 2001: 134–35).

## Acting on What We've Learned: From Aspirations to Reality

This chapter's purpose has been to examine the connections between social inclusion and early childhood education and care. We have argued that ECEC can make a significant contribution to social inclusion by supporting children's development, family well-being, community cohesion and equity. The chapter describes how the goals and objectives of ECEC relate to development and human freedom; it explores how, and under what circumstances, ECEC services contribute to social inclusion — and when they don't. It concludes that in eight key policy areas, Canada does not provide the mechanisms that would enable ECEC to contribute fully to social inclusion. A key question that remains to be asked is whether ECEC services could contribute more to social inclusion than they now do, that is — notwithstanding the present ECEC policy and funding — are there implications for practice in areas that could be improved to strengthen social inclusion? At least four areas for further discussion stand out.

### Quality

We have pointed out that the quality of ECEC programs is key to whether they are effective in developing talents, skills and capabilities and discussed the known elements that contribute to quality. These include staff training, good wages and working conditions and an infrastructure that assures ongoing quality. We have also noted research that shows that Canadian childcare is more likely to be mediocre than high quality. As the OECD study points out, high quality ECEC requires substantial financing, good regulation and well-trained and paid staff. These structural elements clearly require commitment at the policy level. However, even in the absence of commitment to structural changes, there is considerable knowledge with implications for practice at both policy and service levels applicable to improved quality and, therefore, strengthening human development and social inclusion.

A key element that has been missing as an integral part of Canadian ECEC is systematic planning for quality improvement. When quality improvements have been undertaken, they have tended to be time-limited pilot or research projects funded by the federal government (for example, professional development opportunities) or isolated provincial initiatives (for example, wage enhancement or increased training requirements). The OECD study describes systematic approaches to ongoing quality improvement as including consideration of pedagogy, analysis of monitoring systems, qualitative and quantitative approaches to program evaluation, service support and infrastructure, and in-service training and professional development. While ultimately, assuring the high quality ECEC required to truly support social inclusion requires both structural changes at senior policy levels and a coherent systematic approach to quality enhancement, useful lessons about a systematic approach to improving quality can be drawn from this comparative work.

## Disability

A second area to consider is inclusion of children with special needs. As we noted earlier, this is an important equity issue and therefore, fundamental to social inclusion. There are several facets to this issue, with implications for policy and practice. At the most fundamental level is the difficulty of physically including and accommodating children with disabilities in an under-resourced and undeveloped system. While there is no legislative requirement or proactive mandate that would assure that ECEC programs include children with special needs, many centres do so. Barriers to inclusion identified by a national sample of centre directors include: insufficient funds to provide for the required additional staffing, the need to make structural modifications to the centre, the need for additional staff training, the centre already had the maximum number of children with disabilities that it could take or was licensed for, insufficient funds for necessary equipment and limited access to therapists and external resource consultants who could support centre efforts (Doherty et al. 2000a; Irwin et al. 2000).

Research shows that generally, centres that include children with special needs effectively tend to have a proactive director who provides leadership, at least one designated staff person with special expertise in this area, assistance from professionals and positive experiences with parents. These enable positive experiences with inclusion, help staff develop additional skills and reinforce their willingness to accept children with more challenging needs — an "encouraging" rather than discouraging cycle (Irwin and Lero 2001).

Recent observations by Tougas (2002) suggest that expansion of ECEC systems with limited funding support for inclusion may not be sufficient to meet these goals. A more comprehensive approach, including training and ongoing consultations and support seems necessary. Moreover, within centres, training, attitudes and resources must be used to ensure that children with disabilities are not participating separately within the program, but in ways that enhance their development, their participation with others and their acceptance. Current research and best practice examples could be used to enhance capacity regionally and nationally, but will require additional support to be sustainable.

## Policy and service coherence: A systematic integrated approach

The Thematic Review provides evidence about the importance of coherence of policy and service delivery. Systematic integration requires proactive steps at the community and program level, in planning and in funding and policy development. While truly integrated planning would include recognizing and strengthening the links between related services and ensuring that service gaps are filled, even without systemic structural change there is considerable room in ECEC practices and current policy to knit together a more integrated approach to ECEC.

A good example of these possibilities is in the area of ECEC for Aboriginal communities, whose members have historically been particularly underserved by appropriate services. As new services for Aboriginal ECEC have been added in the 1990s, they have tended to remain separate entities at both policy and service delivery levels. Currently, there are four separate federal Aboriginal ECEC programs: First Nations and Inuit Childcare; childcare under the Department of Indian Affairs and Northern Development (DIAND); on-reserve Aboriginal Head Start and off-reserve Aboriginal Head Start. (In addition, some provinces are involved in Aboriginal childcare on reserve; in some cases, this has been negotiated with the federal government and in others, with First Nations. As well, off-reserve First Nations people may participate in non-Aboriginal ECEC programs on the same terms as other Canadians). As Aboriginal communities are under federal jurisdiction, the three federal ECEC programs that provide on-reserve services provide a good opportunity to integrate policy and services to allow First Nations communities to smooth children's and families' participation in ECEC.

A lesson about the importance of an integrated approach that can be learned from the U.S. experience with Head Start should not be lost in the current context. Highly targeted half-day ECEC programs were originally developed in the 1960s for very low-income children whose mothers were not in the labour force. These, however, did not meet the labour force needs of those same families when the welfare reforms of the 1990s required parental employment when children were very young. As the U.S. experience shows, retrofitting programs designed for separate purposes rather than taking a more holistic approach initially can be challenging at best.

## Diversity

Finally, as we described earlier, the fact that Canada is a very diverse country has special implications for the best practice of inclusive early childhood education and care. A study conducted in Canada's three largest cities examined how childcare centres and ECEC training institutions work with families and children from a wide range of backgrounds (Bernhard et al. 1995). Overall, preparation for work in these ECEC settings was less than optimal, and mutual understanding between parents and early childhood educators was not strong. The researchers reported that "we are inclined to believe that there continue to be problems of systemic racism, irrespective of the good will of centre staff" (ibid. 1995: xi). This study and other information suggest that if ECEC programs are to make a strong contribution to social inclusion, there is considerable room for change in current training and centre practices.

# In Conclusion: Towards Socially Inclusive Early Childhood Education and Care

Early childhood education and care services as political, social and economic institutions have an important role to play as agents that support and enhance social inclusion, human development and, thus, freedom. They can enhance children's well-being, development and prospects for life-long learning; support parents in education, training, employment; foster social solidarity and social cohesion; and provide equity for diverse groups in society. Comparative research shows how certain elements of public policy can enable ECEC services to play these roles. It also shows that these elements can be implemented to balance their essential characteristics with cultural and national variations in ideas about children, families and society.

Societies that advance social inclusion are those in which members enjoy equality, participate in a meaningful way, have opportunities for joining in collective experiences, share social activities and attain fundamental well-being. Early childhood education and care contributes to the process of social inclusion by helping to make equality of life chances and a basic level of well-being possible for all children and families. Indeed, some commentators suggest that ECEC is so fundamental to these that it should be a citizenship right (Covell and Howe 2001; Courchene 2001; Ignatieff 2000; United Nations Children's Fund 2001). This right would be consistent with the Convention on the Rights of the

Child and is enshrined and practised in a number of European nations. If ECEC is able to contribute to social inclusion, it is not randomly or by happenstance. The OECD's policy framework makes clear that while there are ways in which current practice can be improved, if ECEC is to make a significant contribution to social inclusion, governments must play a meaningful role. The United Nations Children's Fund (2001) has called on world government leaders to "make children — the youngest most especially — the priority at all policy tables… and to ensure [that this has] the necessary financial and political support." Over the past two decades, nations with a variety of histories, cultures, fiscal capacities and political arrangements have set in motion the enabling public policy for socially inclusive ECEC programs. These examples show us that closing the inclusion gap requires vision, commitment and the political will to turn aspirations into reality through transformative processes of policy and program development.

## Notes

1. Based in Paris, the OECD was founded in 1961 to contribute to economic expansion, growth and employment and a rising standard of living and to the expansion of world trade. Its member countries are Australia, Austria, Belgium, Canada, Czech Republic, Denmark, Finland, France, Germany, Greece, Hungary, Iceland, Ireland, Italy, Japan, Korea, Luxembourg, Mexico, the Netherlands, New Zealand, Norway, Poland, Portugal, Slovak Republic, Spain, Sweden, Switzerland, Turkey, the United Kingdom the United States.

2. Australia, Belgium (Flemish and French communities), Czech Republic, Denmark, Finland, Italy, the Netherlands, Norway, Portugal, Sweden, the United Kingdom and the United States.

3. A Background Report and a Country Note was prepared on each participating country. These are available from the OECD or online at <www.oecd.org> (accessed July 2005).

# Feminist Perspectives on Social Inclusion and Children's Well-Being

*Meg Luxton*

## Putting Children and Their Well-Being on the Agenda[1]

Since 1990 when the United Nations first began issuing its Human Development Index, Canada has ranked among the top countries in the world, a ranking that political leaders have proclaimed proudly.[2] However, on the Human Poverty Index, Canada consistently ranks lower, typically around tenth. And when looking specifically at poverty among children, Canada's rank drops even further. A 2000 United Nations Children's Fund (UNICEF) report on child poverty in twenty-three industrialized countries ranked Canada in seventeenth place, below nations like Spain, Greece, Hungary and the Czech Republic and a mere five above the U.S., which had a child poverty rate of 22.4 percent. The report noted that 15.5 percent of children in Canada live in poverty (UNICEF 2000a). Statistics Canada low-income cut-off figures indicate that child poverty is even higher — 19.8 percent (Vanier Institute 2000: 116–23). These figures pose a challenge: why can't Canada, a country in which so many people have one of the highest standards of living in the world, ensure that all children meet, at a minimum, the criteria measured by the Human Development and Human Poverty indices?

## Defining Social Inclusion from the Perspective of Children

A very limited perspective on children was explicit in the initial formulations on social exclusion, the concept that preceded, and continues to inform, social inclusion. The term social exclusion was coined in 1974 by René Lenoir, the French Social Action Secretary of State in the Chirac government, to refer to those:

> unprotected by social insurance programs, particularly those not covered by employment-based benefits. Originally, the excluded were defined as people with mental and physical disabilities, the suicidal, aged, abused children and youth drop-outs, adult offenders, as well as substance abusers. (Barata 2000:1)

Housewives and other unpaid care providers are strikingly absent, although they fit the criteria. Implicit in this formulation is an assumption that young children, youths in school or making the transition to the labour force, as well as those who care for them, are the private responsibility of their individual families and therefore ineligible for state support. The term social exclusion was quickly taken up in policy debates as an alternative, or successor to the term poverty, but although its focus is more general, proponents of social exclusion paid little attention to children. Social exclusion was considered a more useful concept than poverty because it is multidimensional, going beyond financial or material hardship to include a range of social and political relations of inequality that contribute to both material and social deprivation or oppression. The term encompasses a range of issues such as limited access to an income, housing, education, community services and health care.

In Europe, social exclusion has been understood more broadly as related to limits on the extent to which people are able to participate as citizens in their day-to-day lives and in the workings of their society. Berghman (1995), for example, attributes social exclusion to:[3]

> the failure of one or more of the following systems: the democratic and legal system, which promotes civic integration; the labour market, which promotes economic integration; the welfare state system, promoting what might be called social integration; the family and community system, which promotes interpersonal integration.

Most concepts of social exclusion typically assume its redress is "social inclusion through the exercise of common citizenship rights to employment and to welfare" (Rocke and Van Berkle 1997: xix). This formulation serves to exclude children as most citizenship rights are age-specific entitlements such as participating in the political process (suffrage) or the labour force (stopped by compulsory schooling and anti-child-labour laws).[3] Similarly, most welfare provisions relating to children are family-based; children *per se* have few welfare entitlements. For the most part, debates about social exclusion only relate, indirectly, to children when they discuss the ways in which the social exclusion of particular groups is typically reproduced generationally.

However, social exclusion recognized that some people have only a limited ability to participate in the political process and many face systemic discrimination based on factors such as ethnicity, national origin, language, racism, sexism, age, class ability and/or sexual orientation. As a result, the concept of social exclusion was mobilized by various equality-seeking groups to put their issues on the agenda. Anti-racist feminists came up with the terms "margin" and "centre" and effectively employed a strategy of "decentring" to make claims about the importance of their knowledge that challenge prevailing wisdoms and to insist on the power of marginality (hooks 1984). Patricia Hill Collins (1998: 127) describes decentring as the process of "unseating those who occupy centres of power as well as the knowledge that defends their power." She continues:

when in the 1970s and 1980s Black women and other similarly situated groups broke long-standing silences about their oppression, they spoke from the margins of power. Moreover, by claiming historically marginalized experiences, they effectively challenged false universal knowledges that historically defended hierarchical power relations. Marginality operated as an important site of resistance for decentering unjust power relations. (1998: 127)

In response to such arguments by equality-seeking groups, the term social inclusion came to imply more than the opposite of social exclusion, emerging as a more complicated concept that offers greater analytical scope (Freiler 2001c). Social inclusion offers a complex, interactive model that treats all individuals as social actors and assumes that they play a role in shaping their lives while recognizing that their circumstances impose constraints on what is possible for them. Social inclusion highlights the fact that some people have limited or no access to the social resources available to others and attempts to reduce the barriers to their access to such resources.

However, it recognizes that the solution to inequality is not simply to give those who have been excluded the same formal rights as those who were not excluded. It invites a more intricate analysis by assuming that existing social relations, institutions and cultural practices must also be transformed in order to accommodate everyone. Rather than expecting those "on the margins" to conform more closely to the prevailing norms and practices of those "at the centre," social inclusion implies that the centre must be reconfigured to encompass the practices of those from the margins. One of the values of a social inclusion perspective is that it can allow for the diverse cultural practices and values of various social groups.

Such a perspective is particularly open to children as it asks what is required to ensure that all children, regardless of their circumstances, are accommodated. Activists concerned about disability issues, for example, mobilized such arguments in discussions about whether children with disabilities and special needs are best served by integration into regular schools or by the provision of special schooling. By focusing on inclusion, they were able to ask what needed to change to ensure that children with disabilities or special needs could participate in, and benefit from, the education system as fully as possible.

## A Children's Agenda

Although they do not address efforts to extend social inclusion perspectives to children, international strategies to put children's rights on the agenda offer some important directives. These initiatives crystalized internationally with the 1989 adoption of the Convention on the Rights of the Child (CRC) by the United Nations' General Assembly. The CRC, ratified by 191 nations including Canada, provides a framework for governments to improve the well-being of children. It calls for continuous action and progress in the realization of children's rights based on four general principles:

1. The principle of non-discrimination (Article 2) — by which states commit to respect and ensure the rights of all children under their jurisdiction without discrimination of any kind;
2. The principle of the best interests of the child (Article 3) — in which the interests of the child are recognized as paramount and budgetary allocations should give priority to children and to the safekeeping of their rights;
3. The principle of respect for the child's views and right to participate in all aspects of democratic society (Articles 12–15) — which asserts that children are not passive recipients, but actors contributing actively to the decisions that affect their lives;
4. The principle of the child's right to survival and development (article 6) — which claims the right for children to realize their fullest potential, through a range of strategies from meeting their health, nutrition and education needs to supporting their personal and social development (UNICEF November 1998v; UNICEF 2000b: 46–51).

These principles recognize that poverty is only one measure of the position of children and that policies and practices designed to ensure children's well-being must address all aspects of children's lives. Central to such recognition is an appreciation of "the social" —of the ways in which social structures and practices can shape, and sometimes even determine, the lives of individuals regardless of their own actions. This takes a particularly complicated form with regard to children as they are inevitably subject to their immediate care providers and the larger culture within which they live and their subjectivity changes with their own development and growing capacity to act on their own behalf. The CRC recognizes in Article 5 what a delicate balance is involved in assuring the rights of children while respecting various family, community and cultural practices

The CRC assumes that children's well-being depends on children being fully integrated into their society as social actors, with the right to participate in decision-making proceedings affecting their lives (UNICEF 2000b: 50). More importantly, it assumes that the whole society will accept collective responsibility for the well-being of its children.

Recognizing that adolescents are often ignored by policies focused on children, the United Nations makes a point of extending all their principles to include that sector of the population. Central to this is a commitment to:

> ensure that adolescents participate in decisions that affect their lives, their families and communities, that they support each other as they face the challenges and opportunities of the transition into adulthood, and are actively involved in the development, implementation and monitoring of all of the above activities. (Dick 1999: 4)

The CRC identifies a number of principles for children's rights, deemed essential for ensuring the advancement of children and their well-being. Social inclusion offers a policy orientation that helps implement those principles, by translating abstract assertions of children's rights into more concrete policies and practices. However, efforts to mobilize the concept of social inclusion to advance children's well-being are complicated by the fact that, to date, most of the literature on social exclusion and inclusion is striking for its lack of attention to gender, women, sexism or the feminist analyses intended to correct such inattentions. Most of the social exclusion or inclusion literature takes for granted heterosexual nuclear family forms and gendered divisions of labour, failing to recognize the way such approaches naturalize women's responsibilities for children and obscure what is actually a political debate about the extent to which children's well-being and care is a private family matter or a social responsibility. Such perspectives make it very difficult to formulate policies that both assume and foster children's abilities to become social agents in their own right.

## Feminist Contributions to a Child-Centred Concept of Social Inclusion

The difficulties involved in generating a child-centred concept of social inclusion arise not simply because policy analysts have failed to pay attention to children. Rather they are rooted in the theoretical and political assumptions that underlie current dominant perspectives on social, political and economic organization, which understand children as dependents of their parents, unable to act as independent decision-making agents and not eligible to make citizenship claims in their own right.

Contemporary social and economic policies in Canada still reflect the basic assumptions of classical liberal theory, which understands society as constituted by individuals who interact competitively in markets. In this framework, the individual is always assumed to be a property-owning man with a dependent wife and children; white, western European, heterosexual nuclear families are culturally normative and render other family forms suspect (Lloyd 1984). Heterosexual nuclear families are assumed to be responsible for generating a livelihood sufficient to support their members and are privately responsible for deciding whether, when and how many children to have, and for raising these children themselves. Outside intervention is typically considered acceptable only if parents are deemed to put their children at risk. From this perspective, children are understood as dependents, the private responsibility of their parents. Even when the individual is considered independently of a family and even if individuals are understood as including women, the two main principles of liberalism, that the free and self-determining individual enjoys equality of opportunity and individual choice, are not easily applied to children (Weedon 1987: 5). Infants and young children are inevitably dependent and unable to make decisions for themselves, and most children remain significantly dependent at least into their mid- to late teens. They do not conform readily to the individual as understood by classical liberal theory.

Classical liberal theory is also predicated on assumptions that only consider activities economically productive if they are market-based, thereby limiting "work" to either paid employment or production for exchange in the market. This framework has enormous practical and ideological power. It has formed the basis internationally of economic policies such as the United Nations' National System of Accounts and current World Bank, International Monetary Fund and OECD policies (Waring 1988; Bakker 1994) and in Canada has shaped most federal, provincial and territorial policies (Bakker 1996). This framework means that most childcare — all the unpaid, non-market activities that are involved in caring for children — is not recognized as work. Childcare is not understood as making a contribution to the economy and, therefore, all the rhetoric about motherhood notwithstanding, is not considered socially necessary or valuable (Waring 1988; Folbre 1994; Luxton and Corman 2001).

Children, their generation, care and socialization pose an unresolved contradiction for classical liberalism (O'Neill 1994). Liberal theory fails to recognize children as people in their own right. It renders invisible all the activities involved in bearing and raising children and makes individual children vulnerable to the particular circumstances and personal idiosyncrasies of their caregivers (Waring 1988; Luxton 1997). It tends to produce a policy framework that both takes for granted the existence of, and privileges, heterosexual nuclear families where women are primarily responsible for caring for children. All too often, the results reflect the flawed premises. The policy initiatives do not solve the problems, and nothing in their articulation invites an assessment of why the policies fail.

For example, implicit in much of the literature on social exclusion and inclusion is a confusion of family form with social relations and economic status where single parent or mother-headed families *per se* are identified as problematic for the successful rearing of children. Barata (2000:2) notes that, at the end of the 1970s and early 1980s, many western European countries identified growing levels of child poverty. Policy analysts attributed these to unemployment, cuts to social programs, the breakdown of the nuclear family and children living in families of lone-support parents. While economic insecurity obviously increases the likelihood of poverty, the argument that family form or separation lead to child poverty is based on faulty premises. Nuclear family separations and lone-parent families do not cause child poverty and policies developed on that assumption will fail (Reitsma-Street 1989–90: 527; MacDonald 1997: 10–17). In reality, what causes child poverty are gendered divisions of labour, labour market segregation and segmentation, pay inequalities, the lack of public support for caregiving and men's widespread reluctance to pay child support. It is these social practices which result in women's poverty and by extension impoverish their children. The more that individual families, and particularly women, are made responsible for providing for children, the more vulnerable children are to the particular circumstances of their families, and the greater the chances that children's well-being is achieved at the expense of women (Luxton and Corman 2001). The policies of the current period, which downplay or deny the extent to which children's situations are determined by those of their parents, are informed by an approach which, at base, neither supports the rights of children nor focuses on their well-being.

To counter the basic assumptions of liberalism, feminists have developed a concept of social reproduction that puts children, as both dependents and active members of their society, at the heart of social relations. This concept assumes that children are not a private hobby of their parents, but social actors in their own right. One main goal of social reproduction is bringing up the next generation, that is, to ensure that children grow up to become contributing adult members of their society. The conditions under which they are conceived, born and raised produce not just individual adults, but the population of the next generation. A social reproduction perspective understands children as individuals who have rights to make citizenship claims on the world community and on the particular states, local communities and families in which they live (Luxton and Maroney 1992).

The work of social reproduction — the efforts required to ensure the day-to-day and generational survival of the population — involves two major activities: income-generating work based on market activities such as paid employment or the production of goods and services to sell, and unpaid domestic labour in the home (Seccombe 1992, 1993; Luxton and Corman 2001). From this perspective, women's (and men's) unpaid labour in the home is regarded not as a private service for their families, but an important and socially indispensable labour that contributes to the production of the population in culturally specific ways. It also contributes to the generation of the labour force — that is, produces workers who are ready and willing to sell their capacities to work in the labour market on a daily and a generational basis (Seccombe 1974, 1992; Luxton 1980; Hamilton and Barrett 1986). It is from this perspective that child bearing and rearing are recognized as central to the process of the generational reproduction of a society, its peoples, its economy and its cultures and values.

However, a social reproduction perspective does more than recognize both the importance of children and the contribution of unpaid caregiving to the well-being of society. What is unstated in the CRC's assumption that children's well-being should be recognized as a collective responsibility of the whole world community is made explicit through feminist perspectives on social reproduction. Any efforts to ensure the social inclusion of children must include an analysis of the ways in which the dynamics of social reproduction play out in particular contexts. Social reproduction is a key process that constitutes and reproduces class, gender, national origin, ethnicity, race and age relations in a context that is already constituted by state, law and ideology (Maroney and Luxton 1997). It is central in shaping the lives of children by producing them as members of various social groups with differential access to social resources and thus highlights the shortcomings of assertions such as those on which the CRC depends. In other words, a commitment to social inclusion for children requires its advocates to rethink the premises currently underlying debates about how children are best cared for, by whom, and how to inform policy demands intended to foster children's well-being.[4]

## Children as the Private Responsibility of Their Parents

Throughout most of the twentieth century, Canadian government policies were based on the premise that children were mainly the private responsibility of their parents and that women were wives and mothers with husbands to support them. Social policies assumed mothers would voluntarily provide care for their children and that if mothers were unable to provide such care, it was a family responsibility to make other arrangements (Eichler 1988). A range of social policies provided modest support, such as the family allowance, initiated in Canada in 1945 as a universal benefit to assist families with the costs of child rearing (Baker 1995: 128). Policies were developed for women, especially mothers, who did not have income-earning husbands to support them. These were premised on the principle that mothers would stay at home to look after their children and provided a (limited) means for them to do so (Ursel 1992; Little 1998; Christie 2000).

In the late 1960s and early 1970s, more and more women combined participation in the paid labour force with having small children, and the revitalized women's movement developed the language of social reproduction to explain the constraints such women were under and to justify demands intended to relieve those pressures (e.g., for childcare, pay and employment equity, maternity and parental leaves, benefits for part-time employees and flexible time) (Luxton 2001: 70). Employers and governments came under widespread pressure to increase the support they offered employed parents through a range of measures designed to relieve the pressures involved in managing paid employment and childcare responsibilities (White 1993; Vickers et al. 1993). Canadian governments were under pressure to extend their welfare state provisions but typically responded in a limited manner by using income transfers and tax policies to facilitate parents' choices about whether to keep both parents in the labour force or have one stay home to be with the children.

However, from the 1980s on, governments turned to neo-liberal economic policies aimed at reducing government provisions of social services while fostering private for-profit business (Cohen 1997). They increasingly cut social services and income transfers, assuming that individuals and families would absorb the cuts (*Toronto Star* September 18, 1995: A1).

In all areas of policy, from taxes to social assistance and legislated maternity and parental leaves, and in the face of the absence of a national system of early childcare, governments reluctantly recognized that caregivers could not participate in the labour force without some government support. They also recognized that neo-liberal policies were unsuccessful in reducing either children's poverty or the systemic exclusions suffered by so many. As a result, in the 1980s, neo-liberal governments were challenged by a paradigm shift that focused on investments in children (Beauvais and Jenson 2001). Nonetheless, the policies they developed continued to put pressure on individuals to provide as much care for themselves and others as possible (Bakker 1996; Brodie 1996). Chow, Freiler and McQuaig (1999:1) note the resulting difficulties: "Not knowing whether to support women as mothers, workers or both has led to a form of policy paralysis and an un-developed system of support to families with children."

Such ambiguity, which remains central to the policies that have dominated government practices over the last two decades as neo-liberalism has gained in strength (Luxton 1997), is unsurprising as children continue to be regarded as the private responsibility of their parents. Neo-liberalism assumes that what happens to children in families results from the choices made by the individual adults in those families. The (il)logic of this position was graphically illustrated when, in the face of evidence that children in Ontario were going to school hungry, Premier Mike Harris defended his government's 21.6 percent cuts to welfare benefits. He denied that poverty was the cause of children's hunger and blamed, instead, women's "lifestyles," arguing that many mothers are too busy with their jobs to make breakfast. He contrasted this situation with one he remembered from thirty years before when "mom was in the kitchen with the hot breakfast cooking as everybody woke up in the morning" (Mittlestaedt 1996).[5]

While issuing an overt call for women to leave paid employment and work unpaid at home is unrealistic, neo-liberal political economy continues to depend on much of the work of caring for children being done as unpaid labour in the household economy.[6] The success of their program depends on widespread acceptance of that idea. By creating nostalgia for the days when unpaid domestic labour was largely done by women as housewives, they lay the basis for the notion that it is only a change in "lifestyles" that is creating the problem.

## Using Social Inclusion to Rethink the Position of Children

One strength of a focus on social inclusion is that it reveals a contradiction between current neo-liberal economic policies, which inevitably exacerbate inequalities, and expressions of political intent that aim to reduce social exclusion, especially that of children. A commitment to social inclusion confronts the way social power is situated. It shows that unequal access to economic resources, political power and social status all affect personal behaviour, limiting interpersonal and group relationships regardless of individual intentions. The more individuals and families have to bear the costs of social reproduction, and the more children are the individual responsibility of their mothers in a milieu that assumes women's primary role is as mothers, the more likely children are to risk poverty and other forms of social exclusion.

As a result of neo-liberal policies implemented over the past twenty years, the social and economic resources available to all children — except those with well-to-do parents — have markedly declined (Bezanson 2002). Neo-liberal policies put the majority of families with children at a disadvantage. While enacting legislation that makes their costs higher, they ensure that parents have less time to generate income and are under greater pressures to redistribute what income they have. Neo-liberal policies also reduce or eliminate forms of community support, which exacerbates children's vulnerability to their parents' social position, thereby rendering children more vulnerable to the particular situations of their parents. Without explicit policies of wealth redistribution, children are more likely to be deeply affected by their parents' unemployment. The effects are not just financial: the more stress parents are under, the harder it is for them to give their children the quality of care they may aspire to. Where parents are rendered incapable of caring for themselves, their children are at greater risk of suffering terrible deprivations.[7]

In contrast, policies based on a commitment to social inclusion for children would strive to understand the different rewards and penalties that attach to people in dissimilar social locations. They would also promote the recognition that different groups need to exert different levels of effort to achieve similar goals. The more children are embedded in networks of family, community and other social ties and institutions, and the more childcare is understood to be a social or collective responsibility, the greater are their chances of avoiding poverty and experiencing the benefits of social inclusion. State policies concerning funding for students in post-secondary education illustrate these dynamics. While most post-secondary students are legally adults, their access to student loans is mediated by their parents' presumed ability to pay. In the 1960s and 1970s, the combination of relatively low-cost post-secondary education, scholarship (rather than loan) programs and the availability of summer employment meant that more children than ever before, especially from working-class households, were able to attend post-secondary institutions. In the 1990s and 2000s, as individual students are required to bear a greater proportion of the costs, as loans have replaced grants and as income from student employment covers less of the cost of living, there is growing concern that working-class students, single parents and other people with low-incomes will abandon efforts to get post-secondary education. The more society as a whole accepts some responsibility for caring for children, the more all children will have access to the standards of living and well-being typical for those living in Canada.

## Social Inclusion and the Politics of Diversity

One of the most trenchant criticisms levelled against social policies based on classical liberal theories is that they present culturally specific social relations as universal norms, privileging them at the expense of other cultural forms (Sen 2000). In trying to reduce or eliminate social exclusion, policymakers must exercise great care not to fall into the trap of developing policies aimed at integration, which result, instead, in assimilation. Government and church efforts, in the early to mid-twentieth century, to assimilate Aboriginal children offer a tragic example of the ways in which efforts to eliminate diversity in fact produced greater inequality, the social costs of which are still being measured (*Globe and Mail* December 11, 2000: A3). At the same time, inequalities are produced, reproduced and changed through social differentiation. Policies that accept existing differences uncritically and reify them may easily produce or intensify inequalities. For example, protective labour legislation intended to recognize differences between women and men (such as forbidding women's employment in mining or preventing women from working at night in heavy industry) resulted in discrimination against women, making it hard for them to get well-paid jobs or earn as much as their male coworkers (Luxton and Corman 1991: 84–85; Keck 1998).

Equality-seeking, anti-poverty and anti-oppression activists argue that in recognizing social difference there is a delicate balance between reinforcing and reducing inequality; the challenge is how to ensure and support diversity while eliminating inequality. As Floya Anthias notes:

> The issue of inclusion is not an issue of integration, but involves difficult questions about how diverse cultures and groupings can achieve representation on an equal level and as constituencies of

advocacy, as well as issues relating to individual social and political rights. (1997: 256)

Key feminist demands suggest the kinds of complex policy initiatives that would facilitate such goals. Calling for a multi-pronged approach, feminism advocates "affirmative action" measures that recognize the consequences of systemic discrimination, such as affirmative-action hirings (Abella 1984), while simultaneously pursuing measures that both increase social appreciation of women's traditional attributes and activities (Luxton and Vosko 1998) and foster similar treatment for women and men (Kome 1983). Although it is not couched in the language of social inclusion, the Report of the Royal Commission on Aboriginal Peoples identified guidelines for strategies both to set in motion reparations for past injustices and to foster future dynamics that reduce inequality without eliminating diversity. It calls for the four principles of recognition, respect, sharing and responsibility (Report of the Royal Commission on Aboriginal Peoples 1996: 675–97). Such principles would be appropriate criteria for social inclusion policymaking.

The value of a social inclusion perspective lies, therefore, in its potential to challenge existing inequalities, especially socio-economic disparities, while respecting and promoting diversity. Translated into policy this typically means combining various affirmative-action strategies, designed to overcome the effects of systemic discrimination, with policies developed to transform the mainstream to make it more accommodating of minorities. In Canada, a world dominated by English-language speakers, providing Francophone children with French-only schooling may honour their language rights but result in their subordination in the labour market. Instead, a genuinely bilingual school system may offer greater protection for French-language rights by permitting French-speakers schooling in their own language, ensuring their capacities in English and increasing the number of English speakers who understand French. Full inclusion would require policies that reach beyond the school system to create a climate where French speakers are not ghettoized in particular regions or jobs but rather valued for their language skills. Similarly, in a system permeated by homophobia, providing a gay, lesbian, bi-sexual and transgender-positive school may keep some young people in school and protect them from abuse, but only if it is accompanied by an anti-homophobia program throughout the entire school system will there be any possibility of systemic change.

Feminist pedagogies, for example, have noted the important difference between classroom practices that are non-sexist and non-racist and those that are anti-sexist and anti-racist. Where the former aim for a social inclusion based on the premise that everyone gets treated in the same way, the latter recognize that sexism and racism exist and produce discriminatory and oppressive practices that permeate daily life and that pedagogical practices must therefore consciously aim to counter discrimination. Social inclusion, from this perspective, will only result when systemic oppression is acknowledged, the different social locations of children in the classroom are identified as a source of strength and their diverse experiences are recognized and validated.

The most challenging impact of policies of social inclusion is the fact that efforts to increase social responsibility for children disrupt existing power relations. Social inclusion, if fully realized, means that those who are the main beneficiaries of inclusion are those with the least power — children and women, people with disabilities or who are Aboriginals or First Nations, immigrants, racialized, working class and poor people. Those who currently hold power and are members of groups that have had the benefits of social inclusion for generations stand to loose their relative privileges and may be challenged to share their power in ways that cannot be anticipated by policymakers when they commit themselves to developing and implementing radically new practices.

## Social Reproduction and Social Inclusion: Implications for Children's Policy

The term social reproduction enables us to name processes which are key to what happens to children as they are born, grow up and become full adult members of their society. Any efforts to ensure social inclusion for children have to take account of these processes. There is a long tradition of discriminating against children on the basis of the form of their birth family. Until the 1970s in Canada, children born to a woman and man who were legally married to each other were considered the legal children of those two adults, regardless of the child's actual biological parentage or the adults' actual relationship at the time of the birth. Children born to legally married adults were recognized in law and socially; children born to adults not legally married were considered illegitimate in law and were often discriminated against socially. Over the past thirty years, changing patterns of cohabitation, marriage, divorce and sexual practices have loosened the link between heterosexual marriage and child bearing and significantly altered the relationship between family form and child rearing. In the late 1970s, changes in the law ended the legitimate/illegitimate distinction and widened the range of potential legally recognized parents.

However, a heterosexual and marriage-based morality still plays an important role in the ways children are assessed. It is reflected in the media's use of the coy phrase "love children" to describe children born to parents who were not legally married to each other at the time the children were conceived and born.[8] Likewise, children of lesbian and gay parents are subject to homophobic prejudices (Arnup 1997; Gavigan 1997); children whose mothers apply for social assistance are assumed to live in poverty because they live in single-parent families (Little 1998), and many Aboriginal children whose birth parents are deemed by social service personnel to be unable to provide adequate care are assumed to be without family, even when others in their community are willing or even eager to care for them (Monture-Angus 1995). Current policies presume that biological fathers, regardless of their actual involvement in the day-to-day care of children have a financial responsibility to support their offspring. Following this logic, social agencies put pressure on mothers on welfare to identify the "sperm donor" so he can be forced to contribute to the child's care.

Policies of social inclusion would, in contrast, guarantee that all children have the right to a decent standard of living regardless of their biological parents' willingness or ability to be involved in their support and care. They would ensure that children's well-being does not depend on the marital status of their biological or social parents, emphasizing instead the child's well-being as a member of the community in which she or he is raised, thus bringing to life the vision enshrined in the CRC that childcare is the concern of the "whole world community." In short, to succeed in full, policies aiming to ensure children's social inclusion must continue the trends of the last several decades by working to reduce or eliminate the central role that family form currently plays in determining children's legal and social status.

What such a formulation of social policy also reveals is that, while a specific focus on children in their own right is essential, children's well-being is directly linked to that of the people responsible for raising them. In the contemporary political environment, discussions of child poverty have obscured the fact that children are poor because their parents, usually their mothers, are poor, and just as problematically, have failed to acknowledge that children are well-off because their parents are. Policies aimed at social inclusion for children that do not address the circumstances of their care givers are likely to fail. Yet current social structures and political policies render it inevitable that child rearing is a private responsibility. They are premised on the assumption that individual parents, extended families and the immediate circle of care givers have the major responsibility for the well-being of individual children, an assumption which puts children at risk. As a result, we are caught in a peculiar double-bind in which, as Marge Reitsma-Street (1989-90) notes, young people only have the legal right to adequate care, educational and recreational opportunities if they are actually in the care of the state:

> These rights to food, shelter, and so on cannot be claimed by young people in their own family groups since there are no mandatory provisions ensuring that family groups receive the help they might need to feed, clothe, educate, and develop their offspring. (1989–90: 521)

While state regulations do provide the means to remove children from dangerous familial situations, making a child a ward of the state is neither a measure of social responsibility nor a means to foster social inclusion for the child. Indeed, current evidence overwhelmingly proves that the actual resources provided after a child is removed from a family are rarely sufficient. As Karen Swift (1995: 171) argues, "their futures are far from ensured through these repeated rescue operations." Swift goes on to draw particular attention to the way state intervention hides the actual problems facing families whose children are deemed at risk:

> help offered through child welfare agencies departs in almost every way from our usual professional ideas about what constitutes real help. Procedures through which this help is offered often conceal or distort the very serious problems many of these parents face, and they conceal as well the class-based nature of the concept of neglect itself. (Swift 1995:170)

In contrast, policies premised in the belief that the social inclusion of children requires their society as a whole to share responsibility for their care would invert the current practices. They understand the welfare of children as an effect of the fact that primary caregivers have the resources and support needed to provide adequately for each child. Furthermore, social inclusion recognizes that primary care givers are located in communities and that support and services should be available to them and their children alike. A British study of children's literacy offers an excellent example of the benefits that can derive from policies that are developed out of sensitivity to this fact. It not only found a close association between the literacy rates of parents and children, but recorded that efforts to encourage literacy in the children seemed to work best when parents were included as well:

> Parents' educational levels are important determinants of their children's. Sixty per cent of children in the lowest reading attainment group had parents with low literacy levels; only two per cent had parents with high literacy. Attempts to improve family literacy, parents and children together, look promising. (Sparkes 1999: 3)

It should be clear from my sustained references to the potential enshrined in the CRC's formulation of a community-based system of childcare that I do not support any position which tries to privilege mothers as the primary caregivers of children. Because women are primarily responsible for the caregiving aspects of child rearing, it is impossible not to recognize that children's well-being is closely linked to the specific status of their mothers and, thus, to the more general status of women in the society as a whole. The United Nations has itself made this point:

> It has become increasingly recognized that women's rights and well-being are central to both human development and the realization of children's rights. It is clearer than ever that unequal gender relations and wide gender gaps in social, economic, political and civic spheres do not just deny the individual rights of girls and women — they reduce human capabilities as a whole. (UNICEF 2000a: 6)

There is considerable evidence, in Canada and internationally, that proves that women's education and literacy levels directly correlate to the well-being of their children. Extensive statistical evidence based on historical and comparative studies of countries and regions show clear links between women's education and literacy rates, their ability to earn an independent income, their access to property rights, their general standing in society, and the achievement of lower fertility rates, lower mortality rates of children, increased educational opportunities for children, especially girls, and increased spending on children especially for food, clothing and school supplies (Sen et al. 1994; Prentice et al. 1996: 469–73). The social value or status of the primary care giver appears to have an impact on the status of children as well. Nonetheless, the practice persists whereby, when women work long hours in their homes, their activities are not recognized as work and are not included in the accounting of the respective contributions of women and men to household economy. When women work for pay, their contribution to the family economy is valued differently and becomes more visible. The combination of visibility and economic power increases the status of women and has a direct impact of status of their children — a status that, again, is explicitly gendered, in that their daughters seem especially to benefit (Stiglitz 1998). As the 2000 UNICEF report to the UN General Assembly Economic and Social Council notes:

> the greater a role the woman plays in decision-making, particularly with regard to household expenditure, the better off her children are likely to be. Therefore, future action for children must recognize the importance of increasing women's opportunity for education, employment and reproductive health in order to increase their bargaining power in the household. (UNICEF 2000: 8)

Internationally, women's and children's social exclusion is significantly determined by that fact that caregiving, especially of children, is not valued in current economic and social policy analysis. Despite their recent recognition of "human capital," economists have not paid attention to the relationship between social reproduction and the production of goods and services in the market (Picchio 1992). Their focus on GNP to the exclusion of social reproduction permits governments to reduce health, education, childcare, elder care and all other forms of care to the status of "economic expenditures" and to exclude any consideration of the time devoted to the care and education of the next generation from the macroeconomic category of investment (Folbre 1994). In this formulation, children become "consumer goods" that adults may choose to have, rather than valuable members of society.

To counter this tendency, feminists contend that efforts to put children and their concerns at the top of the agenda require a revaluing of them as well as of those who provide their care. Arguing that social inclusion for women depends on recognizing and valuing the unpaid work of caregiving, they have called for changes to the National System of Accounts so that caring for children is recognized as a vital, socially necessary activity and that women's unpaid caregiving is included in the calculations used to determine economic policies.[9] They advocate a change in priorities, understanding that this requires a complicated and multi-faceted revisioning of current policies and practices. Their suggested changes derive, in particular, from the need to provide the means by which caregivers will acquire the time and resources for childcare, and they include in their ambit a consideration of everything from adequate housing and incomes to maternity and parental leaves, to shorter working days, weeks and years so that caregivers have more time with their children. Their thinking, and the policy proposals to which it gives rise, profoundly challenge existing assumptions that families, usually mothers, can and will act as a reserve army of unpaid labour, taking care of needs that are not met elsewhere (Luxton and Corman 2001).

A commitment to social inclusion requires us to rethink all our current assumptions about the organization of paid employment and unpaid childcare and the extent to which we as a society are prepared to put resources into our children and their well-being. Policies to foster social inclusion would attempt, by socializing caregiving more, to reduce children's dependence on their primary caregivers, give parents more time to be with their children and strengthen community ties among parents, childcare workers and children (Luxton 2001). One such initiative is the provision of childcare from infancy for all children at costs that all parents can afford, while simultaneously publicly recognizing and valuing caregiving by, for example, extending maternal and parental leaves, linking childcare and school hours more closely to hours of employment for parents (or reducing shift work for parents) and increasing the pay of childcare workers (Cleveland and Krashinsky 2001). Could it also mean that non-relatives gain the right to claim parental leave if they are actually involved in looking after an infant? Recognizing the research that shows that a troubled adolescent may need only one caring relationship with an adult to overcome her/his difficulties, could any adult demand paid leave if they were actively involved in helping a distressed teenager?

Just as social inclusion policies combine initiatives to reduce children's dependence on their immediate caregivers with efforts to both free and support caregivers so they have more time and resources for their children, such policies also combine initiatives that recognize children as dependents with efforts to support children as social agents in their own right. This dual position poses significant challenges to social policy initiatives based on social inclusion. As the United Nations CRC recognizes, children embody both the rights of individuals and the rights of their families, communities and cultures. If social inclusion policies hope to centre on children, how might they balance the rights of parents to raise their children within traditions the parents' value with the rights of children to be assured that their upbringing will provide them with the best chances possible to be fully integrated members of their society? And in a multicultural society and an increasingly global society, who decides what is appropriate and what should be publicly supported and funded?

The tensions and contradictions inherent in these circumstances are revealed in the controversies about the adoption of children from impoverished, or from ethnically — or racially — different communities, by white, middle-class Canadians. While some argue that the well-being of individual children is improved by the material and emotional resources and cultural normativity of their adoptive families, others critique such adoptions as a form of either elitism or class, race or cultural genocide. As long as private parenting remains dominant, there will be a logic supporting the claims of those who are closer to the centre and well-to-do that they can provide a better environment for the child than parents on the margins or with fewer resources.[10]

Children raised as whites, who later discover they have Aboriginal roots, have raised troubling questions about the relative weight and value of secure, loving commitment from their adoptive parents and the value of a sense of cultural belonging. A generation of Chinese-born Canadian girls is ten years away from making their contribution to this debate.[11] A focus on the rights of children, independently of their parents, raises important questions about, for example, what an education policy based on social inclusion would look like.

Some might claim that public education ensures that all children have the same educational opportunities and therefore reject both private and home schooling. Others argue that respect for diversity involves parents' rights to choose alternatives to public education. Canada has legally recognized the right of parents to raise their children in the parents' religious tradition, and Ontario has funded Catholic schools. As other religious denominations demand similar funding privileges, some people have raised concerns about the effect of differentiated schooling on public life. Similarly, at present, parents have the right to home schooling as long as they cover basic curriculum, but some critics worry about whether home schooled children learn to work in groups or to relate to other adults effectively. Many parents who take their children out of the public system object to their taxes paying exclusively for public education. Others object to public revenues supporting private schooling.

Similarly troubling questions arise when parents insist on their right to use physical punishment to discipline their children in a society that is struggling to eliminate interpersonal violence and in an international context where peacemaking efforts have increasing importance. What criteria distinguish children's rights to freedom from violence from parents' rights to discipline their children? Do community groups that assume that child-rearing practices affect the quality of their society have any right to intervene? Who decides and on what basis? What criteria can be applied to children who demand their right to determine their own life when the adults in their immediate circle consider their decisions inappropriate? And what kinds of social support might such children be entitled to if their parents make obedience a criterion for support? Should the policy direction encourage children to stay under parental authority or provide the opportunity for children to live independently of parents in supervized group settings or on their own? If a young person rejects her parents' demand that she get married, insisting instead on staying in school, thus forfeiting their support, what social assistance, if any, should she expect — social assistance, tuition, housing? If she decides to leave school, live on the street and work as a squeegee person, should she be entitled to similar support or is public assistance only available to those whose activities are directly linked to future labour force participation?

I suggest that a multi-pronged approach, similar to that advocated for supporting diversity while advocating equality, guide policymaking in this area. Such an approach would recognize the consequences of children's dependency, while simultaneously pursuing measures that both increase social responsibility for children and encourage children's participation in the decisionmaking processes that affect their lives. It would also understand that a measure of the well-being of children reflects, better than any other measure, the well-being of their society.

Efforts to respect children's agency would encourage policies and regulations that incorporate children wherever possible. These might include simple practices such as including children in parent-teacher interviews, thus potentially creating a place for children to raise their concerns. Student councils in schools and community organizations could strengthen children's ability to learn about issues and speak out effectively about their concerns. Various international conferences such as the United Nations' Fourth World Conference on Women have made a point of including child delegates. Another way of developing policies that respect children involves moving away from age-based categories to those based on evolving capacities and abilities. For example, most provinces and territories impose age limits on those applying for drivers' licences, but many children living in rural and northern communities begin driving sooner as they help with farm labour, hunting and bush activities or simply confront the lack of alternative transportation. Skill-based driving tests might provide a more useful screen. Similarly, voting rights are arbitrarily age-specific, a policy that has been criticized by those who point out that young people can join the army and fight in wars several years before they can vote for the government that declares war. Are curious, well-informed ten year olds more or less capable of voting than legal adults who ignore what is happening around them?[12]

Attempts to put into practice principles that support children as social agents in their own rights require a reallocation of resources, first to ensure that all children have access to top-quality childcare, schooling and recreation from infancy to adulthood. Second, fostering children's inclusion includes investing more in community-based services for children, teenagers and their parents or care providers, such as parent-support groups, toy-lending libraries, health clinics, recreation centres and group homes, as well as supporting a whole range of services through which children and caregivers can meet, keep an eye on each other, develop friendship and support networks and enjoy themselves. Such publicly funded programs would have as a central commitment the development of children's physical, intellectual and psychosocial capacities to their full potential. They would also depend on an active commitment by all levels of government and state-funded agencies such as schools, welfare agencies and employment centres to anti-oppression initiatives at all levels from curriculum and programming to service provision, hiring and promotion. This would require greater investment in public education to improve the quality of schools generally and in particular for students with special needs. It would make post-secondary education affordable or free for all qualified students to ensure that social benefits make an impact across generations as much as across existing social classes.[13]

While such proposals complement current policy orientations that advocate investments in children (Beauvais and Jenson 2001), they are contrary to prevailing government policy orientations toward reducing government spending, cutting taxes and expecting individuals and fami-lies to rely more on each other and less on government services. As a result they pose a challenge to children's advocates and policymakers: what levels of social exclusion are we willing to tolerate and for which children? What rates of child poverty are acceptable? Stated positively: what investments of money, time and other resources are we willing to make to ensure the social inclusion of all children in Canada? These are complex political questions that a social inclusion perspective addresses by assuming that at least three criteria that recognize the child as a social agent, should be considered: that children participate in decisions that affect their lives and be involved in turning those decisions into action, based on their evolving capacities; that while children have the right to expect support, care and love from their parents and other immediate caregivers, they also have the right to other sources of support and care if they need them; and that children have the right, as individuals, to make citizenship claims on their society. There are of course no simple answers to the questions I have raised in this chapter, but a public recognition that such questions are not a reflection of the private troubles of individual families, but part of larger social issues about how we maintain and reproduce our society, would at least make the debate more public and invite social, rather than individual solutions.

## Notes

1. The Laidlaw Foundation's initiative and the discussions it prompted have produced a significant contribution that focuses specifically on the usefulness of social inclusion as a policy approach for children. I want to thank the Laidlaw Foundation and especially Christa Freiler for making it possible for me to participate in this discussion. I also thank Christa Freiler, four anonymous reviewers, Kate Bezanson and the members of the Feminist Political Economy study group, Jane Springer and Vee Farr for their comments on previous drafts of this chapter.

2. The Human Development Index measures longevity, levels of education and standards of living. The Human Poverty Index measures the percentage of people expected to die before age sixty, the percentage of adults whose ability to read and write is inadequate and deprivation in overall economic provisioning reflected by access to health services and safe water, and the percentage of children under five who are underweight. See the United Nations Human Development Report for each year from 1990–2000. For definitions of the Human Development Index and the Human Poverty Index, see Human Development Report 1998: 14–15.

3. Robert MacDonald argues that his 1997 book *Youth, the "Underclass"and Social Exclusion* is the first British attempt to investigate "the processes of social exclusion that affect vulnerable young people" (1997: 1), but it too focuses primarily on unemployment, training, the labour market, homelessness and crime, as they relate to teens or young adults. It only addresses parenting in a peripheral way, and the experiences of young children are not addressed.

4. In the course of working on this chapter, I was surprised by comments from several people who took for granted that feminism, both historically and in the current period, has paid little attention to children or that feminist demands for women's equality have been at the expense of children. For example, the initial proposal for this working paper began: "The well being of children had tended not to figure prominently in the 'feminist project' of achieving equality for women." Later, one anonymous reviewer of an earlier draft of this chapter claimed that "children have been largely absent in feminist theory" and suggested that I "discuss the tensions in feminist theory around children a bit more" (Reviewer #3). I completely disagree with such claims. I think children have figured prominently in feminist theorizing and political practice since the eighteenth century. My guess is that prevailing

media discussions of feminism, which tend to present a caricature of a narrow liberal feminism as if it were the only feminism, may explain the prevalence of such ideas.

5.  His language clearly marginalized women who, as they were serving in the kitchen, were not included with "everybody."

6.  In the winter of 2002, treasurer Jim Faherty pushed the logic of the Conservative Party's policy even further when he proposed to cut most or all government funding for childcare.

7.  In 2002, some of the elders in Davis Inlet appealed to the government for help with glue-sniffing addictions among young children. Media accounts of the situation showed that some adults in the community were themselves substance abusers. Their own experiences in residential schools, combined with their inability to rely on the bush for economic subsistence and the lack of effective alternative sources of economic livelihood, resulted in their inability to care for their children (*Globe and Mail* December 7, 2000: A19, *Toronto Star* December 11, 2000: A6).

8.  An example of this hit the media in December 2000 when the newly re-elected major of Toronto, Mel Lastman, was sued by a woman who was his lover for fourteen years and by her two adult sons, who claimed Lastman was their birth father although he had never publicly acknowledged them as such. An article in the *Toronto Star* referred to "The matter of the two love children he allegedly fathered during the affair" (*Toronto Star* December 2, 2000: A5).

9.  This demand was most clearly articulated in the 1995 *Platform for Action*, the official document of the Forth United Nations World Conference on Women, Beijing, China. Initially, objections to collecting such data were based on claims that it could not be collected. Subsequent initiatives have disproved those claims. For example, the United Nations estimates that $11 trillion annually is the non-monetarized, invisible contribution of women (UNDP 1995: 6). The General Social Survey indicates that in 1992 people in Canada performed at least 25 billion hours of unpaid work, 95 percent of which was domestic labour — looking after children and caring for the home. Statistics Canada estimates that this labour is equivalent to about 13 million full-time jobs, is worth about $234 billion, and equals about 4 percent of Canada's gross domestic product — and that women did two-thirds of it (Statistics Canada 1992; Chandler 1994).

10. This has often proved an effective claim in legal custody disputes where the higher income parent, or the father who has remarried and has a stay-at-home wife, is awarded custody in "the best interests of the child" (Boyd 1989).

11. The Chinese government's one-child policy, combined with a preference for boys, has produced a large number of abandoned girls in China. The Chinese government has cooperated with Canadians who want to adopt, so there is now a significant population of Chinese-born girls adopted by Canadian parents. In 2001, the oldest of these was about ten. Many of their parents assume that as young adults, these children will have questions about why they were born, given up for adoption and adopted by overseas, i.e., Canadian, parents.

12. Carl Keast, a grade five student, was studying the *Charter of Rights and Freedoms*. The summary given to him by his school said that the Charter

entitled everyone to vote. He pointed out the error, noting that ten year olds are not enfranchized.

13. The only Canadians to have access to anything like the programs outlined here was the generation of World War II veterans, their partners and children. Many of them benefited from state support such as daycare centres during the war and educational grants and subsidized mortgages after the war. That generation was relatively the wealthiest in Canadian history, suggesting that public investment in social reproduction may be an important way to generate high levels of social productivity and standards of living (Pat Armstrong, personal communication).

# Thumbs Up! Inclusion, Rights and Equality as Experienced by Youth with Disabilities

*Catherine Frazee*

## Introduction: "In Our Own Way... On Our Own Terms"

> Young people are always supposed to listen to adults, we are seldom taken seriously. We are the ones who have to go through school; we are the ones who will have to deal with conflict when we are adult. We have to try out our ideas and practise ways of resolving conflicts. We want to make friends in our own way. We have to do that if we are going to learn about how to relate to each other. We want help from adults but on our terms. I think that all young people need things to change, not just disabled kids. (Mackeith 1999)

"All young people need things to change." Generations of adults have made different interpretations of the need for change to support children's growth and promote their well-being. This chapter — although subject to the inevitable limitations of adult interpretation — seeks to examine the relationship between inclusion and equality, attempting to ground this inquiry in an active consideration of the experiences, perspectives and voices of children and youth.

In particular, this chapter centres upon the experiences of young people with disabilities, seeking to better understand what social inclusion means to them and how its experiential reality links to fundamental concepts and principles of equality. This focus upon disability provides a unique and important opportunity to highlight and reflect upon our responses to the "hard questions" of difference at both individual and policy levels. It is well recognized that the equality status of people with disabilities is jeopardized by deeply entrenched patterns of social exclusion and that unequal treatment in the context of disability most often takes the form of denial of opportunities for inclusive participation. As noted by the Supreme Court of Canada:

> It is an unfortunate truth that the history of disabled persons in Canada is largely one of exclusion and marginalization. Persons with disabilities have too often been excluded from the labour force, denied access to opportunities for social interaction and advancement, subjected to invidious stereotyping and relegated to institutions.... This historical disadvantage has to a great extent

been shaped and perpetuated by the notion that disability is an abnormality or flaw. As a result, disabled persons have not generally been afforded the "equal concern, respect and consideration" that s.15(1) of the Charter demands. Instead, they have been subjected to paternalistic attitudes of pity and charity, and their entrance into the social mainstream has been conditional upon their emulation of able-bodied norms.... One consequence of these attitudes is the persistent social and economic disadvantage faced by the disabled. Statistics indicate that persons with disabilities, in comparison to non-disabled persons, have less education, are more likely to be outside the labour force, face much higher unemployment rates, and are concentrated at the lower end of the pay scale when employed. (*Elderidge v. British Columbia [Attorney General]* 1997)

In this context, it is not surprising that children with disabilities experience social exclusion to an extent greater than that of non-disabled children. According to a Disability Information Sheet recently published by the Canadian Council on Social Development:

They (i.e., children with "special needs') experience more bullying by other children. They are more likely than those with no special needs to feel un-liked by their peers and to feel "left out." They are also less likely to feel safe at school. Although in most cases, the differences between children with special needs and those without special needs are fairly small, the differences do exist and they extend into many facets of the social experience. (CCSD 2001; See also Hanvey 2001)

The presumption that underlies this chapter is that the experience of social exclusion heightens awareness and appreciation for social inclusion and that this heightened awareness and appreciation affords lively and abundant insights well worth the attention of legal and policy theorists. Drawing from accounts provided directly by young people with disabilities and their peers, this chapter therefore contends that through the lens of disability we can most clearly perceive the limitations of an exclusive focus upon rights and legal entitlement and recognize the essential contribution of social inclusion to the challenge of promoting, respecting and protecting lives of dignity and equality for all citizens.

This chapter[1] takes as its starting point a series of e-mail dialogues with six young people from Alberta, ranging in age from fifteen to eighteen.[2] Upon their instruction, these informants will be identified by the following names: Aaron, Brandalyn (Brandy) Lofgren, Kyle, Linda, Lynnsey Harder and Trevor. Two of these young people have disabilities; the other four are involved in some close relational capacity with a disabled peer. Their observations and reflections about inclusion ground the analysis that follows upon a foundation of immediacy and authenticity.

## Inclusion: "To Be Who I Am ... To Do What They Do"

At the outset of our conversations, Aaron, Brandy, Kyle, Linda, Lynnsey and Trevor were each asked the foundational question: "What is inclusion?"

For the most part, these young people defined inclusion in terms of opportunity: the opportunity to participate; the opportunity to achieve; the opportunity to be seen and understood; the opportunity to belong:

> Lynnsey: Inclusion to me is giving each child, teen and adult the opportunity to join in and be included in whatever activity is going on despite anything (disabilities, I.Q., etc.).[3]

Some defined inclusion in terms of basic ethical principles:

> Trevor: Inclusion means friendships and treating each other with caring and respect.[4]

Other definitions were fundamentally experiential:

> Aaron: Inclusion is being able to be with kids my own age and do the things they do and go where they go. Inclusion is being with them. Inclusion helps people see that there is a lot more to me than autism. It helps them see that I'm just a regular teenager. Inclusion is important because it allows me to be who I am and to be with my friends and do what they do.[5]

Some recognized and articulated the crucial element of support to the exercise of individual agency:

> Kyle: Inclusion is — being provided with all the supports that I need to be in a regular classroom at school, do all the activities in Scouts or anything else that I'd like to try to do.[6]

For some, there is a transcendent quality to inclusion — a recognition of self in the other and an affirmation of universal human needs and aspirations:

> Linda: Inclusion is seeing the abilities, not disabilities, of everyone and supporting every individual as to help them achieve their optimal potential. Inclusion is to look at someone's soul and to see them as a fellow human with emotions, feelings and desires like all of us. Inclusion is all this and so much more, but most importantly, inclusion is to make those who may feel un-included or isolated, included.[7]

Most striking was the emphasis that most contributors placed upon the twin values of participation and acceptance:

> Brandy: To me inclusion is belonging... being with everyone else, and feeling a part of what they're doing. It is acceptance, and knowing that you "fit in" (I guess). You're no different than any of the others. You feel safe, secure, strong there. You can be yourself. True inclusion does not come in degrees. It's either there or it's not.[8]

In her recent feminist text subtitled *Experiencing and Understanding Disability*, Thomas (1999) has highlighted a duality of restrictive forces operating in the lives of persons with disabilities. On one hand are multiple barriers and restrictions that impede disabled persons' opportunities to act in the social world. Much attention has been paid by activists, policymakers and commentators alike to the removal of such barriers and to the promulgation of legal and regulatory standards that guarantee access by disabled persons to public places, services and opportunities. Although much remains to be done in terms of the implementation of such standards and the dismantling of physical, structural and systemic barriers, this notion of access is well recognized — a straightforward matter of bricks and mortar or lumber, nails and elbow grease, a matter of design and accommodation, an issue of how resources and priorities are allocated.

Kyle's entreaty for supports to "do all the activities... that I'd like to try to do," Aaron's desire to be with his peers "and do the things they do and go where they go" and Lynnsey's urgings for everyone to be "included in whatever activity is going on" speak to a highly prevalent phenomenon of exclusion from mainstream activity and opportunity — and suggest that inclusion demands vigilant attention to barrier removal. An inclusive community, our informants tell us, is one in which opportunities to act in the social world are not, as the Supreme Court noted in Eldridge, "conditional upon [the] emulation of able-bodied norms."

On the other hand, according to Thomas, "there are additional, often intangible, dimensions to the social exclusion of people with impairments." The language and mechanisms of these restrictions are much less well understood, as are the forms of "access" that counter them. For disabled persons, a full notion of access must go well beyond the mechanical challenge of entry into buildings or the bureaucratic challenge of eligibility for civic opportunities. Access must also be about making one's way into citizenship and human community and about feeling secure and worthy. Framed in this way, inclusion calls for engagement within a dynamic of access to respect, access to a sense of oneself as a whole person and access to identity as a valued contributor, a bearer of rights, knowledge and power.

The notion of "belonging" that Brandy identifies as synonymous with inclusion elicits an imperative of feeling "safe, secure, strong... [so that] you can be yourself." These same intangibles appear as well to underlie Trevor's emphasis upon "caring and respect" and Linda's insights about truly "seeing" individuals with disabilities through the lens of our common humanity. Aaron concludes: "Inclusion is important because it allows me *to be who I am* and to be with my friends *and do what they do*" (emphasis added).

His conclusion resonates strongly with Thomas's argument that:

> The focus should include not only a concern for what "we do" and "how we act" (are prevented from doing and acting) as disabled people, but also a concern for "who we are" (are prevented from being), and how we feel and think about ourselves. (1999)

Upon this foundational account of inclusion as promoting freedoms both *to do* and *to be*, we can now consider a set of "inclusion narratives." From the accounts that follow, it may be possible to begin some preliminary sketching of how inclusive experiences shape not only "what we do" and "how we act," but also "who we are," and "how we feel and think about ourselves."

## Inclusion: "Sharing, Sharing, Sharing"

> Kyle: I care about inclusion because it affects my future. I have dreams and if I am not included I will not be able to develop into the person I want to be and to achieve my goals.

Kyle is fifteen years old and a grade nine student. He describes his disability in the following terms: "When I was three, I had a drowning accident that left me with a brain injury, so now I use sign language or my Dynavox[9] machine to speak to people."

When asked to describe his earliest memory of inclusion, Kyle has considerable difficulty. According to his father, Kyle has "always been included." With some effort, however, he recalls the following experience:

> My earliest memory of being included was when I was five years old and I was included in Beavers. I was still in a wheelchair. There were lots of boys my age; we began each meeting with a chant "Beavers, Beavers, Beavers. Sharing, Sharing, Sharing.' We also made a sign at the same time with two fingers. I loved being with the others boys; we played games and did crafts. One of the boys would help me to do my craft and there was always someone to push my wheelchair so I could join in the games. No one knew how to find a way for me to communicate at that time. But one day my mom was eating some toast and I wanted some. I remembered the sharing sign from Bea-

> vers and I made that sign to my mom. It took her a while but she finally
> clued in and figured out that I wanted to share her toast. After that
> Mom decided that maybe we should learn some sign language to-
> gether. It worked.

Kyle's communication breakthrough is recounted as a direct, albeit serendipitous, outcome of an inclusive Beavers program. Without diagnostic or clinical interventions, this "eureka" moment belonged to Kyle and his mother. Anecdotal accounts of this kind of agency-enhancing triumph are a recurrent motif in disability narratives. Children — and adults — discover latent capacities and resolve problems that confound the experts. While it is beyond the scope of this chapter to draw conclusions of an empirical nature about this phenomenon, we can appreciate — at least intuitively — a link between inclusion and the broadening of exposures; between broadened exposures and aug- mented individual repertoires of possibility; between expanded reper- toires of tools and ideas and an increased likelihood of their successful application. As Kyle concludes, "It worked."

For Kyle and for the other young people featured in this article, inclusion worked in more generalized ways as well. Almost without exception, these young people defined inclusion as primarily not a concept but an experience — an experience of growth and discovery universally regarded as both personally emancipatory and socially rewarding. For each of the young contributors, inclusion confers the valued prize of friendship, and with that prize, a coming into being of a self connection to others, known, honoured and cared for.

Aaron, for example, presents the depth of his understanding of friend- ship in terms that resonate with empathy and compassion:

> I feel sorry for other people who don't have friends ... I can have fun
> and be happy and be myself with my friends ... I like being with them
> and I am happy when they are happy and sad when they are sad and
> I smile at them and give them hugs and I like them to be with me all
> the time ... They say hi to me and include me in their activities and
> help me if I need it and sit with me and look after me when I need it
> and they care about me when I am happy or sad or mad or upset and
> they hang out with me.

Aaron's friend Brandy, in her articulation of what makes a "REAL friend," draws mature insights from the wellspring of inclusion. Her friend Aaron is "different," but the difference that counts for Brandy is ethical, rather than functional or performative. On this scale, Aaron rises above his peer group and enters into valued relationships of unconditional friendship:

> Brandy: Aaron is a REAL friend. The best friend that a person could

ask for. He doesn't care what your marks are, how well you can play basketball, if you wear Nike shoes and Tommy jeans, if you have crooked teeth or zits on your face. He is the best kind of friend because he shows unconditional friendship, no strings attached!

As young people recount their experiences, it becomes clear that while mere physical proximity is a precondition, it is in no way determinative of the experience of inclusion. Friendship is the distinctive and defining feature of inclusion — friendship that is expressed freely as a dimension of being and exchanged without measure or consideration:

> Trevor: I don't understand why [Kyle's mother] thinks I give so much to our relationship. She is always telling me that I am giving so much to Kyle, but it never seems that way. I am just being myself — the best way I can. Even after a year and a half I still don't get it.

It is a rough and tumble friendship, rather than the "kid glove" variety — friendship in which both Kyle and Trevor can explore and express a fullness of selfhood, at work and play, in school and beyond, active and passive, in good or bad temper:

> Kyle: Some friends are just nice to you in school; they help you with your work or eat lunch with you. Then there's Trevor, he's my best friend. We hang out together, have sleepovers, go to the mall, listen to music, play video games, watch movies, tease each other and laugh a lot. Trevor and I accept each other just the way we are. Most of the time when Trevor and I are together we joke and have a good time but we do bug each other sometimes — that's OK. It's part of being a good friend.

Notably, the quality of friendship that defines inclusion is quite distinct from the dreary alliance of fellow captives, as Maresa Mackeith (1999) recalls in her remembering of childhood experiences in segregated facilities for disabled children:

> I have been to all types of schools. In the special school I was treated as if I didn't understand anything. I tried to make friends but we were all so badly treated that it was impossible to ever talk to each other. I don't want to see those people now because I get so sad.

In the experience of the young people interviewed for this chapter, the link between one's own sense of well-being and inclusion is straightforward and irreducible. For Kyle and Trevor and Aaron, the question of "how we feel and think about ourselves' is inextricably linked to feelings of being included:

Kyle: It feels THUMBS UP to be included and it feels really bad when you are not.

Trevor: It feels good to be included because you know that somebody cares about you, you have someone to trust and rely on.

Aaron: [If I were not included] I would be at home all the time and would be lonely and sad and angry.

Research by Jenkins and Keating (1998) confirms that robust networks of social relationship such as peer friendships correlate strongly with the development of childhood resilience and ability to cope with external stress. Operating as a kind of "natural intervention," feelings of connection to others have been demonstrated to contribute to a sense of security, integration and purposefulness. For Kyle, the stress of peer harassment is kept in perspective through a healthy sense of self forged in the mint of inclusion:

The worst thing about being in school is when kids ignore you or call you a loser but I think that happens to everyone not just to kids with special needs.... Some people worry about everybody being in the same classes together. I know that I belong with my friends and they belong with me.

The youths who contributed to this chapter highlighted themes of cooperation, trust and mutual support in their enumeration of the benefits of inclusion. Aaron's commentary below illustrates how inclusive friendships not only support confidence in his present identity, but enable him to push past fear at developmental thresholds. Inclusive friendships, we see, support not only *being*, but also *becoming*:

I can have fun with [my friends] and encourage them and concentrate better with my friends around.... I would not have the friends I have if I was not included. They are always there for me and are encouraging, supportive and helpful. They give me confidence in myself. I didn't think I could take the big step of high school because I was so afraid, then I found out all my friends were afraid too and it wasn't so hard after that. We were all the same.

In their reflections upon inclusive friendship, the young people who participated in this study did not appear to divide and differentiate along lines of physiology or demonstrable intellectual capacity. Norms of behaviour, physicality and communication appear more fluid, with the process of defining self and other founded instead upon values and standards of conduct. A true friend, as Brandy declared above, is one who does not judge you by the logo on your sneakers or the "zits" on your face.

In another comment she illustrates the value of acceptance in inclusive friendship in relation to the delicate unfolding of adolescent identity:

> When someone ignores you or yells at you we usually tend to stay away from that person, but not Aaron, we always come back and try again. Many people don't intend for anything to become of their first contact with Aaron but it always does. People are drawn to him and always want to be around him. Especially when they're having a bad day. Just being with him brings you all the comfort in the world. He gives us reassurance without saying a word. He seems to have an aura of acceptance about him.

The stranger, the alien in their midst is not the one whose speech patterns or behaviour mark him or her as different, but the one who does not share in the value system of inclusion — the "smart ass" new kid who makes a "big deal" out of the autistic boy's behaviour is quickly and definitively put in his place by his peers, and the bullying is stopped short.

> Brandy: I would feel really sorry for the kid that decided to pick on Aaron, because everyone stands up for him under all circumstances. When a new kid came to school and figured that he'd mention something negative about Aaron, every single one of the guys in the class stood up for Aaron and the subject didn't go any farther. If Aaron had been in a different class from ours or hadn't grown up with these kids and had such a close relationship, this situation could very likely have been quite different.

The meaning of inclusion to these young people is therefore bound together with the quest for identity. "Who we are" evolves and is nurtured through self-affirming relationship. Indeed, reciprocity is perhaps the single most important element in the inclusion testimonials provided. The relationships described are untainted by the charitable impulse of broader societal responses to disability, being instead characterized by mutuality and respect:

> Trevor: Kyle is fun to hang out with, he never stresses out on only one thing to do, and he takes things into consideration.

> Tamara: Aaron made the classroom more fun and more exciting to learn. He is one of the best friends I have had because of his autism. He listens to my problems and he will not tell anyone. He is very fun to be with and he is very smart. I am sure the other kids in my class that knew Aaron will agree that he is very bright and a very good friend. I think there should be more people like Aaron. The one thing I missed when I left Centennial school was Aaron. (from a letter to Mr. Herbert Seder, Deputy Superintendent, Wetaskiwin Regional Public Schools, 20 August 1997)

From these narratives we see that inclusion arises from an ethic not of tolerance, but of active valuation of difference. In the inclusive subculture from which Aaron and his classmates offer their reflections, Aaron's growing confidence takes root in a rich ground of peer respect, support and affection. In his easy camaraderie with Trevor and others, Kyle masters and manifests an identity of spirited self-assurance and irrepressible vitality. In high school environments that critics of the system have decried as "the most dysfunctional institutions yet devised by the developed world" (Wente 2000), clusters of Edmonton youth co-create oases of mutuality and engagement. The meaning of inclusion is quick and vibrant, suggested — even if never fully captured — in these images of mutual *being* and *becoming*.

## Equality and Exile: Lunch in Room 20

Belonging. Such an achingly simple word. It conjures up some of our deepest yearnings, and for some of us, perhaps our most painful memories. Equality claims begin and end with a desire for belonging, for community. Ideas of equality lie at the heart of the Canadian promise of community. Yet we know that communities are built in two ways: by welcoming in, and by keeping out.

The desire to belong is intense and profound. Each of us has a deeply personal experience of that, which has been built since childhood ...

Equality law seeks to protect and promote belonging; to allow others into the fold, and to encourage and cement our bonds of community. It is meant to do this by a subtle and complex mix of burden and benefit: the iron hand in the velvet glove. (Pentney 1996)

Kyle: The one thing I don't like about my school is that all the kids with special needs eat lunch in room twenty.

Aaron is sixteen years old and a grade ten student. Aaron has autism. From kindergarten through grade six, Aaron was included in all of the regular programming in his neighbourhood elementary school. Toward the end of Aaron's sixth grade year, he and his family were advised that Aaron would be grouped with other disabled youth and placed in a separate class in junior high school, with specific "inclusive experiences" to be provided in designated areas, such as physical education. On Aaron's behalf, his family took legal action to challenge this decision and to have Aaron continue to attend classes with his non-disabled friends. Throughout the course of this legal process, Aaron pursued his grade seven education at home. Aaron's friends from elementary school came to his house after school and did their homework with him. They visited for lunch occasionally on school days and kept in touch through weekend activities at church, the local arena and swimming pool. They wrote letters to the school board, supporting Aaron's right to a fully inclusive education:

> Dear School Board,
>     I think that Aaron should be in a regular class. He has been in one up until now so why switch?
>     Aaron is my best friend and it is important that he is in a regular class because otherwise he will not learn as much as he is able to. Aaron needs to be in a regular class so he will have lots of friends.
>     Aaron has taught me lots of things and I think it is important that he is in the right class. My class.
>     Yours truly,
>     Tanner

After an academic assessment at the conclusion of his seventh grade year, Aaron was permitted to join his friends in junior high school. According to his mother, "Aaron not only adjusted to the changes from home to junior high, he sailed in and never looked back."

For Aaron, his family and friends, as for many other Canadian families whose disabled children are denied fully inclusive educational services,[10] the issue is one of entitlement and rights rather than one of "professional" judgment and institutional policy. Aaron's friend Brandy sees it this way:

> We all have our differences. Some kids have difficulty writing, others (like me) understanding things like weird poetry or stories. Whatever the case, we all struggle with different things — some more than others, but that is no reason to single them out from everyone else. Society would not consider dividing people up by their hair colour, or whether they wore glasses or not, so why should kids like my friend Aaron be any different? Some people may call it specialized learning, but I call it prejudice.

Enter the iron hand in the velvet glove. Canadian equality law, expressed in section 15 of our Charter and in federal and provincial human rights legislation, has taken us a good distance toward exposing the prejudice that Brandy refers to and uprooting deeply embedded patterns of discrimination and disadvantage. Equality rights jurisprudence has provided important legal and analytical tools for remediation and redress, whenever discrimination — either direct or indirect — is found in public or private actions, policies and systems. Upon closer examination, however, we encounter inherent limitations to the rights/equality paradigm in uprooting the "persistent social and economic disadvantage" (*Eldridge v. British Columbia [Attorney General]* 1997) faced by disabled persons. Rights, it seems, are oriented toward what "we do" and "how we act," offering legal recourse to persons excluded from mainstream activity and opportunity. On the other hand, questions of "who we are" and "how we feel and think about ourselves" may be less readily justiciable, particularly in a social, legal and policy context characterized by an unconscious but pervasive majoritarian bias — a climate that makes "entrance into the social mainstream ... conditional upon [the] emulation of able-bodied norms" (ibid. 1997).

What does our justice system offer to children and/or families of children who have been excluded from community participation? Although it is beyond the scope of this chapter to fully map developments and precedents in Canadian human rights and equality jurisprudence likely to bear upon such claims, it will be instructive for the present purpose to review two significant cases where young people with disabilities have been directly involved as plaintiffs. The first of these is *Youth Bowling Council of Ontario v. McLeod*, a 1990 decision of the Ontario Divisional Court (C.H.R.R. Ont. Div. Ct. 1990).

The complainant in this case was Tammy McLeod, an eleven-year old girl with cerebral palsy who, beginning at the age of six, had participated in recreational bowling at an alley near her home in Strathroy, Ontario. Tammy bowled with the assistance of a wooden ramp, the top end of which rested in her lap while she sat on a chair behind the foul line. Her mother would place the ball at the top of the ramp and Tammy would line up the ramp to direct the ball, then push it down the ramp.

Tammy was registered with the Ontario Youth Bowling Council and in 1985 qualified with other children from her area to compete in the Council's zone tournament. However, Tammy was not allowed to compete in the tournament because the Council ruled that Tammy was ineligible as long as she used a ramp to deliver the ball.

A Human Rights Board of Inquiry in 1988 ordered the Council to allow Tammy to compete using the ramp and to enact a new rule that would provide for the accommodation of young disabled bowlers. The Council appealed this decision, arguing that "for a tournament to represent a fair contest, a fair comparison of the skills of the participants, it was essential that the participants make use of the same physical attributes" (ibid. 1990: para. 32).

In dismissing this appeal and upholding the Board of Inquiry decision, the Court noted:

> The integration of handicapped and non-handicapped bowlers achieves a major aim of the public policy of Ontario as enunciated in the preamble to the [Human Rights] Code. To exclude the handicapped from the tournament setting when they are welcome... in the non-tournament setting is not acceptable in the absence of an over-riding reason. The suggested reason is the

effect upon the fairness of the tournament but on the evidence such an effect from Tammy's participation — or a dozen Tammys for that matter — would be minuscule.

The unspoken premise underlying the Council's argument is, I think, as follows: that the degree of organization of the tournament, its prestige, its nation-wide scope and its declaration of a champion preclude participants employing assisting devices. I cannot accept the premise that a sporting tournament however organized, however widespread, however prestigious, is thereby exempt from the reach of the remedial effects of the Code. The use of otherwise sanctioned aids in the tournament setting is not an undue hardship to the Council.

There is no evidence of hardship to the competitors. They are not required to alter the manner in which they bowl in any way. The evidence is clear that Tammy's device gives her no competitive advantage over others. Her ball speed is low. She cannot significantly vary the velocity of the ball — an important competitive element; nor can she impart spin to it, which according to the Council's expert is one key to success.... No evidence was given by any competitor complaining of Tammy's device. The children appear to be completely accepting of her. (Ibid. 1990: para. 33–35)

For Tammy, the outcome of a three-year process of litigation was an affirmation of her right to participate in the inclusive recreational activity of her choice. For Aaron, the outcome of a one-year process of advocacy and home schooling[11] was an affirmation of his right to participate in a fully inclusive high school setting. In both cases, cherished principles of equality were invoked successfully "to protect and promote belonging." But in neither case, however, was an absolute right to inclusion affirmed. For Tammy, the court's judgment appears to attach considerable significance to:

- the absence of complaints by Tammy's peers;
- the absence of any necessity for others to adapt their manner of play; and
- Tammy's continued competitive disadvantage.

For Aaron, as we have seen above, a lengthy trial process was circumvented by a formal assessment that demonstrated academic parity with his peers. Although at times his behaviour and methods of communication departed from social norms, his academic aptitude — to his benefit — conformed to those same norms. In ways that directly parallel the success of Tammy's claim, we can see that the support of Aaron's peers, the fact that he would require no — "special treatment" that might be interpreted as privileging and the absence of any necessity for major overhaul to the high school program" — all of these factors weighed significantly in the success of his claim for an inclusive school placement.

Aaron's experience contrasts sharply with the second case presented here for review: *Eaton v. Brant County Board of Education* (1995). This case centered upon the educational placement of Emily Eaton, a twelve-year-old child with multiple disabilities. For the first three years of her education, Emily, with the assistance of a full-time educational assistant, had attended regular classes alongside her non-disabled peers in the local public school. Upon the identification of concerns over Emily's increasing isolation within a "theoretically integrated setting," the Identification, Placement, and Review Committee of her county's school board had determined that Emily — like Aaron — should be placed with other disabled children in a segregated special education class. Emily's parents opposed this decision, arguing for Emily's continued access to inclusive education and pursuing the case through several levels of appeal, up to the Supreme Court of Canada. The Ontario Court of Appeal ruling of Madame Justice Arbour in *Eaton* examined the meaning of exclusion in a broad social context:

> In all areas of communal life, the goal pursued by and on behalf of disabled persons in the last few decades has been integration and inclusion. In the social context, inclusion is so obviously an important factor in the acquisition of skills necessary for each of us to operate effectively as members of the group that we treat it as a given. Isolation by choice is not necessarily a disadvantage. People often choose to live on the margin of the group, for their better personal fulfillment. But forced exclusion is hardly ever considered an advantage. Indeed, as a society, we use it as a form of punishment. Exile and banishment, even without more, would be viewed by most as an extremely severe form of punishment. Imprisonment, quite apart from its component of deprivation of liberty, is a form of punishment by exclusion, by segregation from the mainstream. Within the prison setting, further segregation and isolation are used as disciplinary methods. Even when prisoners are segregated from the main prison population for their own safety, the fact that they will have to serve their sentences apart from the main prison population is considered an additional hardship. (*Eaton v. Brant (County) Board of Education* 1995, 22 O.R. (3d) 1 (C.A.): 15)

The Ontario Court of Appeal ruled that the decision to educate Emily in a special classroom for disabled students — against her wishes as expressed by her legal representatives — was discriminatory within the meaning of section 15 of the Charter. The Court directed that "unless the parents of a disabled child consent to the placement of that child in a segregated environment, the school board must provide a placement that is the least exclusionary from the mainstream and still reasonably capable of meeting the child's special needs" (*Eaton v. Brant County Board of Education* 1997, 1 S.C.R. 241: 40). In her decision, Madame Justice Arbour noted the reciprocity of benefit that is the characteristic endowment of the inclusive relationships highlighted earlier in this chapter:

> Inclusion into the main school population is a benefit to Emily because without it, she would have fewer opportunities to learn how other children work and how they live. And they will not learn that she can live with them, and they with her.
> ... The loss of the benefit of inclusion is no less the loss of a benefit simply because everyone else takes inclusion for granted. (*Eaton v. Brant (County) Board of Education* 1995, 22 O.R. (3d) 1 (C.A.): 15–16)

Regrettably, the decision of the Ontario Court of Appeal was ultimately overturned by the Supreme Court of Canada, and the Tribunal's placement of Emily in a special education class was upheld. Mr. Justice Sopinka, writing for the majority, endorsed the principle that "integration should be recognized as the norm of general application because of the benefits it generally provides" (*Eaton v. Brant County Board of Education* 1997, 1 S.C.R. 241: 69).[12] He framed his judgment, however, in terms that placed Emily's "differences" central to the analysis, concluding that her "actual personal characteristics" (i.e., her impairments) were such that she required a special educational placement "in order to achieve equality." Disability discrimination, unlike other forms of discrimination, according to Justice Sopinka:

> will frequently require distinctions to be made taking into account the actual personal characteristics of disabled persons....
> [D]isability, as a prohibited ground, differs from other enumerated grounds such as race or sex because there is no individual variation with respect to these grounds. However, with respect to disability, this ground means vastly different things depending upon the individual and the context. (Ibid. 1997, 1 S.C.R. 241: 66, 69)

Within a framework described by Justice Sopinka as "the difference dilemma," what amounts to discrimination against one person with a particular kind or degree of impairment (such as Tammy or Aaron) may amount to equal treatment of another person with a different kind or degree of impairment (such as Emily). According to the Court, exclusion or segregation might be "both protective of equality and violative of equality depending upon the person and the state of disability" (ibid. 1997, 1 S.C.R. 241: 69).

Within such a framework, difference matters profoundly. Distinctions must be made along lines of demonstrable physical and intellectual function in order to determine "suitable" routes to equality. The more fluid norms and the value-based categories modeled by Aaron, Brandy, Kyle, Linda, Lynnsey and Trevor stand far removed from this analysis. The question identified by the Court as pivotal in *Eaton* was whether "the individual [in this case, Emily] can profit from the advantages that integration provides" (ibid.). Emily herself, rather than her school environment, became the focus of interrogation. At the end of the day, given the particular nature and extent of her impairments, the Court assessed that the Tribunal had balanced Emily's "various educational interests... taking into account her special needs, and concluded that the best possible placement was in the special class" (ibid. at 76). The Court determined that no equality rights violation could be found in Emily's involuntary assignment to an exclusionary school placement.

While the Court in *Eaton* acknowledged a qualified "right" to inclusion, the Court's exploration of the roots of *exclusion* may be traced back to the more conventional conceptions of disability disadvantage related to "acting" and "doing," but perhaps eclipsing those related to "being" and "belonging."

> Exclusion from the mainstream of society results from the construction of a society based solely on "mainstream" attributes to which disabled persons will never be able to gain access. Whether it is the impossibility of success at a written test for a blind person, or the need for ramp access to a library, the discrimination does not lie in the attribution of untrue characteristics to the disabled individual. The blind person cannot see and the person in a wheelchair needs a ramp. Rather, it is the failure to make reasonable accommodation, to fine-tune society so that its structures and assumptions do not result in the relegation and banishment of disabled persons from participation, which results in discrimination against them. The discrimination inquiry which uses "the attribution of stereotypical characteristics" reasoning as commonly understood is simply inappropriate here. It may be seen rather as a case of reverse stereotyping which, by not allowing for the condition of a disabled individual, ignores his or her disability and forces the individual to sink or swim within the mainstream environment. It is recognition of the actual characteristics, and reasonable accommodation of these characteristics which is the central purpose of s. 15(1) in relation to disability. (Ibid. at 67)

A critique of the *Eaton* decision must begin with some recognition that Emily's functional capacities might be directly relevant to the kinds of accommodations needed in order for her to communicate, to participate and to learn in a classroom environment. To this extent, her actual characteristics, like those of the blind person or the wheelchair user in Justice Sopinka's examples above, do perhaps merit taking into account "in order to achieve equality." This first phase of analysis would indeed be essential background to the interrogation not of Emily's eligibility for inclusion, but rather of the appellant school board's practices — framing the question around whether the Board had in fact forced Emily "to sink or swim within the mainstream [classroom] environment," enabling or obstructing her opportunities to act in the social world.

Whether or not this different framing of the question would have led to a more favourable outcome in the *Eaton* case is moot — as, ultimately, was the decision itself. Following the Tribunal's initial move to consign Emily to a segregated class, the Eaton family had undertaken the transitions necessary to transfer Emily to an inclusive class within the separate school system. Indeed, although the factual record before the Court included little or no evidence of this, at the time of the court's decision Emily had already enjoyed several years of the same kind of positive and successful inclusion described in Aaron's story. Perhaps, like Aaron, Emily "sailed in and never looked back."

Nevertheless, the legal outcome in Emily Eaton's equality claim highlights certain fundamental inadequacies in a rights analysis that preserves what Martha Minow (1990) coincidentally also described as "the dilemma of difference." Superficial implementation of a kind of "exclusionary inclusion" — placing disabled children unsupported and without creative intervention in classrooms that are already too large and under-resourced — leaves them vulnerable to an equality analysis that sees their differences as "residing in themselves" (Minow 1990). Such an analysis perpetuates their disadvantage by imposing conditions upon inclusion, once again holding out the offer of equal participation as contingent upon their capacity to emulate valued social norms.

Instead of focusing upon the kinds of relationships that need to be cultivated to ensure a young person's well-being, leading to a critical exploration of resources and methods most likely to yield this result, conventional rights discourse may relegate to Lunch in Room 20, children whose differences confound the imaginations of those empowered to affirm and protect their being and belonging. Distinctions made on the basis of "actual personal characteristics" are surely neither relevant nor appropriate in the context of determining an individual's access to relationship, mutuality, respect and selfhood.

The equality rights framework clearly and properly gives those who seek to challenge barriers to full participation a persuasive language in which to frame their assertions and a legal forum in which to advance their arguments. Rights-based mechanisms, however, may be better suited to remedy restrictions upon activity than they are to remedy restrictions upon "being" and "belonging." Moreover, the effectiveness of equality doctrine in securing a right to inclusion in hotly contested cases remains far from certain. The unfolding of both Tammy and Aaron's claims, however, suggests that prior inclusive experiences enhance the likelihood of success in the assertion of rights-based claims. To the extent that inclusion forges relationships of mutual regard and respect, these relationships may accord some level of resilience and surety to rights entitlement.

## Conclusion: An Appetite for Involvement

> To rescue our children we will have to let them save us from the power we embody: we will have to trust the very difference that they forever personify. (Jordan 1978)

As this chapter began with the voices of youth, fleshing out meanings of inclusion drawn from the pulse of experience, it is appropriate to turn again to the same contributors in shaping the study's conclusion. As we listen for guidance and correction, seeking to mobilize "the power we embody" as educators, analysts, policymakers, electors and decisionmakers, we must do so in a manner that supports youth's quest for justice and inclusion.

How has the exercise of adult governance influenced the experiences of inclusion described by these young people? What impact and contribution do they attribute to adults in positions of authority?

Lynnsey is seventeen years old and a grade-twelve student. Lynnsey's youngest brother has Down Syndrome and some hearing difficulties. Lynnsey regrets that her brother has been denied the opportunity to receive his education in an inclusive classroom. Her sensitivity to this injustice informs many of her interactions and social encounters:

> When I was younger I was attending a Christmas Party and there was a bunch of kids there — one with Tourette's, a son of my mother's friend. There was a group of us who were going to go swimming in the pool — me and this other girl suggested we should invite him to swim with us.
> That's when an adult spoke up and said that probably wasn't a very good idea because we might have a hard time getting along with him. Being surrounded by children with disabilities my whole life I thought this was a weird thing to say. Needless to say, me and that girl never went swimming but made a friend!

For Lynnsey, the adult's cautionary injunction was simply "a weird thing to say," irrational, but happily circumventable. For a number of the other youth contributors, adult prohibitions to inclusion were seen as more seriously problematic:

> Linda: I personally think that many teachers fear inclusion, they fear that it is something too expensive, too difficult and somehow they feel they don't know how to react or even approach students with developmental disabilities, and so they react to these feelings by stating they are against it or don't believe in it.

Linda's analysis of adult behaviour in response to unspoken, unacknowledged feelings is acutely perceptive. Her observations invite us to critical self-reflection regarding the extent to which arguments based on economic "realities" or logistical "impracticalities" may mask deeper feelings of inadequacy and inexperience, vestiges perhaps of the very system of exclusionary practice through which many adults grew to maturity.

She reminds us that she and her peers are ready to take up the challenge — and the opportunity — that we deny them: to lead, from the place of our hindrance:

> I believe fellow students in a high school would like to figure out how to help out a fellow classmate with a disability if they are given the chance. It appears the attitudes of teachers and principals act as major obstacles to our having this opportunity.

Kyle speaks convincingly of adults who chronically underestimate his abilities. He highlights the recurring interference of rigid thinking and other adult inhibitions to creativity — patterned tendencies that are fatal to the project of inclusion:

> Sometimes inclusion is difficult at school because sometimes people do not believe that I can do things and don't even give me a chance. When people's expectations are set it gets in the way of inclusion happening because they don't use their imaginations to find ways to make it happen.

For Lynnsey, Linda and Kyle, the exercise of adult authority in the lives of disabled children undercuts the compelling logic of inclusion with the blunt violence of stereotype, foreclosure and devaluation. Their observations are supported by research that explores the experiences and perspectives of disabled children. Shakespeare et al. (1999) highlight the extent to which adult behaviour and social settings define, reinforce and legitimize categories of difference and inferiority that disabled children must actively resist in their attempts to construct autonomous, competent and interdependent identities. They suggest that "the institutionalization of difference seemed to be an unconscious justification of the segregated practices found in many schools" (Shakespeare et al. 1999). Antle and Frazee (1999) noted in their study of transitions to independence that young people with disabilities were compelled to "blast away at low expectations," especially in educational systems, mirroring the experience of American disability activist Ed Roberts forty years earlier. Middleton (1999), as well, documents the extent to which disabled youth in her study "felt written off and patronized," deprived by low expectations and lack of opportunity.

Social inclusion can be understood as either a process or an outcome. As a *process*, social inclusion invokes us to cultivate in all children an appetite for involvement, self-expression and self-discovery, along with a well-founded expectation that their participation will be welcomed, their choices supported, their contributions valued and their integrity safeguarded. As an *outcome*, social inclusion shows itself in communities that afford a range of meaningful and respectful opportunities for children's involvement, expression and discovery, consistently and concurrently promoting children's "being" and "becoming," as well as their "doing" and "acting."

The relationship between inclusion and equality can be seen, through the lens of disability, as a relationship of two distinct, integral and complementary principles, both operating in the service of just social outcomes. Just as the principle of equality is expressed in the currency of rights, the principle of inclusion is expressed in the currency of relationships. Standing like pillars of equal weight and proportion, they command us to equal attention and regard. Each is weakened in the absence of the other; each reinforces the imperative of the other for the securement of human dignity and well-being.

This chapter has attempted to highlight the role of children and youth as social agents, seeking to exercise autonomy and choice, to assert values and identity and to influence the institutional and political culture within which their dreams for the future must take root. The extent to which rights and rights discourse can be used as tools to support these processes will depend in large measure upon our capacity to abandon hierarchies of difference and to negotiate new relationships of mutuality, empathy and respect.

> The question of equality is the meaning of equal moral worth, given the reality that in almost every conceivable concrete way we are not equal but vastly different and vastly unequal in our needs and abilities. The object is not to make these differences disappear when we talk about equal rights, but to ask how we can structure relations of equality among people with many different concrete inequalities. (Nedelsky 1993: 21)

We conclude this chapter with the suggestion that although we may be vastly unequal in our needs and abilities, we are much more like one another in our need, desire and capacity for human connection.

## Notes

1. The author extends her appreciation to a number of young Canadians who presented in a panel entitled "Inclusive Education" at the Canadian Association for Community Living First National Family Conference in Edmonton, Alberta, on October 21, 2000. Much of the content of this article reflects upon their presentations. The quotations come from the presentations and from e-mail exchanges with the author following the conference. Thanks also to Heather and Paul Kohl, Brian Lillo and Vanessa Grimm for their assistance in facilitating these dialogues.
2. Age at time of research interviews.
3. At time of interviews, Lynnsey was seventeen years old and a grade-twelve student.
4. At time of interviews, Trevor was fifteen years old and a grade-nine student.
5. At time of interviews, Aaron was sixteen years old and a grade-ten student.
6. At time of interviews, Kyle was fifteen years old and a grade-nine student.
7. At time of interviews, Linda was eighteen years old and a first-year college student.
8. At time of interviews, Brandy was sixteen years old and a grade-ten student.
9. A computerized augmentative communication device for non-speaking individuals.
10. See, for example, the Ottawa case of nine-year-old Zachary Bonnah, whose father was charged with trespassing after making repeated attempts to take Zachary to school on days when special education assistants (allocated by the Board for only two days a week) were not available (Rupert 2000).
11. According to Aaron's mother, neither she nor any of Aaron's teachers knew that he was capable of working at grade-level curriculum until his year of home schooling. The academic assessment that demonstrated this fact proved to be crucial in negotiating his acceptance back into school, without the necessity of a lengthy trial process.
12. It is worth noting, as was pointed out by O. Endicott, in an unpublished paper entitled "Key Trends in Case Law Pertaining to Supports for Persons with Disabilities," that:

> The Supreme Court continued to endorse inclusion as the constitutional norm in 2000, when Justice Binnie in the Granovsky judgment re-asserted Justice Sopinka's words and reinforced them with a quotation from Justice Thurgood Marshall's dissent in the U.S. Supreme Court decision in *Cleburne v. Cleburne Living Centre Inc.*, where he wrote that exclusion "deprives the [disabled] of much of what makes for human freedom and fulfilment — the ability to form bonds and to take part in the life of a community."

# Social Inclusion as Solidarity: Re-Thinking the Child Rights Agenda

*Michael Bach*

## Introduction

A few months back a story[1] came to me across cyberspace attached to an email message. The story goes like this:

> In Brooklyn, New York, CHUSH is a school that caters to learning disabled children. Some children remain in CHUSH for their entire school career, while others can be main-streamed into conventional schools. At a CHUSH dinner, the father of a CHUSH child delivered a speech that would never be forgotten by all who attended. After extolling the school and its dedicated staff, he cried out, "Where is the perfection in my son Shaya? Everything God does is done with perfection. But my child cannot understand things as other children do. My child cannot remember facts and figures as other children do. Where is God's perfection?" The audience was shocked by the question, pained by the father's anguish and stilled by the piercing query. "I believe," the father answered, "that when God brings a child like this into the world, the perfection that he seeks is in the way people react to this child." He then told the following story about his son Shaya:

> One afternoon Shaya and his father walked past a park where some boys Shaya knew were playing baseball. Shaya asked, "Do you think they will let me play?"
> Shaya's father approached one of the boys in the field and asked if Shaya could play. The boy looked around for guidance from his teammates. Getting none, he took matters into his own hands and said "We are losing by six runs and the game is in the eighth inning. I guess he can be on our team and we'll try to put him up to bat in the ninth inning."
> Shaya's father was ecstatic as Shaya smiled broadly. Shaya was told to put on a glove and go out to play short center field. In the bottom of the eighth inning, Shaya's team scored a few runs but was still behind by three.
> In the bottom of the ninth inning, Shaya's team scored again and now with two outs and the bases loaded with the potential winning run on base, Shaya was scheduled to be up. Would the team actually let Shaya bat at this juncture and give away their

chance to win the game?

Surprisingly, Shaya was given the bat. Everyone knew that it was all but impossible because Shaya didn't even know how to hold the bat properly, let alone hit with it. However as Shaya stepped up to the plate, the pitcher moved a few steps to lob the ball in softly so Shaya should at least be able to make contact.

The first pitch came in and Shaya swung clumsily and missed. One of Shaya's teammates came up to Shaya and together they held the bat and faced the pitcher waiting for the next pitch. The pitcher again took a few steps forward to toss the ball softly towards Shaya. As the pitch came in, Shaya and his teammate swung at the bat and together they hit a slow ground ball to the pitcher. The pitcher picked up the soft grounder and could easily have thrown the ball to the first-base man. Shaya would have been out and that would have ended the game. Instead, the pitcher took the ball and threw it high to right field, far beyond the reach of the first baseman.

Everyone started yelling, "Shaya, run to first. Run to first."

Never in his life had Shaya run to first. He scampered down the baseline wide-eyed and startled.

By the time he reached first base, the right fielder had the ball. He could have thrown the ball to the second baseman who would tag out Shaya who was still running. But the right fielder understood what the pitcher's intentions were, so he threw the ball high and far over the third baseman's head. Everyone yelled, "Run to second, run to second." Shaya ran towards second base as the runners ahead of him deliriously circled the bases towards home. As Shaya reached second base, the opposing short stop ran to him, turned him in the direction of third base and shouted, "Run to third." As Shaya rounded third, the boys from both teams ran behind him screaming, "Shaya run home."

Shaya ran home, stepped on home plate and all 18 boys lifted him on their shoulders and made him the hero, as he had just hit a "grand slam" and won the game for his team.

"That day," said the father softly with tears now rolling down his face, "those 18 boys reached their level of God's perfection."

I was very moved by this story. One of the lines that struck me most was the father's belief that "perfection" lies not in his son, or in any child, but in the ways people react to his child. This insight shifts our view about what matters. We turn from a child's disability to the ways in which the child is recognized by others, to the way others "react" and know the child. The shift in view the story records is central, I believe, to understanding what social inclusion is all about. My aim in this chapter is to formulate a notion of social inclusion that could help to advance a political and public policy agenda for the well-being of children in Canada, with a particular focus here on children with disabilities and their families.

The paper is organized around the following contentions. Social inclusion is more a normative than descriptive term. I suggest that one of its core notions is that societal institutions should be organized to provide *valued recognition* to diverse groups, to the "others" often marginalized by a dominant political culture. Calls for inclusion as valued recognition are growing as the dilemma of the "rights revolution" becomes clear — a context where rights are expanded and exclusion is entrenched. A social inclusion agenda could address this dilemma by promoting social solidarity across expanding social, ethnic and cultural differences that increasingly characterize and divide so many societies, often in destructive ways. I argue that policy analysis should reveal ways that social, economic and political arrangements systematically undermine social solidarity by devaluing certain people and groups, even though their rights are assured. Fostering solidarity across differences in our society is an important step in creating a culture where citizenship rights people hold can be more fully realized in their daily lives.

In the final section of the chapter, I show how a social inclusion analysis could be applied to the exclusions facing children with disabilities to generate a public agenda for change. It would bring to light a number of the rules and practices by which the devaluation of children with disabilities is constructed. Stereotyping of children, practices to "cleanse" the human genome of genetic disability and indicators for measuring and monitoring child development at a population level that equates disability with ill-health and abnormal development are the priorities that I suggest for analysis.

# Calling for Inclusion and Facing the Dilemma with the Rights Revolution

## Defining social inclusion

A large body of literature on social exclusion details various ways in which particular population groups are denied participation in, and access to benefits and advantages of political, social and economic institutions. Social inclusion names a goal that brings exclusion into view and into question. It expresses an aspiration that the arrangements between us be inclusive — whether in our personal relationships, a neighbourhood baseball game like the one Shaya joined or in our social, political and economic institutions in the public and private sectors. "Social inclusion" names an ideal that arrangements not disadvantage certain "others" because of their differences from the dominant norms; that arrangements not allocate benefits, status and advantages in ways that misrecognize, devalue or stereotype certain groups in relation to others. It means that arrangements should not foster or fund forms of recognition that deepen and entrench the social distance between certain groups (e.g., residential and education segregation of disabled persons would not survive such a test). Socially inclusive arrangements would help to nurture paths of mutual recognition that close the distance in ways that bring respect and value for the differences that define us.

When social inclusion is viewed in this way, we can understand how the term might sometimes be used as a political claim for full citizenship or as an ideal to which societal organizations and institutions should aspire, or to name the process of reform of such arrangements. There are many institutional arrangements to which the claims, ideal and process of social inclusion could apply — for example, early childhood development services, recreation services, education, family support services, labour market training, arrangements that provide benefits through the tax system and by other means, and even those institutions that regulate, fund and undertake social and health research on human populations (e.g., the Human Genome Project), etc. Simply stated, such institutional arrangements should be inclusive, we should be able to examine the extent of their social inclusivity, and we should be able to launch a process of reform that we might call social inclusion.

## Calls for inclusion from the disability rights movement

Disability rights movements have helped to formulate this understanding of social inclusion. Over the past few years there have been many calls from disability movements nationally and internationally to advance a new agenda of inclusion with its variants of education inclusion (Bunch and Valeo 2000), labour market and workplace inclusion (Roeher Institute 1993), or community inclusion (Roeher Institute 2000a, 2000b and 2001). A call for inclusion is particularly resonant in the disability movement because it speaks directly to the problem of recognition and misrecognition of others. Many are seeking not only the *integration* of children with disabilities in the education system (usually a mix of regular and "special" or segregated classes and schools). They seek their *inclusion* — by which is meant an understanding of the child as a child first; education fully in regular classrooms; valued recognition that we expect all children to obtain from teachers and peers; inclusion in the activities and personal relationships in which children come to be known personally; and the needed physical, curricular and other accommodations to make this happen. It also means that difference and diversity will be taken seriously — communication systems will be developed that enable communication among children, even when some children do not communicate through spoken or written language. In this sense, social inclusion is not an agenda for homogenization, it is one that seeks to forefront the challenges of articulation and alliance and communicative capacities across the social and physical and communicational differences that define us.

Similarly, with labour market and workplace inclusion the issue is not simply provision of paid work opportunities to working-age adults with disabilities. Sheltered workshops have provided that for a number of years, but at the cost of many adults, particularly those with intellectual disabilities, not being recognized as capable of participating with co-workers in regular workplaces and the labour market, nor as deserving of basic labour rights. In this context, inclusion is the process of adapting workplaces, accommodating individuals and ensuring that labour market information is provided to individuals with disabilities in ways that enable their access to training and paid work opportunities in the mainstream.

Community inclusion has been conceptualized as a multi-faceted process involving personal, institutional and societal dimensions. It is the process of fostering valuing personal relationships for people marginalized by a disability status, securing rights protections, ensuring economic and educational inclusion and reconstructing community institutions (education, recreation, social services, etc.) to enable full participation by people with disabilities (Roeher Institute 2000b).

The vision of citizenship that a call for inclusion appeals to goes beyond the exercise of political rights and social and economic claims on the state. It demands social, cultural, political and economic participation in all institutions of society. The calls expand the arena for realizing citizenship from state provision to include civil society (that sphere of association, free press, public forums and community institutions), "emancipatory inasmuch as it liberates the individual from entrenched social hierarchies and allows interaction across formerly separated spaces" (Chandoke 1995: 198). Calls for educational, workplace and community inclusion are consistent with the shifts in theories of citizenship that Kymlicka and Norman (1994), Young (1990 and 2000), Chandoke (1995 and 1999) and others point to — citizenship is fundamentally about full and democratic participation and inclusion in the institutions of society. Such calls speak to a desire to go beyond the juridically defined individual of liberal theory whose rights realized may still encounter exclusion. The calls from the disability movement for inclusion envision forms of social identity, reciprocity and solidarity that provide a foundation for rights to be realized in relation to others, for a life well-lived in community.

## Why Call for Inclusion now? Dilemma of the "rights revolution"

Why these calls now? In their historical context, calls for inclusion appear at the cusp of the disability rights movement, mobilized most strongly in Canada over the past two decades. Part of the answer, it seems to me, lies in the assumed relationship between rights granted and valued recognition realized. In his recent tracing of "the rights revolution," its history and current achievements, Ignatieff (2000: 140) suggests that the "political and social history of Western society is the story of the struggle of all human groups to gain inclusion" in a political community where everyone has an equality of rights. It is true that an impressive framework of constitutional and statutory rights has been established in Canada at the federal, provincial and territorial levels. Canadians now have protections to equal benefit and advantage of the law without discrimination on the basis of disability, written into our constitution. We have rights to freedom from discrimination on the basis of age, disability, gender, race, etc. — in access to employment, housing and services available to the public — written into our provincial/territorial and federal human rights codes. International human rights instruments have also expanded. The Universal Declaration on Human Rights, and various subsequent conventions, hold the promise that the state's granting and protection of human rights will redress economic and social inequality and denial of freedoms. For children, the 1989 UN Convention on the Rights of the Child signifies the recognition of children as full citizens — deserving of comprehensive human rights protection.

This array of rights, Ignatieff suggests, requires of us all the "recognition, empathy, and if possible, reconciliation" with others who we understand bear equal rights to our own. Yet Ignatieff seems a little more sanguine than me in assuming that rights institutionalized will bring recognition and empathy across the boundaries of gender, race, ethnicity, religion and ability that continue to divide us. We have secured inclusion for many under the banner of human rights, but have we gained full inclusion for those who, nonetheless, through various policies and practices seem to be less recognized and valued than others? That the extension of human rights is a condition of valued recognition does not mean that valued recognition necessarily follows. This dilemma — of rights without recognition — we might call the dilemma of the rights revolution.

Evidence abounds that exclusions persist for many groups despite an expansion of rights. For example, there exists a litany of exclusions of children and youth with disabilities and their families, including endemic discrimination faced in access to life-saving treatments, to health care, to childcare services, to education (Roeher Institute 2000a); the sexual abuse of children and youth with disabilities — 50 percent of children and youth who are deaf; 60 percent of young women with an intellectual disability (Roeher Institute 1988; Sullivan et al. 1987); access to the justice system denied because they are often not considered credible witnesses to their own victimization (Roeher Institute 1995); inadequate integration into national child development schemes in many countries — children miss out on key developmental opportunities and are often not seen worthy of the investment (Alur 2000); continual downgrading of parents' labour force participation — for many to unemployment because they cannot obtain the workplace flexibility or outside supports they need (Irwin and Lero 1997; Roeher Institute 2000c); the over-representation of children with disabilities among those neglected and maltreated and who are in the child welfare system (Trocme et al. 2001).

For children and adults with disabilities, and their families, a rights-based approach to citizenship finally gives people a claim to press on the state, finally gives a promise of equality to challenge the violence, the poverty, the education exclusion so many face. But like so many others they face the harsh realities of the rights revolution of the latter part of the twentieth century. We have largely been getting what we asked for in terms of human rights instruments — but people are still excluded. The advance on social and economic rights and human rights law for children, for people with disabilities and others, has come with three main problems.

First, exit systems are in place where the law imposes obligations on the state and others to secure human rights for people with disabilities — granting to governments, employers and providers of services ways of exiting from their responsibilities and obligations when the costs seem too high — for instance, when inclusive education imposes an "undue hardship" on the school board, or when the rights of children with disabilities under Article 23 of the U.N. Convention on the Rights of the Child are limited to the extent that states have resources to deliver on them.

Second, in the Canadian legal context at least, the application of human rights law tends to provide individual compensation rather than the systemic and proactive policy change called for by the disability movement. As human rights are more and more institutionalized, fewer cases based on disability are coming forward. A small subset of cases of disability are proceeding, usually not those related to developmental or intellectual disability.[2] For those who do persist with a complaint, the process is long, and the outcome often provides little in return — certainly not "inclusion" as the disability movement expresses that ideal. Often the discrimination is based on stereotypes and devaluing attitudes, which the individual compensation does little to address (Mosoff 2001).

Third, human rights laws are still fragile structures when it comes to addressing discrimination and disadvantage faced by people with disabilities. These laws still need embedding in our legal and political cultures and in our policy frameworks if they are to be instruments of change. In Canada, children with disabilities have no entitlement to the disability-related supports they require to live at home with their families, though a medical diagnosis might give them an entitlement to long-term institutional care. Moreover, attempts to institutionalize greater entitlements meet resistance and those won remain fragile. For example, the Government of Ontario repealed the provincial Employment Equity law when the Conservative Party came to power in the 1990s. This law required that large employers simply identify and plan to address the barriers in workplaces to the employment of people with disabilities, women, racial minorities and Aboriginal or First Nations peoples, that they provide reports on the progress of removal of barriers and report on the numbers of people among these four groups who were employed in their organizations. This fragility is as true in the Western industrialized countries as it is in the South. Writing in the Indian context, Sheth suggests that political, social and economic rights provisions, as advanced as they might be on paper, prove of "limited utility for those without entitlements and outside of the organized sectors" (1991: 34).

Many in the disability movement believe that these dilemmas can only be resolved if we make integral to securing citizenship and human rights the process of recognizing and supporting others in ways that make their inclusion possible and valued. But how do we get there from here? How do we confront the dilemma of the rights revolution where rights granted do not mean recognition secured? If universal human rights provisions on their own do not secure inclusion for all among those who are recognized with value and status, and if our inclusion and value depends to a significant extent on recognition from others (e.g., school teachers, employers, community service providers, other citizens), the first step is to better understand this process of the denial and the granting of the recognition we seek.

## Jurisprudence and Theories of Equal Recognition

How is it that children with disabilities come to be recognized as something less than fully human, less deserving of the same moral and legal status as others? How are we to understand what is at the root of the various forms of exclusion, the various ways in which children with disabilities are misrecognized? Where do we turn if a human rights strategy cannot on its own address these exclusions? In *Making All the Difference: Inclusion, Exclusion, and American Law*, Minow (1990) suggests that the social and economic boundaries that define status according to class, race, age, ability, sexual orientation, etc. — are rooted in some way in law. While statutory and case law define and grant rights, they also define conditions for exercising those rights and for being known and recognized as a person or group able to exercise those rights. This is where the formula that equates the granting of rights, with securing equal and valued recognition, breaks down. Along with the rights granted, the exit systems the law also establishes can, in fact, mobilize kinds of recognition that devalue certain groups. We cannot fully understand the nature of exclusion of children, and of children with disabilities in particular, or how we might secure their inclusion among those fully valued, unless we bring into view this relationship between human rights, law and state policy, and the forms of knowledge and recognition they command.

## Social inclusion as valued recognition — what the jurisprudence suggests

Issues of recognition by others and who is included among those obtaining valued recognition and who is not are central issues in recent jurisprudence in Canada concerned with interpreting constitutionally protected equality rights. In the 1989 *Andrews v. Law Society of British Columbia* case, for example, a non-Canadian citizen argued that a provincial statute regulating the legal profession infringed his equality rights because it restricted him from practising law in Canada, simply on the grounds that he had not received his legal education in Canada. His nationality, he claimed, was used by a Canadian institution to recognize him and his capacities in devaluing ways. Writing the majority opinion for the Court and striking down the provision, MacIntyre J. wrote that equality rights under the Canadian *Charter of Rights and Freedoms* require:

> the promotion of a society in which all are secure in the knowledge that they are recognized at law as human beings equally deserving of concern, respect, and consideration. (*Andrews v. Law Society of British Columbia* 1989, 1 S.C.R. 143 at 171)

In the 1998 *Vriend v. Alberta* case, a man brought a human rights complaint on the basis that he had been fired from a teaching position because he was gay. The Supreme Court of Canada eventually ruled on the case, where the Court quoted a minority judgement in the *Egan* case:

> A discriminatory distinction is one capable of either promoting or perpetuating the view that the individual adversely affected by this distinction is less capable or less worthy of recognition or value as a human being or as a member of Canadian society, equally deserving of concern, respect, and consideration.

In the *Law v. Minister of Human Resources Development* (1999) case a thirty-five-year-old woman, denied a surviving spouse pension under the Canada Pension Plan because she was not sixty-five, claimed she had been discriminated against on the basis of her age. In a judgement rejecting her claim, the Supreme Court of Canada reviewed cases under the equality rights section of the Charter and wrote:

> It may be said that the purpose of s. 15(1) [the equality rights provision in the *Charter*] is to prevent the violation of essential human dignity and freedom through the imposition of disadvantage, stereotyping, or political or social prejudice, and to promote a society in which all persons enjoy recognition at law as human beings or as members of Canadian society, equally capa-

ble and equally deserving of concern, respect, and consideration.

These cases suggest that what we come to know of one another, how we come to know it and the institutionalized distinctions on which our views of one another rest, matter fundamentally. We might call the process of securing the equally valuing recognition characterized in these judgements as the process of social inclusion — inclusion among those recognized and valued "as a human being or as a member of Canadian society, equally deserving of concern, respect, and consideration." Guided by the language of the *Law v. Minister of Human Resources Development* case, this process of social inclusion is one of constructing forms of knowledge and institutional rules and boundaries that confer recognition and respect on individuals and groups as valued members of society and that do not systematically undermine that respect.

We cannot take for granted that rights instituted mean that valued recognition follows. Despite the legal requirements to ensure equal recognition under human rights law there are instructive cases where exclusions seem enforced because of whose knowledge is given status, whose act of recognition matters. For example, in the *Eaton v. Brant County Board of Education* case, the Supreme Court of Canada ruled that a school board was not required to accommodate Emily Eaton in a regular classroom because of the extent of her communication and other needs and that a segregated environment did not impose a burden on Emily (*Eaton v. Brant Country Board of Education* 1997, 1 S.C.R. 143 at 171).

In the Court's view, what came to be defined as Emily's physical, intellectual and communication competencies marked her as so different than other children that the instruction she was deemed to require was considered impossible in a regular classroom. Segregation was thereby justified (for a detailed analysis of this case, see the Canadian Association for Community Living 1999). The Court ruled that knowledge about Emily's "actual characteristics" resides only with those who know by the means of a bio-medical account of disability — where a "characteristic" comes to light only by its deviation from what is presumed to be "normal."[3] Moreover, this particular form of knowledge was validated as the only foundation for defining best interests of the child in this case and for making the educational placement. The knowledge of Emily Eaton's parents was consigned to the category of parental preference and choice. The struggle over whose knowledge, whose form of recognition of Emily was to count, and questions about the extent to which different forms of recognition bring dignity, were not addressed, were not adjudicated. Nonetheless, the court did decide whose knowledge of Emily was to be valued, what attitudes about Emily mattered and what forms of recognition were to count in determining where she would go to school.

## Resolving the dilemma of the rights revolution — at least in theory

If there is no simple equation between rights granted and forms of recognition that secure value and inclusion, then what other variables matter? In his analysis of the rights revolution, Ignatieff suggests that recognition of others:

> is something more than a process of concession and negotiation alone. Properly considered, recognition is an act of enlargement that enables both sides to envisage new possibilities of living together. We don't simply recognize each other for what we are; we recognize what we could become together. (2000: 136)

Honneth (1995) seeks to articulate a theory of recognition to make explicit how this "enlargement" happens. He does so by making problematic the ways in which, and the practices with which, we come to know one another. He does not assume that rights possessed lead simply to valued recognition. Rather, he understands an extension of human rights as one strategy in weaving bonds of recognition in society. In developing a multi-layered theory of recognition, he begins with the assertion that the value of "human dignity" emerges as a mobilizing force throughout history in response to forms of personal degradation. In asking what then must constitute human dignity, Honneth suggests that it depends upon intersubjective, mutual recognition. Hegel's and Mead's theories of intersubjectivity provide the starting point for Honneth — the self develops in "a process in which the individual can unfold a practical identity to the extent that he is capable of reassuring himself of recognition by a growing circle of communicative partners" (Honneth 1995: 249). He proceeds to identify three distinct forms of degradation and disrespect, and corresponding forms of recognition.

Physical maltreatment of another person's body is the first and most basic — sexual exploitation, trafficking in children, torture, other forms of physical abuse. Such actions by others bring many harms. For Honneth, one of the most profound is denying the person a recognition that personal control over and care for his or her body is, to others, worth preserving. Its converse is a form of mutual recognition that gives one self-confidence from an early age. It comes in the attachment to one's intimate circle and brings an understanding that one's physical and emotional needs can be heard and responded to by others; that others will take care with respect to one's body and grant respect to the boundaries it establishes. Such forms of recognition are granted by one's "concrete others" (Benhabib 1987), those in a relationship of personal knowing and attachment. Honneth calls this form of recognition simply — love. But, as we have seen, love is not enough to make sure a child can get into school, or that an adult will have a job, have friends in the community or exercise the right to vote.

So Honneth turns to the history of a second kind of disrespect — a disrespect that denies a person possession and enjoyment of legally established rights within a society. Refusing to recognize a person as a full member of society, as "a full-fledged partner in interaction who possesses equal moral rights" (Honneth 1995: 251), can bring a loss of self-respect. It denies the opportunity to view oneself, according to Honneth, from the standpoint of the "generalized other," in Mead's terms, who is institutionalized in established rights. The corresponding form of mutual recognition is a condition in which a person "learns to see herself from the perspective of her partners in interaction as bearers of equal rights" (ibid.: 254). As we have seen, even as people obtain their rights as citizens, they face exclusion. Such forms of recognition are not enough.

A third form of disrespect comes in others devaluing the ways in which persons or groups realize themselves, the form of life they establish or participate in, "within the horizon of the cultural traditions of a given society" (ibid.: 251). Such denial of recognition for the social contributions and forms of life of others undermines the value that a person or group can attach to their own abilities, their own ways of life. Honneth sees the counterpart form of mutual recognition as "solidarity" — an approval for "unconventional lifestyles" and valuing of people's uniqueness and difference. Such approval across cultural, racial, linguistic and genetic difference, for example, provides individuals and groups a cultural vantage point with which to affirm and value their own differences and those of others.

These three types, or "patterns," of mutual recognition — love, right and solidarity — each correspond to different levels of society: those concrete others in intimate relation to a person; the institutional framework of a society; and the broader set of cultural values and social forces. I find in Honneth's framework a key source for conceptualizing social inclusion as a multi-faceted and dynamic process for constructing at interpersonal, institutional and societal levels the valuing forms of knowledge and recognition the Supreme Court of Canada suggests are central to realizing human dignity and equal recognition of worth.

## Towards a social inclusion as solidarity agenda

I would argue for a social inclusion agenda to focus more clearly than it has on Honneth's third level of recognition — that of building a social solidarity that can bring value and recognition across differences of gender, language, communication, culture, age, ability, etc. This is not to leave aside a concern for fostering capacities and conditions for nurturing and attachment (level 1 in Honneth's framework), or for strengthening protection, participation and provision rights for children (level 2). Rather, it is to acknowledge that the solidarity that brings recognition across deeply divided social spaces is weak in certain respects in Canadian and other societies. Formulated in this way, solidarity is not simply about coalition-building or forging alliances for a particular political struggle. Following Honneth, it is much more about bringing to critical light the extent of recognition granted to different forms of life, the breadth of diversity that a particular set of cultural and institutional arrangements allow and the forms of knowledge that fortify exclusionary divides.

Advancing solidarity, in the way that Honneth defines the term — as valuing forms of life characterized by many social differences, including race, ethnicity, language and disability, can be read as a guiding purpose in recent political philosophy. In *Inclusion and Democracy*, Young (2000), for instance, suggests that solidarity is now a much-needed goal to pursue in securing inclusion for disadvantaged groups defined by culture, race, gender and disability in the benefits and resources allocated by state and society (housing, for example). She also advances solidarity as a goal to guide strategies and designs for political inclusion in processes of decision-making in local, regional, national and international governance. She frames the ideal as "differentiated solidarity" to account for the fact that valued recognition of others can mean supporting groups to form and support one another on the basis of particular affinities of race, ethnicity, etc. For Young, solidarity creates an obligation to "constitute and support institutions of collective actions organized to bring about relations of justice among persons" — where she defines justice as obtaining the conditions for self-development and self-determination (2000: 224). By bringing focus to solidarity as the test for the inclusiveness of social, economic and political institutions, Honneth and Young provide a vantage point for thinking about the possibilities and limitations of granting rights protections. Human rights can also serve as a test of inclusiveness — i.e., do all individuals and groups have adequate rights protections to enable them to access social, economic and political institutions? The test of solidarity shifts the obligation for securing inclusion exclusively from those who must press their rights claims in order to get access to the education system or to paid employment or to the political process. A focus on solidarity creates the obligation on others to enable those claims to be made and realized. It establishes the obligation, for example, to create education systems where all children can be included, fully recognized by others in ways that value them, and thereby thrive.

A conception of solidarity can also be rooted in the intellectual contributions to understanding societal recognition of different groups made by Canadian philosophers. For instance Taylor (1992) called the politics of our times a "politics of recognition"; Tully (1995) refers to the "politics of cultural recognition" in his study of the constitutional misrecognition of First Nations in Canada; Kymlicka's (1995) study advances proposals for securing recognition of diverse and disadvantaged cultural communities through constitutional and legal protection of minority rights; and O'Neill's (1994) study of children demonstrates their absence from the visions of liberal political theory. Honneth's work and

that of Canadian political philosophers are informing theories and proposals for recognition of diverse and marginalized religious, ethnic and
cultural communities in the U.S. (Gutmann 1994), in India (Chandoke
1999) and in the European Union (Habermas 1998) to name a few of the
applications. Much of this work seeks to account for the struggle for
recognition of diverse groups in a political age so defined by individual
rights.[4]

Solidarity is O'Neill's answer to the question about what can ground a
full citizenship for children in an age defined by liberal individual rights.
As he writes in *The Missing Child in Liberal Theory*, for an earlier Laidlaw
initiative on children, "any form of sustainable society is grounded in a
vast lore/law that requires us to extend ourselves in a community of civic
obligation towards others whose recognition simultaneously affords us
our own moral worth" (1994: 86). And, he confirms, solidarity is a means
by which this kind of recognition is mobilized in a society, it is the basis of
"any adequate concept of citizenship" (111).

Solidarity is also one way of answering Tully's question about the
"spirit" appropriate to an age of cultural diversity. After his detailed
analysis of the conventions for a constitutionalism that could account for
that diversity in the Canadian context, and after his argument that "mutual
recognition" among cultures must be a guiding convention for such a
constitutionalism, he quotes Vaclav Havel to answer his question: "if the
world today is not to become hopelessly enmeshed in ever more terrifying
conflicts, it has only one possibility: it must deliberately breathe the spirit
of multi-cultural co-existence into the civilization that envelops it." Still
quoting, Tully writes "the 'basis' of this 'new spirit' is for different peoples, religions, cultures' to learn to 'respect each other,' to 'respect and
honour each others' differences'" (1995: 212).

Taylor suggests that in the midst of our contemporary diversity, what
makes us equally worthy of respect is a "… universal human potential,
a capacity all humans share. This potential, rather than anything a
person may have made of it, is what ensures that each person deserves
respect." Moreover, "our sense of the importance of potentiality reaches
so far that we extend this protection even to people who through some
circumstance that has befallen them are incapable of realizing their
potential in the normal way" (Taylor 1992: 41–42). Taylor argues that this
"presumption" of equal worth should guide our "approach" to others
different from us and help guide us through the contemporary struggles
and "politics of recognition." With Habermas, I would say that solidarity
names the acts of approaching, recognizing and honouring others in ways
that bring an equal worth and respect, even to the strangers in our midst:

> Equal respect for everyone is not limited to those who are like us;
> it extends to the person of the other in his or her otherness. And
> solidarity with the other as one of us refers to the flexible "we" of

a community that resists all substantive determinations and extends its permeable boundaries ever further. This moral community constitutes itself solely by way of the negative idea of abolishing discrimination and harm and of extending relations of mutual recognition to include marginalized men and women.... The "inclusion of the other" means... that the boundaries of the community are open for all... and most especially for those who are strangers to one another and want to remain strangers. (Habermas 1998: xxxv–xxxvi)

There is yet an adequate study to be done in political philosophy that would consider how people with disabilities might be considered a cultural community whose status is deserving of the recognition, collective rights and constitutional protections that Kymlicka, Taylor, Tully, Chandoke and others consider necessary for other cultural communities more conventionally defined. In studies extending the analysis beyond ethno-racial-cultural-linguistic communities, there should be no simple equation with differences defined by gender, as Wolf (1994) has argued, and I suspect the same holds for disability. But there are useful links and equivalencies to be drawn. Certainly, the negative stereotyping and construction of people with disabilities as diseased, as deficits, as abnormal, to be rehabilitated or genetically cleansed suggests disadvantages and cultural harm similar in scale to other groups for whom claims to cultural and political recognition have become so urgent. And certainly within the disability movement claims for recognition of rights to self-determination, to escape institutional confinement, etc. echo in many ways calls of other groups. Moreover, without more collectively defined rights to needed disability-related supports and accommodations in education, the labour market, etc. there is little doubt that the citizenship of this group remains diminished and neglected.

There is no uniform answer to the constitutional and human rights guarantees necessary to recognize cultural diversity, and indeed the solution is undoubtedly place and nation specific. While they disagree to some extent on what the rights regime might look like, and some focus on actual proposals more than others, Taylor, Tully, Chandoke, Honneth, Habermas, Young and others look beyond particular frameworks of rights for solutions to the misrecognitions and failures of recognition in our age of diversity. They theorize and seek to establish principles for the acts of solidarity, the modes of dialogue, the cultural means of recognition which might ground and help to negotiate an adequate framework of rights in different settings. Either implicitly or explicitly they distinguish the recognition that comes with rights granted, from the social solidarity and political culture that makes those rights manifest and that hold a promise for cultural recognition. It is an atrophied or absent "spirit" and political culture of recognition, or solidarity, that helps to explain the negotiation of an unjust framework of rights and a daily disrespect in so many lives. I believe that useful implications for a social inclusion agenda for children with disabilities can be drawn from Honneth's analysis of how institutionalized rights are inadequate on their own to ensure valued recognition. Understandings of other theorists in social and political philosophy about the need for solidarity and mutual recognition to ground a just framework of rights can also contribute to such an agenda. Collectively, their work brings me to an assessment and to a question: The current framework of constitutional and statutory rights do not yet secure inclusion for Emily Eaton among classmates in a regular school where possibilities for her valued recognition might have a fighting chance. So what other strategies might a broader solidarity agenda point toward?

## A "Social Inclusion as Solidarity" Agenda for Children with Disabilities

Given the dilemma of rights and recognition I have outlined above, I would argue that we need a focused public agenda to advance solidarity with children with disabilities and their families. Undoubtedly, there are numerous issues to confront. But the analysis I have laid out in this chapter suggests the challenge is to build a broadly based valued recognition in society of children with disabilities on which the numerous issues can then be better addressed and on which the full citizenship of children with disabilities will rest. Otherwise, the citizenship of all of us — who withhold that solidarity — will be diminished. In Ignatieff's terms, our sense of self and community will not be englarged to the extent it might if we more widely wove the bonds of recognition and reciprocity.

I suggest three priorities for a public agenda to build solidarity for social inclusion of children who are marginalized and devalued because they do not measure up to physical and intellectual norms. These priorities are distilled from three aspects of exclusion that the current rights discourse has not fully addressed: i) institutionalized forms of knowledge that stereotype and objectify on the basis of disability; ii) misrecognition and devaluing of different forms of physical and intellectual life (i.e., genetic differences read as genetic deficiencies and abnormalities); and iii) a naturalizing of certain kinds of capacities and developmental paths over others (i.e., particular, dominant forms of communication and mobility that devalue other forms of communication or mobility, and thereby undermine justifications for investment in developing alternative capacities). Formulated in this way, these issues go beyond education, or the need for disability supports or child poverty *per se*. When the question is about the forms of recognition that result in various exclusions of children with disabilities then new, and I believe deeper, issues rise to the surface.

## Stereotyping and objectification in public policy

It is clear that Emily Eaton was excluded from a regular classroom because of the way in which the conflict over different forms of knowledge was adjudicated. Forms and technologies for producing knowledge based on a typology of disorders and capacities that construct disability as a fixed and absolute quantity ruled the day. The social and economic relations by which those technologies were deployed were occluded in the adjudication (the professional interests, the institutionalized requirements for an either/or educational placement process, the history of the constructs that informed the categorical assessments of Emily). Thus disability came to be seen as an ontological feature of an individual life rather than a social relation, a status ascribed by others. In a very different judgment by the Supreme Court of Canada, which dealt with a right to interpreter services in order to effect the right to access health care services, this social construction of disability was a central element of the ruling and led to a very different conclusion by the Court:

> It is an unfortunate truth that the history of disabled persons in Canada is largely one of exclusion and marginalization. Persons with disabilities have too often been excluded from the labour force, denied access to opportunities for social interaction and advancement, subjected to invidious stereotyping and relegated to institutions. The historical disadvantage has to a great extent been shaped and perpetuated by the notion that disability is an abnormality or flaw. As a result, disabled persons have not generally been afforded the "equal concern, respect and consideration" that s.15(1) of the *Charter* demands. Instead they have been subjected to paternalistic attitudes of pity and charity, and their entrance into the social mainstream has been conditional upon their emulation of able-bodied norms. (*Eldridge v. British Columbia (Attorney General)* 1997, 141 D.L.R. (4th) 577 at 613)[5]

The conflict over whose knowledge should matter, and how, is at the core of what moral philosopher Lorraine Code (1987) refers to as "epistemic responsibility" — the moral responsibility for knowing others well. This requires, she suggests, that we do not objectify others beyond recognition as humans. We have a responsibility not to use stereotypes in knowing others — because that is the source of hate, of devaluation of others (Code 1989). She suggests, along with other philosophers (MacIntyre 1981; Benhabib 1986; Taylor 1989; Kearney 1998) that we can only know another well if we know them narratively — or through their personal story. We become valued in the eyes of others, and our "self" is born — only in stories written and re-written by ourselves and those who know us — stories of the past, of hopes for a future. Research has shown, in fact, that people's attitudes about those with disabilities change most clearly when they come to know them personally, and coming to know someone personally is to know them through their personal stories of struggle, of hope, of pain, of misfortune, of likes and dislikes, of family and friends (Roeher Institute 2000).

Kearney (1998) writes of the "moral-transformative" nature of witnessing the personal narratives of others in public spaces and forums. In their witnessing, such narratives are the source of empathy and the stuff of new social bonds. In the stories heard lies a critique of structures of domination that exclude. In the moral visions they point to are utopias for the future. The report of the Law Commission of Canada (2000) on abuse of children in institutions considers whether such an approach — through a Truth Commission, for example — might be needed to bring about valued recognition of and restitution for victims of abuse. Truth and reconciliation commissions in South Africa, the Nuremburg trials and the work of the War Crimes Tribunal in gathering testimony from refugees fleeing Kosovo are all examples of the work of building solidarity, on which a new foundation for affirming and asserting rights was established, even if in the midst of horrific abuses of those rights.

Knowledge is not a neutral affair, and state and other interests in regulating the status of different accounts about a child with a disability are determinative in a child's life and possibilities. A social inclusion as solidarity agenda for children must confront the question of whose knowledge counts in public policies regulating educational placement and other allocation decisions (such as triaging of health services for children whose projected quality of life might be considered inadequate to justify heart surgery; long-term institutionalization of children, etc.). It must also consider how to nurture new forms of social knowledge that bring to life the narratives of those systematically excluded by disability, by poverty, by institutionalization. I suggest three possible directions to explore in such an agenda.

First, clear principles are needed to guide public policy to ensure that personal, narrative knowledge of a child's capacities, hopes, forms of communication, needs, etc. — often the knowledge with which parents and family members have most expertise — is granted priority status in educational placement decisions for children with disabilities.

Second, there is a need to critically examine and revise eligibility criteria for access to needed health and social supports at home, in the community and at school in order to question the forms of knowledge making that require parents to have their children labelled with "severe" deficits and syndromes as a condition of gaining access to any supports at all. In the education system, the examination might look at the "catch 22" many parents encounter: have a child labelled as severely as possible in order to gain access to supports, but then face the prospect that the child may not be placed in a regular classroom because those responsible for gathering knowledge to determine educational placements will likely find the child too severely disabled to benefit from, or to be accommodated in, a regular classroom. Efforts to restructure relationships and status between different forms of knowledge would be driven by the insight that children with disabilities will come to be known by others as children first, only if they are borne through personal narratives about their possibilities and not confined by labels and stereotypes.

Third, consideration might be given to the creation of a public sphere where children, youth and adults with disabilities (including the disproportionately high proportion who live in poverty), and their families, can document and widely share their own personal stories (their hopes, their accomplishments, the barriers they face in accessing services, jobs, food, adequate income). The forums and public media that might constitute such a public space could help shape a political culture strong enough to advance a full citizenship agenda for people with disabilities and their families (through reforms in social assistance, income tax, labour market policy — e.g., paid leave for caregiving — and disability supports policy, for example). Without such a public sphere, Canadians are unable to witness and come face-to-face with the realities of a growing proportion of the population. The creation of an inclusive public sphere does not replace the need for a human rights agenda. A social inclusion as solidarity strategy would supplement the agenda. It would focus on the apparent lack of political will to advance anti-poverty and social support policies; on the need to foster a more supportive political culture; and on the need to form bonds of solidarity to nurture such a culture. That solidarity is only possible if Canadians come to hear and witness the faces and stories of disability and poverty in Canada. One might argue that Canadians have heard, and they won't listen, but such an argument should not be accepted uncritically. It may be that our strategies for solidarity-building — for giving testimony and witnessing — have not been compelling enough and that they need re-thinking.

## Public policy and genetic value

There are growing concerns in the disability movement about the eugenic potential of the genetic technology revolution, and the implications for public policy are just now being articulated. As standards of good pre-natal care in some jurisdictions now require publicly funded genetic testing (Weir 1996) and as the (in part) publicly financed Human Genome Project draws the boundary around what it means to be genetically "human," the status of those with genotypes outside of the norm comes into question, and human value tends to be reduced to genetic make-up (Wolf 1995). Recent legal judgements confirm such outcomes. Damages for "wrongful birth" are being awarded to parents of children born with disabilities, because the mother's physician did not make available genetic testing that would have identified Down Syndrome, for example, or give the woman information on which to base a decision about selective abortion. Genetic screens and tests are technologies for knowing others as genetically deficient and therefore as something less than human. As technologies for knowing and judging the possibilities and shape of human life, they should be a central concern in an agenda for the valued recognition and status of all children. The information they generate can present a divide in a social solidarity that is difficult to overcome without a conscious re-thinking of how the knowledge is produced and used. Otherwise, the technologies will sustain and supplement forces of exclusion. Their very existence, for example, has been used by insurance companies to suggest that parents who knowingly bear a child with so-called "genetic deficiencies" should not be eligible for the extended benefits for that child (Wolf 1995).The possibilities of genetic knowing makes the bearing of a child with a disability a private affair and therefore makes the financial responsibility for care a private matter as well.

Who benefits from the genetic technology revolution? The biotechnology research and development industry clearly benefits with the equation of genetic normalcy and good maternal health care. The value of "gentech" stocks skyrocket, and health care systems in Canada and elsewhere absorb the burgeoning costs of purchasing genetic screens, and physician charges for applying the tests. The insurance industry benefits as it divests itself of responsibility for the costs of care where women make decisions to bear children who might have a disability. The industry also benefits as the costs of medical insurance balloon in the wake of recent decisions like that by highest appeal court in France to award damages against a physician that did not genetically test a fetus for Down Syndrome prior to the child's birth.

But at what cost? The cost, the disability rights movement and some ethicists are arguing, is the perpetuation of the stereotype of disability as abnormal, as a burden, as a genetic failure that should be cleansed (Wolf 1995; Asch and Geller 1996; Cole 2001). Just as decisions to selectively abort on the basis of sex are understood to do harm beyond the fetus involved, to do harm to women as a whole, so too selective abortion on the basis of disability has been argued to bring harm to people with disabilities as a whole. The availability of the technology and its systematic use threaten a eugenics that makes mutual recognition across the differences between us that much more difficult to nurture.

What might a social inclusion as solidarity agenda entail were it to address the divides being established among humans on the basis of their genotypes and screened genetic conditions? Caulfield et al. (2001) suggest the need for an analytic framework of "tests" to determine whether public funding or access to a genetic test is justified. The first analytic test is whether a particular genetic service is "morally acceptable." Such a framework provides a useful place to begin, depending of course on how the criteria for moral acceptablility are determined. To deal with the concern that disability might be left as morally irrelevant, a framework to regulate both research and applications in the health care system might also require that groups who may be adversely affected by genetic research or applications (e.g., through the stereotypes it might perpetrate, or through the inattention in research to the ethical and legal questions genetic technologies raise) be part of the ethics approvals process. This could be fairly simply addressed by requiring that representatives of national or regional disability rights organizations be part of ethics review committees at major research institutions (universities, Canadian Institutes for Health Research) and be part of any technology assessment process that guides development of purchasing and practice guidelines in the health care system. Their participation would ensure that the perspectives of people with disabilities are part of the ongoing dialogue about the potential for a new eugenics that genetic research and testing/screening raises and about the guidelines to be developed for minimizing such risks.

Ensuring an inclusive design for the national monitoring mechanisms on genetic research and applications in Canada, called for under the recent UNESCO Declaration on Human Rights and the Human Genome to which Canada is a signatory, could also help to advance solidarity across the genetic divides now being etched. The monitoring mechanisms should engage disability, First Nations and other groups who stand to be substantially disadvantaged through basic and applied genetic research (e.g., by patenting of genetic sequences, or by the hierarchy of human value that comes with the enterprise to establish normal and abnormal genotypes). The national monitoring mechanisms could be structured to ensure that groups are resourced to participate in the monitoring of impacts of genetic technologies and in the consideration of regulatory frameworks to ensure that the research accords with the commitments in the UNESCO Declaration to ensure a recognition of and respect for human diversity, dignity and rights. Solidarity emerges through understanding that often comes with face-to-face dialogue. Ongoing dialogues between geneticists and people with disabilities could be organized to resist the genetic reductionism that has come with much of the new wave of genetic research under the Human Genome project.

These specific strategies would not address all of the citizenship and inclusion issues raised by the spectre of the genetic revolution. A human rights agenda is also clearly needed to ensure that adequate protections are in place to prevent discrimination on the basis of genetic differences — in access to insurance coverage, health care, education, training and the paid labour market, etc. But, on their own, such human rights provisions will likely be as inadequate in securing full citizenship as are existing human rights provisions in ensuring equality and prevention of discrimination on other grounds. A social inclusion as solidarity agenda would help to bridge the gulf of understanding between the scientific community and the truths it bears (which often seem invulnerable to human rights provisions) and the disability community, which bears the narrative knowledge of human life well-lived in the midst of genetic diversity. At its core, the solidarity agenda must confront the forms and technologies of knowledge-making used to establish hierarchies of human value and give greater status to forms of knowledge borne by those near the bottom of the hierarchy.

## Measuring healthy child development

Psychoanalytic theory, theories of cognitive development and social psychology all emphasize that healthy, "normal" development occurs as infants, toddlers, young children and adolescent youth reach and pass through certain developmental stages or benchmarks. Failure to reach certain stages (in terms of language and communication abilities, cognitive, and motor skills, and ego and identity formation) is usually regarded as a sign of "abnormal development." When failure is first noticed, assessments are often called for to determine the nature of disability and to assign a particular bio-medical status.

The systematic exclusion of children with disabilities from a conceptual and monitoring framework of healthy child development is evident in a growing body of literature on the importance of ensuring that adequate investments are made in the zero-to-six age group so that they are "ready to learn" upon school age (McCain and Mustard 1999). Indicators of readiness to learn usually include:

- physical well-being and appropriate motor development;
- emotional health and a positive approach to new experiences;
- age-appropriate social knowledge and competence;
- age-appropriate language skills;
- age-appropriate general knowledge and cognitive skills (Doherty 1997).

Many children with disabilities are simply unable to meet some of these developmental outcomes. They may communicate in different ways than the majority of children raised in a hearing and English- or French-speaking culture. They may not be able to move in the same ways or have the same kinds of agility as those who fall within the statistically "normal" range. When viewed from the perspective of children with disabilities, the cultural bias of these outcomes is clear. They mark a group of children that education systems, in their current design, are most able to include and educate. They are based on a narrow theory of development in which verbal language skills are associated with cognitive development, readiness to learn and healthy development.

Establishing a framework of developmental outcomes is not simply an exercise of academic value. With the recent adoption by the federal and provincial/territorial governments of the Early Childhood Development Agreement, the federal government has committed a transfer to provinces and territories of $2.2 billion a year for five years for early childhood services. Both levels of government have committed to monitoring their investments in early child development and the outcomes for children. How outcomes are conceptualized and the benchmarks selected for developmental progress will help to determine which children are seen to most benefit from investments. Concerns have been expressed that some children with developmental and other disabilities are losing access to early childhood services such as speech and language therapy because these children are considered unable to adequately benefit from this investment. It is believed that the scarce dollars and services would better be invested in other children (Roeher Institute 2001b).

Mackelprang and Salsgiver (1999) review some of the intellectual foundations for a broader view of developmental theory that would begin to address the cultural biases of predominant approaches and make possible the development of a more inclusive set of outcomes and indicators. This work suggests we need to shift from measuring the gap between age and expected developmental achievements, to focus on the conditions that enable people with disabilities to carry out "developmental tasks" that are culturally shared and defined. To be able to communicate with others, for instance, is a developmental task whose achievement need not be measured by verbal language skills in the dominant language. Moving into adulthood need not be defined by the capacity for independence, which would exclude from successful adult achievement those who require ongoing personal supports. It can also be defined by the control one is given over one's supports and the opportunity to develop and pursue a wider range of goals.

A more inclusive developmental framework for children would pay more attention to conditions that enable access to needed resources and which structure opportunities for development, for social interaction and for exercising control over one's environment. Novick (1997), drawing on the work of the Laidlaw Foundation's Children at Risk Programme, and a wide body of research in the field suggests that an adequate theory of child development must incorporate an understanding of the various domains that structure opportunities, social interaction, control and access to resources. Novick includes the structural domain (broad societal cultural forces), institutional, personal, familial, and communal domains. This approach shifts the focus from one of strict age-related developmental stages to be achieved, to an understanding that every child has a unique "developmental path" (or unique ways of realizing different developmental tasks, whether they be managing communication and interaction with others, developing personal identity or moving from adolescence into adulthood). The task of public policy, social investment and community development is to ensure that across all domains of development children have access to the life chances they need to pursue and realize their unique path. How different domains structure and distribute life chances, in ways that account for differences of sex, race, economic class and disability becomes a question for research and a matter of public monitoring.[6] Taylor's formulation, of each person's unique potential as the basis of worth and equal respect, provides the ethical foundation for a public policy that values diverse developmental paths. It provides an ethical foundation for choosing self-anchored indicators in measuring a child's development.[7]

How could a social inclusion as solidarity agenda be struck to confront the divides structured in a developmental investment strategy that values children with certain physical, intellectual and developmental characteristics over others? First, it is essential that an inclusive framework of developmental outcomes be established as the basis of public investments and monitoring. Second, population survey instruments are needed to gather data on indicators consistent with outcomes and domains of development incorporated into the framework, with a particular emphasis on the extent to which children obtain the needed supports and opportunities to develop and exercise communicative and other capacities. Third, disability organizations could be supported to engage in the public monitoring of child outcomes so that perspectives of children and youth with disabilities are adequately represented. Population survey instruments could then be designed to incorporate evolving understandings of needed supports and the various ways children develop and exercise learning, communicative and other capacities. Finally, given the importance of communicative capacities to a child's intellectual and social development, it is essential to critically review the breadth of communication systems funded and used in early childhood services and the education system (e.g., written and spoken language, sign language interpretation, augmentative communication technologies and the child's unique gestural and behavioural sign systems where spoken language is not used).

A social inclusion as solidarity agenda asks what knowledge, whose knowledge and which communicative competencies are left outside of the public sphere and public discourse. Bridging social, economic and cultural differences that bring valued recognition to those who are devalued and excluded, requires that we promote dialogue and understanding across public spaces previously silent to their voices and their realities. The agenda would not be about ensuring everyone's access to every benefit and advantage Canadian institutions have to offer. Rather, it would ask that distinctions made in the rules and practices of institutions, services and organizations not systematically undermine the recognition and status of any group based on age, capacity, sexual orientation, gender, etc. Moreover, it would be about fostering forms of knowledge and recognition that value others and about questioning forms of recognition that distance, that devalue, that cast aside. At an institutional level it would add to the rights protections associated with citizenship, a prescription to identify and transform policies and practices that violate human dignity through stereotyping and discrimination. At a personal level it would call for a "virtue" of citizenship practised through knowing and recognizing others in ways that bring human dignity.

## Conclusion

Women's movements, disability rights activists, child poverty action groups,[8] First Nations and groups based on distinct ethno-racial-linguistic differences increasingly claim exclusion of one form or another. These are important voices. They speak from outside institutions and organizations of power, privilege, and advantage in Canadian society. They tell us something about ourselves, about how we are "reacting" to the differences in our midst, about our collective state of imperfection. At their roots, these claims of exclusion are about the denial of valued recognition in Canadian society and speak to the ways that some come to be known by others. The denial of valued recognition is organized in concrete ways through our political culture, legal systems and public policies and practices.

In this chapter I have suggested that we can usefully understand social inclusion as a political claim, as an ideal for social institutions and as a process for building solidarity and valued recognition across diverse persons and groups in the spaces structured by the state and civil society — schools, labour markets, health care institutions, community associations, public governance, etc. Social inclusion is about re-writing the rules, re-casting our cultural images and resources, and instituting practices to bring equally valued status to those who have been assigned a place of lesser value and status in Canadian society. Social inclusion does not demand that we assimilate and homogenize social and cultural differences in our education, health care, political and other systems. Valued recognition of others entails respecting their differences and identities in ways that enable them to speak their voices, exercise their rights, and secure their own path to well-being. Social inclusion also demands reciprocity. Groups that seek status and public space, but whose mission and practice involves stereotyping and devaluing others, are not deserving of equally valued recognition and status by their broader society.

What are the policy implications of this understanding of social inclusion for advancing the well-being of children in Canada? First, it brings focus to the ways in which knowledge about children and about certain groups of children is made. It asks about the status that different kinds of knowledge are given in gaining access to these different settings and institutions. Forms of knowledge that stereotype children as so different from other children that they are refused access to education, for instance, is challenged in such an agenda.

Second, an agenda for social inclusion raises a challenge to create new public spaces where the lives and realities of children and their families can be witnessed, where testimony can be given, where a new commitment to invest can take root. It is in these acts of recognition that the other, Kearney (1998) argues, comes to make an ethical difference, where new social bonds can be woven across the differences that divide. Surely this is the promise of a citizenship that values belonging, dignity, reciprocity and respect — where rights claims and aspirations obtain not only legal but broad social recognition and commitment. Only then are needed policy investments likely to follow. I believe the analysis outlined above applies not only to issues facing children with disabilities and their families; they have provided a case study with which to explore the notion of social inclusion as solidarity. The analysis, it seems to me, applies also to other issues affecting children. Persisting and deepening child poverty in Canada, for example, is not a consequence of a lack of resources or labour markets and policies that cannot be restructured. It is a lack of will and commitment, where the fact of poverty does not seem to matter enough. A social inclusion as solidarity agenda focuses, for example, on building a much wider recognition of the realities of children and families who are poor, of making their realities matter to all Canadians in a way that commitment to address the structural roots of poverty will follow. A solidarity agenda does not on its own put bread on the table. It creates the public consciousness and commitment for public policies and practices to make sure it gets there.

A social inclusion as solidarity agenda should be paramount if we are to move forward on the kind of covenant for children that O'Neill (1994) calls for and address the exclusions that persist. The covenant does not need to be written. It is already expressed in many national and international human rights instruments — most clearly for children in the Convention on the Rights of the Child. It could be articulated anew, but the sources for its expression and for legal and moral obligation are there. What is missing is the commitment to realize it. What is missing is the process of social inclusion that will bring all children within the ambit of moral consideration, worthy of securing the personal and collective obligations they are due. So many children and families are absent from the public sphere — children with disabilities and their families, Aboriginal children, children growing up in poverty, victims of abuse and violence. Commitment for the covenant will grow only as their testimonies are more widely witnessed, their realities and possibilities more clearly documented in population surveys and by other means, and in ways that make their concerns and aspirations resonate in Canadian political culture. By these means we might shed better light on the absences in our collective social imaginations.

Social inclusion as solidarity does not deny the need for a strong framework of rights for children. It does require that we look at how children and youth come to be known, at the policies and practices of genetic differencing, of educational segregation, of communicational straightjacketing. A solidarity agenda would not seek to eradicate diversity. It would make problematic the organization of advantage and disadvantage across the differences that define us. With such an agenda we would not be satisfied with a simple extension of rights, safe in the knowledge that children and adults can then press claims to battle the walls that exclude them. It would demand that citizenship virtues of reciprocity, or knowing others well, be actively fostered. It would sound a call to mobilize personal and collective forms of recognition that bring dignity and value to *all* children.

I have sought throughout this chapter to draw the links between human rights, full citizenship, social inclusion and solidarity. The notion of citizenship and what it requires has evolved historically through many political and intellectual struggles. The calls for social inclusion have been made in its shadow — calls to be included as citizens from those not yet seen by the light it sheds. Hence, the strategies for social inclusion have evolved and changed as the concept of citizenship has been re-written. In the past fifty years, a human rights agenda has been the most compelling strategy to advance an inclusive citizenship. While that agenda has clearly not yet been fulfilled, it is becoming increasingly clear that, on its own, it still leaves some in the shadows. I have suggested that solidarity should now constitute a major agenda for socially inclusive citizenship — one that fully accounts for and recognizes all children in equally valuing ways. In the arguments I have laid out here a solidarity agenda need not depart from a human rights agenda. Rather, they represent different orders of analysis and critique in a common cause to secure valued recognition of devalued groups.

Institutionalizing human rights has been one means to fuel the social inclusion of devalued groups among those who obtain valued recognition and citizenship in society's institutions. Solidarity agendas must also be struck to complement establishment of human rights if we are to more fully confront the refusal by some to include others in ways that bring value, respect, and dignity. Social inclusion is not the aim. Valued recognition, respect and dignity that make full social, economic and political participation possible, name the core elements of citizenship and the aspirations to which human rights instruments intend. Social inclusion names social and political struggles to realize these aspirations in the lives of people and groups so often mis-recognized, de-valued and denied. It offers an ideal for institutional arrangements. Criteria for inclusivity could also help guide institutional reform.

In these times we find ourselves in, a commitment to social inclusion must include steps to bring understanding across the divides that establish race, language, gender, ability, creed, genotype, economic class and nationality as grounds of status and value. To bring inclusion where it has so often been denied, we must forge a solidarity that listens across these divides of status and then questions their roots in law and in domestic and foreign policy. We must question the institutionalized refusal to know and respect others well. Thereby, the daily realization of children's rights might become a much deeper concern and commitment for governments, communities and citizens. The evidence makes clear that a solidarity and political culture valuing all children is certainly not a given in our society; it is yet to be woven.

# Notes

1. Editors' note: Our research in preparing this book for publication indicates that several versions of this story are currently circulating in both print and Internet forms. We are including this story as originally published with the Laidlaw Foundation Working Papers because it is integral to the author's contribution, but without further information we cannot vouch for the authenticity of any particular version.
2. This may be because the link between reason and citizenship remains firmly entrenched in our political culture, statutory law and legal reasoning — making human rights claims by people with intellectual disabilities that much harder to press.
3. In constrast, a "social model" of disability is being advanced by those who find in the bio-medical account a reductionist tendency — reducing the disability to individual characteristics defined as deficits (Barnes 1991; Rioux 1994; Oliver 1996). In a social model, disability arises from the discrimination and disadvantage individuals experience in relation to others because of their particular differences and characteristics. This shift in thinking finds a primary source in feminist theories of difference — where the challenge is to recognize differences of gender, race, sexual orientation, physical and intellectual characteristic, etc. without assigning social or economic value on the basis of these differences (Minow 1990).
4. Kymlicka's (1989) analysis of liberal and communitarian theories of the self helped enormously in resolving the theoretical impasse between liberal accounts of the political and ethical primacy of the individual, and communitarian accounts of the person that emphasize the importance of community, tradition and culture (e.g., MacIntyre 1981; Sandel 1982). Kymlicka addressed the impasse by revealing the link between the self-development and self-determination that liberal political philosophy so values, and the availability of cultural resources that a community provides an individual — resources of language, modes of thought, horizons of meaning, etc. Recognizing the centrality of community and culture to individual self-development and freedom begs the question of how to provide recognition and protection for diverse communities, some of which may be threatened by cultural genocide, that face systematic discrimination by dominant cultures or that come into being with the massive dislocations and migrations that are unlikely to subside in these times.
5. In confronting directly the issue of recognition of people with disabilities in Canadian society, the Court moved in this case to clearly articulate a "right to effective communication," establishing that in order for deaf citizens in Canada to access their right to health care, they were entitled to interpreter

  services in the health care system.

6.  The Roeher Institute has drawn on this work and related literature, as well as a series of consultations with disability and family organizations, children's services providers and government policy analysts, to re-conceptualize a framework of healthy child development for monitoring public investments and their impact on children. The framework includes a set of seven developmental outcomes, framed to be inclusive in their basic conceptualization (e.g., *all* children could meet the developmental targets with adequate supports). The outcomes include: physical well-being, emotional and mental well-being, social well-being (membership, participation, social relationships), spiritual well-being, communicative capacity, learning capacity and a positive future for a child envisioned by others. The domains of development that should provide support and opportunity for children to pursue and reach these outcomes include family, school, community, paid labour market (for parents), public policy (for investment in needed developmental supports). This framework is presented and discussed in Roeher Institute 2001d).

7.  Self-anchored indicators measure a child's progress in reaching their own potential. Rather than measuring a child against a fixed norm or criterion of capacity, self-anchored indicators measure the progress over time in a child meeting his or her unique communicational, motor, relational, learning and other goals. Self-anchored indicators are already in use in some population surveys. For example, the National Population Health Survey, asks people to rate their own health status. Such a survey leaves the definition of health up to the respondent. For a discussion of self-anchored indicators and a critique of norm-referenced assessments as the sole basis for assessing child development, see Roeher Institute 2001d).

8.  I am not suggesting here that "poverty" represents a difference that should be valued, or that those living in poverty constitute a unique cultural identity of their own choosing. We need a sustained attack on poverty that addresses its systemic roots in inequitable access to education, labour markets, income support, health care, social supports, transportation and decent housing. I am arguing, however, that those living in poverty tend to be constituted by *others* in stereotyped and devaluing ways, where their poverty is seen as an individual rather than structural problem. Building a much broader solidarity with those living in poverty is required, I suggest, in order to foster a political culture where the will might be borne to address the systemic roots of poverty. Until people living in poverty matter more to Canadians in general, the political and cultural forces that demonize them and justify political inaction will win the day.

# Immigrant Settlement
# and Social Inclusion in Canada

*Ratna Omidvar and Ted Richmond¹*

## Introduction

In recent years the Laidlaw Foundation has been working to develop the notion of social inclusion as a framework for a more progressive approach to social policy questions in Canada. As well, the issue of immigrant settlement is evolving as one of the most important questions of public policy in Canada. Canada is experiencing serious and increasing difficulties in making full use of the skills and talents of our newcomers in both the economic sphere and in public life in general. Simultaneously, immigrant and refugee communities and their spokespersons are expressing a growing sense of frustration, even despair, at the barriers they encounter to full participation in all domains of Canadian life.

This chapter then is an attempt to bring together these two important issues and to pose the following questions. What does the concept of social inclusion offer for a better understanding and ultimately a better resolution of the problems of immigrant and refugee settlement in Canada today? More specifically does the concept of social inclusion offer new perspectives and help us formulate improved policies in the vital area of immigrant settlement?

Social inclusion involves the basic notions of belonging, acceptance and recognition. For immigrants and refugees, social inclusion would be represented by the realization of full and equal participation in the economic, social, cultural and political dimensions of life in their new country. In a simple but useful sense, therefore, social inclusion for immigrants and refugees can be seen as the dismantling of barriers that lead to exclusion in all these domains.

As many commentators have noted, the definition of "social inclusion" remains fluid and open to debate and is ultimately shaped by political and ideological convictions. Within the framework of our own beliefs, we will attempt to address different dimensions of the notion of inclusion: as a process, as an outcome and as a metaphor or means of re-conceptualizing fundamental issues.

Recently there has been much discussion and debate with the goal of refining the concept(s) of social inclusion, both inside and outside the dialogue promoted by the Laidlaw Foundation, and it is well beyond the scope of this chapter to adequately address all the issues that have been raised. We are working with a more practical focus, which is to test the potential of social inclusion as a policy framework against what we know of the reality of immigrant and refugee settlement in Canada today.[2]

## The Economic Status of Newcomers in Canada

During the last two decades there has been a dramatic, downward shift in the economic status of newcomers to Canada. The groups of immigrants and refugees who have arrived in the last twenty years — overwhelmingly non-European visible minorities — are experiencing severe difficulties in the Canadian labour market and associated problems of individual and family poverty.

During roughly the first forty years after the Second World War, newcomers to Canada, with some initial settlement support and over a period of time, generally were successful in the Canadian labour market. Their employment participation rates were as high or higher than the Canadian-born, and their wages and salaries rose gradually to the level of the Canadian-born. However recent research indicates persistent and growing difficulties in the labour market integration of immigrants, especially recent immigrants. Rates of unemployment and under-employment are increasing for individual immigrants, as are rates of poverty for immigrant families. As well, there is a substantial body of evidence indicating income discrimination against visible minority workers (both immigrant and Canadian-born) as well as gender-based wage discrimination for female immigrants. The general trend is summarized by Shields:

> The great difficulty is that since the 1980s immigrant performance in the Canadian labour market has deteriorated precipitously, dampening the possibilities of economic integration and expanding the dimensions of immigrant social exclusion. (2002: 21)

These general trends have been documented in numerous studies, including Devoretz (1995), Kazemipur and Halli (1997; 2000), Reitz (1998; 2001), Lo et al. (2000), Ornstein (2000), Pendakur (2000), Galabuzi (2001), Harvey and Siu (2001), Mwarigha (2002) and Shields (2002). Some of the main trends were summarized in the much-cited HRDC bulletin (2001), which revealed that immigrants to Canada in the 1990s have not fared as well as previous cohorts of immigrants in terms of earnings and employment outcomes, in spite of the fact that these recent immigrants are more highly educated and skilled than previous cohorts. The bulletin noted that this is contrary to historical trends, in which the pattern has been that immigrants earn less on arrival but their incomes rise rapidly and catch up or surpass the Canadian employment earnings average after ten to fourteen years. In previous periods economic principal applicants selected on the basis of education and skill have had earnings higher than the average of the native-born more quickly, starting one year after arrival. However recent immigrants have lower rates of employment, which declined markedly between 1986 and 1996. The result is that Canada's immigrants exhibit a higher incidence of poverty and greater dependence on social assistance than their predecessors, in spite of the fact that the rate of university graduates is higher among all categories of immigrants, including family class and refugees as well as economic immigrants, than it is for the Canadian-born.

These trends are accompanied by a general increase in poverty for immigrants, particularly recent non-European immigrants, which impacts on families as well as individuals. For example Harvey and Siu (2001) found that poverty levels for all immigrants increased between 1991 and 1996, with visible minorities in Toronto showing the largest increase, from 20.9 percent to 32.5 percent. The study also shows that visible minorities are much more at risk of experiencing persistent poverty for thirty-five years than immigrants who are not visible minorities. It confirms earlier findings by Ornstein (2000), based on 1996 Census data, of increased unemployment, under-employment and individual and family poverty for recent immigrants and visible minorities in Toronto, the destination of about one-half of Canada's newcomers. The Ornstein research revealed that non-European groups in Toronto are burdened with family poverty rates at twice the levels of families of European and Canadian origin, and that for some groups such as Latin Americans, African Blacks, Caribbeans, Arabs and West Asians the rate is more than 40 percent, or roughly three times higher. This academic research is confirmed by accounts in the popular press, which reveal a dramatic increase in the use of food banks by highly educated newcomers (Quinn 2002).

A significant factor in these trends is the underutilization of immigrant skills within the Canadian labour market. Reitz (2001) has looked at the quantitative significance of this issue using a human-capital earnings analysis, which identified immigrant earnings deficits as arising from three possible sources: lower immigrant skill quality, underutilization of immigrant skills or pay inequities for immigrants doing the same work as native-born Canadians. He concluded that in 1996 dollars, the total annual immigrant earnings deficit from all three sources in Canada was $15.0 billion, of which $2.4 billion was related to skill underutilization, and $12.6 billion was related to pay inequity. He observed as well that employers give little credence to foreign education and none to foreign work experience, that discrimination specific to country of origin or visible minority status is mainly related to pay equity rather than skills utilization, and that the economic impact of visible minority status and immigrant status is very similar for both men and women. In addition Reitz noted that race appears to be a more reliable predictor of how foreign education will be evaluated in Canada than the specific location of the origin of the immigrant from outside Europe.

These trends must be considered in relation to structural changes in the international economy and Canadian labour market in the past several decades, specifically the trends towards globalization of markets and liberalization of world trade making both labour and capital more internationally mobile and domestic (Canadian) employment less secure. Historically, during the first decades after the Second World War, the majority of immigrants gained employment in relatively high-wage, low-skill industrial jobs. Now in Canada as in other advanced economies the service sector is replacing industrial production as the main source of employment, and immigrant employment is more concentrated in the relatively high-wage and high-skill (public) service sector as well as in low-wage, low-skill (private, retail) services.

For example Shields (2002) concludes that during the 1950s and 1960s male immigrant labour market success was mainly a product of the wide availability of jobs and relatively high wages in the manufacturing and construction sectors, which did not demand high levels of formal schooling. With the decline of this sector and the rise of the service sector the labour market is much more challenging for recent immigrants. As well Lo et al. (2000) note in a study of Toronto that while immigrants are still over-represented in manufacturing they are concentrated in unstable, lower waged and disappearing sectors.

Pendakur (2000) provides a comprehensive historical analysis of these trends, covering the period from the end of the Second World War to the 1990s, during which the source of immigration shifted to predominantly non-European countries and the work done by immigrants in Canada moved from factories and construction sites to retail stores, hospitals and classrooms. Historically, this period included two very different immigration paths, one emphasizing family reunification and the other stressing labour-force requirements as well as family reunification. It was also a period of major transformation from a manufacturing-based economy to a largely service-based one.

For Pendakur (2000), changes in skill and education requirements meant that immigrants were likely to perform labour force roles different than either the Canadian-born or previous immigrants, but their options were also determined by prevailing labour market conditions within a relatively rigid Canadian labour market. As the relatively high-wage and low-skill jobs in manufacturing disappeared, new immigrants were recruited into both high-wage and high-skill positions in social services and business, and low-wage jobs in the retail sector. Differences in the occupations of the new immigrants were also related to whether they were employed for wages or self-employed, and whether they were male or female. It appears that male immigrants are more subject to labour market discrimination as visible minorities, while female immigrants experience more discrimination both as immigrants and as women. Pendakur's study also confirms the penalties in income and occupational status paid by immigrants whose education has been acquired outside of Canada, as well as the existence of substantial income penalties in the Canadian labour market rooted in ethnicity and colour.

## Other Groups of Newcomers

While the economic analysis summarized in the preceding section reveals many of the barriers to social inclusion for Canada's newcomers, we must also take account of a number of other groups facing both economic and social exclusion. Attention to these groups is particularly important because for various reasons they often do not receive as much attention in official statistics and current research.

Among the temporary immigrants admitted to Canada, for example, there are agricultural workers imported on a seasonal basis to labour under harsh conditions with minimal legal rights. Historically as well domestic workers, while enjoying the right to an eventual claim to Canadian citizenship, have endured both economic exploitation and workplace and sexual harassment to earn this privilege. As well in Canada there are small but growing numbers of female temporary immigrants recruited for the illicit sex trade, and victims of international immigrant smuggling schemes abandoned without any legal status.

At the present time, there are also a number of undocumented immigrants such as failed refugee claimants or visitors who have stayed beyond their permitted time. The exact numbers are not known; the reports come from social service and health agencies who provide emergency supports to these people without provision for funding for these services. These people make silent contributions to our economy, often through exploited labour, while being denied basic social and health services for lack of documentation. Many are parents, including parents of Canadian-born children, whose children may be denied the right to schooling and access to healthcare. All of these vulnerable groups of newcomers are excluded in various ways from access to basic legal protection and economic justice.

To understand the multiple dimensions of both economic and social exclusion for Canada's newcomers we must also consider the gendered experiences of immigrant and refugee women (James et al. 1999; Mojab 1999; Preston and Man 1999; Chard et al. 2000). To a large degree newcomer women in Canada continue to be streamed into lower-wage jobs in the growing service sector as well as in the declining manufacturing sector. At the same time due to factors related both to their conditions of arrival in Canada and to the socio-cultural traditions of their country of origin, newcomer women carry very heavy burdens of domestic responsibility in terms of housework, family maintenance and socialization of children.

Finally, from the perspective of newcomer social inclusion one of the most important issues in Canada is the extended period during which thousands of refugee claimants remain in a "legal limbo." Although Canada's inland refugee determination system and the quasi-judicial nature of the Immigration and Refugee Board (IRB) are seen as progressive by the rest of the world, there are serious problems within the system. The determination of the status of refugee claimants is legally and administratively complex and can create significant backlogs (delays). For refugee claimants this can mean an extended period during which they face significant barriers in access to social services and the labour market, as well as a postponement in potentially acquiring rights such as sponsorship of family members and eventual citizenship. They can't get a bank loan, or vote, or work in certain professions (e.g., education and health care); they can't travel internationally, even to the U.S.; and they can't get loans for post-secondary education. Currently it is common for this situation to last five years, or more.

The situation of refugee claimants in legal limbo is creating a new underclass of persons without status composed of those who most need our help, those who left their own countries under conditions of great stress and with tremendous hopes for their new life in Canada (Mohamed 2002). It has a very negative impact not only on the individuals concerned but also on the family and friends, and this negative impact is occurring during the first few years of their life in Canada — the years most important to successful settlement. And during those years, Canada is losing the opportunity to benefit from the education and skills these people have brought to their new country.

## Immigrant and Refugee Children and Youth

One of the more comprehensive studies of newcomer youth is that by Kilbride et al. (2000), which integrates a number of research projects involving community collaboration focused on diverse groups of adolescent newcomers in different cities of Ontario. The researchers found that the challenges of adolescence were greatly compounded by the stresses of settlement. They found as well that immigrant and refugee youth felt pulled in opposite directions, between what seemed to be irreconcilable values or cultures and a desire to adapt and fit in to their new homeland. The tensions between parents and youth associated with the challenges of settlement were very important. Feelings of isolation and alienation were linked to perceptions of cultural differences and experiences of discrimination and racism. Support from friends, family and institutions was key to overcoming the challenges of settlement.

One of the particular findings from this study was that lack of (Canadian English) language facility creates barriers for newcomer youth in education, employment and general social adaptation, including for those (for example from the Caribbean) who speak English with a dialect. The study also found that newcomer youth who arrived while younger had a less difficult process of adaptation than those who arrived as older adolescents, because they had a longer period of time to adapt to the education system and adjust to Canadian social and cultural values.

This study also revealed that the stresses of the settlement process experienced by their parents had a great impact on the newcomer youth. Parents who had to work longer hours for lower pay had less time for involvement in family activities, and youth were often obliged to take up correspondingly greater obligations such as staying home alone, caring for siblings, doing grocery shopping and cooking, finding paid employment and translating and interpreting for their parents.

Other reports and research studies emphasize the particular experiences of refugee youth and children. Omidvar (2002) emphasizes the fact the immigrants and refugees have different experiences, while supporting the observations of Kilbride et al. (2000) that racism and discrimination are real factors and complicated by intergenerational issues. She notes as well that there are special issues for female newcomer youth. For Kaprielian-Churchill and Churchill (1994) one of the main points from a study of Ontario schools is that refugee children have special needs and that teachers and schools have not developed the training and programs of intervention to deal with these needs.

Sadoway (2002) emphasizes that children are at risk around the world, particularly when they are separated from their parents and families due to war, poverty and oppression, and also when their caregivers have become their oppressors. Sadoway asserts that the community and the state have often been reluctant to intervene to protect children because of deeply ingrained paternalistic notions of children as property, as chattels or extensions of their parents, rather than persons in their own right. Children lack power in our society and therefore are dependent on adults to recognize their needs and ensure their care and development as well as safety and protection. The issue of what constitutes "persecution" of children, in terms of the U.N. Convention for the determination of refugee status, continues to challenge adjudicators. Issues like forced conscription, sexual exploitation and female genital mutilation are beginning to be recognized, but other more common-place issues such as domestic service in private homes receive less recognition.

Montgomery (2002), in discussing the status of unaccompanied minors in Canada, states that in principle the *Charter of Rights and Freedoms* grants equal rights to all persons residing in Canadian territory, but in practice all residents are not treated equally. Minority and immigrant communities experience forms of exclusion related to the immigration process, access to services and discrimination. Unaccompanied minors (youth under the age of eighteen who have been separated from parents and who arrive in Canada unaccompanied by a legal guardian) are particularly vulnerable due to their dual status as minors and as refugee claimants. In Canada in 2000 the number of unaccompanied minors was estimated at around a thousand, most living in Ontario, Quebec and British Columbia. However, NGOs report that numbers are rising, probably because parents in conflict zones try to get their children out first or may only have the resources to get their children out.

Montgomery's analysis reveals that unaccompanied minors, particularly older youth, experience settlement problems similar to those of immigrants in general and refugees in particular. For example in the labour market employers often refuse to hire persons without a regularized immigration status. As well refugee claimants are excluded from most government-sponsored employment and training programs because of their immigration status, and although they have a right to language training in practice it is difficult for them to access this service. As well, there is discrimination in obtaining housing, such as the requirement of supplementary proof of identity or additional proof of capacity to pay rent. Access to health services is also a problem, as the Interim Federal Health Program (IFHP) provides only "essential" services and not routine medical, dental or mental health services. Montgomery emphasizes as well that the process and lengthy period of resolving status creates great mental stress.

A social inclusion perspective on newcomer integration therefore must include sufficient attention to the particular and complex needs of immigrant and refugee youth. Recent findings as outlined above suggest that the settlement challenges of newcomer youth are compounded by the barriers of social exclusion faced by their parents and indeed are often essentially the same. We must note as well that newcomer youth not only face particular challenges as immigrants and refugees but also confront the general barriers of youth in today's Canadian society with respect to changing socio-economic conditions and opportunities. Tyyska (2001) for example demonstrates convincingly that the age status of the young in Canada has become a factor of disadvantage (or risk, or marginalization, or social exclusion) along with related factors such as gender, poverty and visible minority status.

## Settlement Services and the NGO Sector

Many immigrants and refugees require settlement services when they first arrive, as well as linguistically and culturally appropriate health and social services throughout their years of adaptation. The provision of these services is essential both to ensuring the effective settlement of newcomers and maintaining public support for the continuing high levels of immigration required for our labour force. Indeed, Reitz (1998) has shown in a comparative study of different countries that the level of public support for settlement is vital to immigrants' economic success and socio-political inclusion.

Currently most funded settlement services are devoted to initial support for newcomers, including language training, assistance with labour market integration, individual and family counselling, translation and interpreting, and referrals to health and social services. The funds for these services come from a variety of sources, including federal and provincial governments, municipalities and community charities and private foundations. However the delivery of these services (in Ontario and across Canada) is provided mainly by non-governmental organizations — community-based immigrant service agencies (ISAs).

One of the most serious problems of the current system lies in the fact that settlement funding and programming is focused on the initial stages of adaptation, in spite of the fact that the process of settlement continues throughout the life of the newcomer. Mwarigha (2002) notes that after the initial or first stage of adaptation, in the middle or intermediate stage newcomers require assistance with access to various Canadian systems and institutions including municipal services, with their principal needs usually centred around timely and equitable access to the labour market. Other important needs in the intermediate stage include housing, health services, legal assistance and advanced or employment-specific language instruction. In the long term or final stage of settlement, immigrants and refugees strive to become equal participants in Canada's economic, cultural, social and political life. It is no exaggeration to state that settlement policy in Canada is currently in a state of crisis, due largely to the lack of a pan-Canadian and long-term perspective that takes into account all three stages of settlement.

A second grave problem, directly related to the first, is that the NGO sector delivering settlement services is in a precarious state due to a combination of funding cutbacks and imposed restructuring. The situation of the ISAs in Ontario, including Toronto, has been documented in numerous studies, including Richmond (1996), Owen (1999), Simich (2000) and Shields (2002). The effect has been that many community-based providers of settlement services, particularly the smaller "ethno-specific" agencies, have been forced to curtail their services drastically or even to close their doors. Those that are still functioning are operating under conditions of extreme stress due to a combination of overloaded service demand and limited funding.

This situation, however, derives not just from inadequate funding but as much or even more from a restructuring of the conditions of government funding. The transition for most government funders from "core" to program-specific funding favours the larger agencies with more administrative resources for the management of programs delivered on a contractual basis and leaves all remaining ISAs with extremely limited resources for community education, needs assessment, program planning and advocacy. This kind of imposed restructuring as noted by Evans and Shields (2002) is part of a general trend towards neo-liberal restructuring of the relationship between government and the non-profit or third sector. These authors point out that the expansion of the welfare state has been based not only on a growth in government social support services but also the growing role of the third sector, and that this symbiotic relationship is threatened by restructuring, which compromises the basic mission of third sector organizations and therefore their ability to contribute to social inclusion.

One of the essential mechanism of this restructuring is the imposition on the ISAs, as part of the new contractual terms of service, of so-called "evaluation" schemes, which are really nothing more than administrative mechanisms to maintain state control of third-party (and third sector) service providers (Chambon and Richmond 2001). While this issue may appear to be purely administrative, in reality it is political because our frameworks for evaluation are directly linked to our visions of accountability in a democratic and pluralist society (Hanberger 2001). This type of restructuring has particularly serious and negative implications for the ISAs, which historically have used their legitimate autonomy as community agencies to play a leading role in the development of an anti-discriminatory and anti-racist framework for human services (Richmond 1996).

## Urban Issues and Newcomer Settlement

To understand the dynamics and challenges of newcomer settlement in Canada today from a social inclusion perspective, it is essential to recognize that immigration is principally, indeed overwhelmingly, an *urban* phenomenon. Currently about 70 percent of immigrants to Canada settle in the three largest cities of Toronto, Vancouver and Montreal, with about half of them eventually arriving in Toronto alone.

For the past five decades immigration has become a primary force not only in broad economic and demographic terms, but also in shaping the Canadian urban environment, impacting on residential housing development, neighbourhood and street life, the delivery of municipal services, urban politics and cultural life (Troper 2000). Siemiatycki and Isin (1997) point out as well that transnational migration has generated new claims to urban citizenship in Toronto. Newcomers have dispersed their residences and developed and transformed their neighbourhoods, laying claim to public space, challenging cultural traditions, creating organizations and getting involved in civic politics.

Unfortunately one of the most disturbing and indeed dangerous trends associated with the urbanization of immigration is the growing risk of the racialization of urban poverty. For example Shields (2002) observes that there is a strong correlation between recent immigrant status and elevated levels of family poverty and notes the real danger that a process of racialization of poverty is underway. As well, Galabuzi (2001) confirms the development within our major urban centres of an underclass of visible minorities, many of whom are recent immigrants, concentrated in racial enclaves of poverty. Kazemipur and Halli (2000) found that larger urban centres — Montreal, Winnipeg, Quebec City, Toronto, Saskatoon, Regina and Vancouver — had large concentrations of visible minority immigrants in neighbourhoods with a poverty rate of 40 percent and higher. The latter study also revealed that in Toronto, immigrants are more likely than non-immigrants to live in neighbourhoods with high rates of poverty. Mwarigha (2002) suggests that one of the most disturbing consequences of the current settlement service system is that it is ineffective in combating the accelerated emergence of an immigrant underclass, concentrated primarily in the poorer neighbourhoods of Toronto.

It must be emphasized however that the issue here is not simply the fact of the concentration of ethno-racial groups within particular neighbourhoods. Qadeer (2003) has concluded that the concentration of an ethnic group in a particular urban neighbourhood can facilitate the development of religious, cultural and community institutions. According to his studies, once a community has formed, it tends to persist and evolve, as on the basis of a segmented housing market, as a socio-ecological grouping. These "ethnic enclaves" are largely expressions of preferences, common interests, social networks and common cultural and/or religious needs of their residents. They can be especially helpful to women, children and seniors, especially those not fluent in English and who are accustomed to the supportive presence of friends and relatives. For Qadeer there is a risk however that ethnoracial residential concentrations can act as a barrier to the residents meeting and networking in the mainstream society and economy, and the risk is particularly high if the segregation coincides with low incomes, poverty and poor housing. Nevertheless, Qadeer suggests that this process gives a new meaning to social integration: constructing a "common ground" of institutions and services for civic engagement of diverse communities. Residential space then, along with schools, workplaces, recreation and sports and political participation, is one of the many sites for social inclusion.

The issue then is the degree to which concentration in neighbourhoods of *poverty* acts as a barrier to social and economic integration of new immigrants and their children. Living in areas of concentrated poverty has adverse impacts on a whole range of life experiences, and in the case of new immigrants it leads to family conflicts, loss of self-esteem and a sense of despair about future prospects in the new country of settlement. Young immigrants who grow up in such conditions can develop a culture of alienation both from their parents and their community of origin, and from that of the host society (Mwarigha 2002).

## The Social Inclusion Perspective

The notion of social inclusion originated in Europe in response to the crisis in the health and welfare programs in Europe in the 1970s and 1980s. In the period from the Second World War to the mid-1970s, most European governments developed comprehensive health and social insurance programs to protect their citizens (Guidford 2000). This was followed by a period of fiscal restraint and cutbacks in the United States, Canada and most European governments, which not only proved to be unpopular, but also in many ways aggravated the problem of poverty among the most disadvantaged groups. The increasing number of people experiencing long-term poverty became a big problem for the welfare system, especially in Europe. Initial measures to limit benefits through increased means-testing only meant that more and more people ended up living outside the system, jobless and homeless.

Social inclusion was initially started by the French to effectively re-integrate the large numbers of ex-industrial workers and a growing number of young people who right from the start did not have the opportunity to join the new economy labour force of the 1980s and 1990s. As the concept gained credence in the rest of Europe, it incorporated non-traditional target groups, such as racial minorities, elderly, youth and people with disabilities, as sections of the population in need of deliberate social inclusion programs.

The social crisis caused by the unfettered growth of the new economy in the 1980s and 1990s provided an opportunity for governments to not only revisit the traditional notion of universal welfare, but also to add in new values of inclusion, "characterized by a society's widely shared experience and active participation, by a broad equality of opportunities and life chances for individuals and by the achievement of basic level of well-being for all citizens" (Sen 2001). In essence, social inclusion became a vehicle to enhance access and equity in the field of social policy and programming.

The notion of social inclusion also gained acceptance in countries that did not proceed as radically towards the dismantling of their post-war social welfare system. In Sweden, for example, whose welfare system remained relatively intact in the new economy age of the 1980s and 1990s, there was recognition that:

> the system had not fully succeeded in guaranteeing the welfare of young people, immigrants and single parent providers. These groups were hit particularly by the employment crisis at the beginning of the 1990s. And as a result they also suffered most as regards other aspects of welfare. At the same time there were groups in the 1990s, as before with significant problems such as substance misuse and homelessness. (Government of Sweden 2001)

At a broad policy level, the goals of social inclusion are pursued on the basis of the following key principles: 1) structuring policy interventions around a life cycle approach, where necessary to meet individual need; 2) tackling failing communities and the needs of other excluded groups of people; 3) mobilizing all relevant actors in a joint multi-agency response; 4) tackling discrimination in all its forms, wherever it occurs; and 5) ensuring all policy formulation is evidence-based. These principles enable a multi-dimensional approach to confronting the problems of social exclusion and promoting social inclusion.

Evidently, the notion of social inclusion is the antithesis of social exclusion. Social exclusion is a way of understanding the impact of existing social economic systems on marginalized groups, while social inclusion is about finding out what works and mobilizing resources to resolve the problems brought about through social exclusion.

Within this general framework, however, the notion of social inclusion can be developed in different directions. One focus can be the incorporation of access and equity principles into a traditional agenda of national (universal) social inclusion, based on a universal social security system for children and families, and universal human development such as early learning for all. Such an approach would see the problems of social exclusion as being resolved by returning to the traditional post-war welfare state, which was dismantled by neo-liberal governments in Europe in the last three decades and more recently in Canada. A second focus, typical of the European approach, emphasizes the basic notions of capacity building and focusing resources to those at the bottom end of the social spectrum. This approach would target traditionally marginalized workers like retrenched workers and the long-term unemployed as well as racial/ethnic minorities, people with disabilities, children in poverty and the homeless.

A third focus would emphasize social inclusion as a fundamental capability, in a "rights-based approach." According to Sen (2001), an inclusive society is characterized by widely shared social experience and active participation, by broad equality of opportunities and life chances for individuals, and by the achievement of a basic level of well-being for all citizens. This approach emphasizes the need for policy to improve capabilities through legal human rights protections that ensure that all have the opportunity and ability to be included. It shifts the focus away from the individual who is for example living in poverty or dependent on social assistance, and thus away from blaming the victim.

Ultimately the test of the relevance of these notions of social inclusion lies in their ability to shape progressive and practical social policy reforms and initiatives. They must therefore be grounded in and shaped by the complex realities of growing social exclusion for Canadian newcomers.

## Social Inclusion and Canada's Official Multiculturalism

Any consideration of social inclusion in the Canadian context must take into account the fact that Canada is an officially multicultural and anti-racist society, with what is considered to be one of the most open and welcoming immigration policies in the world.

Canadian policies of multiculturalism, however, are rooted within and limited by their specific historical origins. Canadian multiculturalism evolved within a process of political bargaining among the two "founding nations" of English and French and the more established immigrant communities of European origin (Wayland 1997), without the political participation of the overwhelmingly visible minority immigrant arrivals of the past two decades. Furthermore, official Canadian multiculturalism and its derivate formal anti-racist policies have not been adequate to resolve the demands for Quebec independence, Aboriginal claims to land and autonomy, or anti-racist mobilization by visible minorities both immigrant and Canadian-born (Winter 2001).

Indeed, Canada has one of the world's most inclusive policies of citizenship acquisition, and this must be recognized as a legitimate and important factor of social inclusion. Newcomers are able and encouraged to become citizens after three years of settlement of Canada, and the vast majority do acquire Canadian citizenship. As documented previously in this chapter, however, the immigration status of newcomers (immigrant, refugee, refugee claimant) represents a hierarchy of rights with both legal and practical implications for social exclusion. Furthermore, the actual possibilities for economic, social and political inclusion of all newcomers, regardless of their formal immigration status, are too often in contradiction to the formal and official promises of multiculturalism, anti-racism and citizenship acquisition.

The contradictions between Canada's official policies and the reality of social exclusion for Canada's newcomers are well-documented. Richmond for example (1994 and 2000) reports on a system of "global apartheid" in which controls on international migration continually increase for the most vulnerable while becoming more flexible for the international business elite. Galabuzi (2001) speaks of a looming crisis of social instability and political legitimacy for Canadian society based on the growing trends towards the racialization of poverty for visible minorities and recent immigrants. Henry and Tator (2000) speak of "democratic racism" in reference to the deep tension in Canada between two competing value systems: the reality of pervasive racism and a commitment to the ideology of democratic liberalism. And Lo et al. (2000) talk of the failure of immigrant settlement and integration policies because of the persistence of high unemployment, low income and poverty for specific immigrant groups, and the incongruity between immigration selection policies and integration policies.

We are witnesses, therefore, to a real and growing contradiction between Canada's official policies of multiculturalism, anti-racism and immigration citizenship acquisition, and the growing reality of social exclusion for Canada's newcomers. The resolution of this contradiction involves at least two fundamental issues.

One of these issues, which is explored more fully by Saloojee (2002), concerns the fact that a social inclusion framework must incorporate an anti-racist perspective, taking into account the limits of multiculturalism and the realities of systemic racism in contemporary Canada. Within this perspective, of course, we must recognize that the vast majority of recent newcomers are non-European "visible minorities" experiencing systemic barriers of exclusion within the process of settlement.

The second issue addressed by others including Jenson (2002) involves our basic notions of citizenship. Jenson suggests that the Canadian diversity model can incorporate a notion of shared citizenship, in which unity and diversity are not mutually exclusive, and that we can rely on democratic institutions to choose between competing social values. Such a perspective might allow us to move beyond the limits of multiculturalism as the conservative preservation of "cultures of origin" and move towards a creative public dialogue incorporating the progressive values imported by our newcomer communities along with the democratic traditions of the host society. In exploring the relationship between citizenship values and the impact of newcomer settlement there is much to be learned from our colleagues in Quebec, where the debates and experiments have taken place in the context of a commitment to the social dominance of the French language and a critical distance from official Canadian multicultural policy (McAndrew 2001). One important lesson of the Quebec experience is that there is a considerable tension between a focus on individual rights, which tends to co-exist with more traditional notions of citizenship values, and an emphasis on collective rights, which tends to be supportive of an anti-racist perspective and notions of deep diversity.

## Policy Perspectives within a Social Inclusion Framework

There can be no doubt of the importance of including newcomers to Canada in the development of a social inclusion perspective on public policy reform. Canada has one of the highest proportions of immigrants to total resident population of any country in the world, and (both) newcomers and visible minorities make up more than half the population in our largest cities like Toronto. The role of Canada's newcomers is therefore central to any meaningful development of the notion of social inclusion.

But do the concepts of social inclusion "work" for newcomer settlement in Canada? Do they resonate? Do they offer new perspectives? Can they be useful tools for developing policy?

At the most basic level the notion of social inclusion certainly provides a powerful metaphor for addressing the challenges of newcomer settlement in Canada today. Immigrants want to be included, especially in the labour market. Refugees want to be included though resolution of their status. And all newcomers want to be included as full and equal participants in the economic, social, political and cultural life of their new homeland, while fearing that public policy debates will exclude their particular issues and interests as immigrants, or refugees, or visible minorities. The notion of social inclusion therefore provides an important starting point as an alternative to the currently dominant concept of focusing immigration policy exclusively on recruitment of "the best and the brightest," of continually raising the bar for admission to Canada while secondarizing the needs of family reunification and refugee resettlement and ignoring the barriers of social exclusion experienced by those who have already begun the settlement journey within our country.

We contend that the three possible focuses of a social inclusion perspective identified earlier are not mutually exclusive, but rather essential and overlapping elements of the application of a social inclusion perspective to the challenges of newcomer settlement in Canada. The restoration of government responsibility for universal social programs in the face of the neo-liberal tide for example is a necessary pre-condition for the social inclusion of both newcomers and the Canadian-born. Furthermore the targeting of social programs to the most disadvantaged is of obvious necessity for immigrants and refugees excluded from equitable participation in the Canadian labour market as well as in areas of exclusion for newcomers such as housing, education and access to health and social services. At the same time a rights-based approach to social inclusion is an essential perspective for dealing with the reality of differential legal and practical rights for Canada's newcomers based on immigration status (citizen versus immigrant versus refugee; selected immigrant versus family class; sponsored refugee versus refugee claimant, etc.)

We would argue as well that the five elements of a social inclusion perspective as previously identified can be applied directly, and productively, to the policy challenges posed by the growing social exclusion of Canada's newcomers. The notion of structuring policy interventions around a life cycle approach, for example, relates directly to the reality of the settlement process extending over the newcomer's lifetime and continuing (at least) into the second generation. The necessity to deal with failing communities and the needs of other excluded groups of people is directly relevant to the reality of economic, social and political exclusion for large groups of newcomers as documented in this chapter. The need to mobilize all relevant actors in a joint multi-agency response speaks to both the necessity to involve all levels and relevant departments of the federal, provincial and municipal governments in tackling the challenges of newcomer settlement, and the necessity to incorporate all stakeholders, including settlement agencies, mainstream institutions, employers and private foundations, in a policy response. Tackling discrimination in all its forms, with respect to newcomer settlement, means nothing more nor less than the necessity of an anti-racist perspective in dealing with the social exclusion of immigrants and refugees, the majority of whom are visible minorities. Finally, the notion of ensuring that all policy formulation is evidence-based speaks directly to the need for practical and transparent mechanisms of public accountability for the various sectors of government responsible for combating the exclusion of Canada's newcomers from full participation in the economic, social, political and cultural life of their new homeland.

Within this perspective, we offer the following suggestions for policy reform. While they vary considerably in scope and complexity, they all represent concrete examples of the potential of a practical and incremental approach to the application of the social inclusion perspective to the challenges of newcomer settlement.

## Access to trades and professions

An example of the immediate relevance and practical applicability of the notion of social inclusion is the issue of access to trades and professions (ATP). There can no longer be any doubt that the economic contributions of immigrants and refugees would be significantly higher if Canada were capable of properly utilizing their foreign-based experience, education and skills. In the next few decades, Canada will reach a point where net immigration accounts for 100 percent of both population growth and labour market replacement. Effective utilization of the experience, education and skills of newcomers is therefore key to economic success in an increasingly competitive global economy. As a result there is growing pressure for real progress in this area based on a recognition by multiple stakeholders that we are quite simply wasting the talents of our new citizens (Brouwer 1999; Reitz 2001; Alboim and Maytree Foundation 2002). It is particularly and bitterly ironic for newcomers, and for those who try to assist them, that the various licensing and professional bodies as well as Canadian employers appear to deny the legitimacy of the very skills and education that gained them admittance to our country.

Fortunately the vital importance of this issue is gaining increasing attention at various levels including the federal government. The Canadian Innovation Strategy for example is a federal policy initiative that focuses on the necessity to develop the skills, talents, knowledge and creativity of Canadians in an increasingly globalized, technological and knowledge-based economy (HRDC 2002). It is significant that this policy includes specific objectives related to immigration and that in addition to attracting and selecting highly skilled immigrants, the goals also include developing an integrated and transparent approach to the recognition of foreign credentials, supporting the integration of immigrants into Canada's labour market and helping immigrants to achieve their full potential over the course of their working lives.

Nevertheless, as noted by Couton (2002), the non-recognition of foreign credentials remains one of the most serious challenges to making effective use of the increasing numbers of highly skilled and highly educated newcomers attracted to Canada by our current immigration policies. Furthermore as documented in detail by Alboim and Maytree Foundation (2002), real progress on the issue of access to trades and professions requires a series of complex and detailed policy reforms involving multiple stakeholders. Progress in this area would represent a major "win-win" situation from the perspective of both newcomers and the Canadian-born, but the realization of this progress remains a vital testing ground for the practical application of a social inclusion perspective, particularly with regards to the development of effective partnerships and successful, incremental policy reforms.

## Local autonomy and immigrant settlement

One progressive trend in the urban environment is the growing demand for municipal autonomy. Across Canada there is growing pressure from municipal governments for a "new deal" in their relationship with federal and provincial authorities. Among the demands of municipal governments are increased resources for immigrant settlement and a greater political voice in immigration policy (Chief Administrator's Office 2001; Commissioner of Community and Neighbourhood Services 2001; Mwarigha 2002).

Historically, issues of immigration and settlement have been the responsibility of the federal and provincial governments. In recent years however the major urban centres have not only increased their role in providing support services to newcomers, but also been obliged to deal with all the multiple aspects of an increasingly ethno-racially diverse population with respect to municipal programs and policies. In recent years extra pressures have been placed on municipalities because of the effects of downloading of responsibilities to municipalities by senior levels of government, severe cutbacks to public spending, the amalgamation of municipalities and the lack of an integrated and effective pan-Canadian policy for newcomer settlement. In Toronto for example city planners warn that the municipality requires more resources to respond to the growing need for housing, employment and community services for newcomers, and that services currently provided to many new immigrants are not adequate (Commissioner of Community and Neighbourhood Services 2001).

Greater involvement by municipal governments in the settlement process and in consultations over immigration policy could provide real benefits. Local governments could make essential contributions to the development of long-term planning for newcomer settlement and could also play a key role as "brokers" in bringing other partners to the table, including federal and provincial departments with no direct mandate for short-term settlement, as well as the voices of NGO service providers and immigrant and refugee community leaders.

There is, of course no guarantee that municipalities will be any more responsive to, or representative of, newcomers and visible minorities than other levels of government. The outcome of the current drive for urban reform with respect to newcomer settlement will depend on political mobilization, particularly on mobilization of the immigrants and refugees who now constitute such a significant portion of the population of our major cities. Nevertheless the drive for urban reform provides an important impetus for the active political involvement of newcomer communities in urban politics, just as the mobilization of these communities is essential to ensuring that urban reform results in improved newcomer settlement. The prospects of linking urban reform to newcomer settlement therefore has real potential for the policy application of a social inclusion framework.

### The immigrant dispersion policy

One very contemporary and controversial policy debate in Canada involves the proposals by former Minister of Citizenship and Immigration Denis Coderre to regulate the dispersion of a portion of Canada's newcomers to our smaller cities.

These proposals are motivated by legitimate policy concerns. On the positive side, there is no doubt that our smaller or "second-tier" cities could benefit economically and otherwise from increased immigration. On the negative side, there are doubts — within the framework of existing settlement policy — about the capacity of our three largest cities to successfully absorb the overwhelming majority of immigrants and refugees who currently choose to reside in Toronto, Vancouver or Montreal.

The problem with the proposals as currently formulated however is that they will contribute to the exclusion rather than the inclusion of a segment of Canadian newcomers (Siddiqui 2002). Their mobility rights will be restricted, in comparison both to rights of the Canadian-born and previous immigrants, and in possible violation of our *Charter of Rights and Freedoms*. Furthermore, they will be denied the very benefits that have attracted previous newcomers on a voluntary basis to our largest cities: economic opportunities, social and cultural diversity and support from communities of their own ethno-racial origins.

Within a social inclusion framework, the same policy challenges could result in new solutions. Dispersion of recent newcomers could be developed on a voluntary basis, with appropriate material incentives. Newcomers could be attracted to second-tier cities through the development of improved settlement services within these urban centres. Furthermore, the process of developing these incentives and improving local settlement services would involve a generally beneficial increase in collaboration between federal, provincial and municipal governments.

## Newcomer children and youth in the schools

There is clearly a need for improved and extended settlement services for both newcomer youth and their parents, and recent research and program developments suggest that the school system is the natural location for such programs. Along with its importance for the education of increasingly large numbers of newcomer children and youth, the school system provides opportunities for interaction with these children's parents and their ethno-racial communities, for experimentation and innovation in the development of anti-racist curriculum and for more effective coordination of support services. Kilbride et al. (2000) emphasize the importance of schools as a location for integrated, supportive programs with a focus on anti-discrimination and anti-racism. They note as well that programs and interventions must be targeted, taking into account the differences experienced by newcomer youth according to country of original, ethno-racial and cultural and religious background, immigration status and gender.

One example of the development of such programs is in Ontario, where Citizenship and Immigration Canada during the past few years has funded pilot programs for school settlement workers working in collaboration with both school boards and local settlement agencies (Centre for Applied Social Research 2002). The program began in Toronto in 1998 as a partnership of the Ontario Administration of Settlement and Integration Services (OASIS), the Toronto District School Board (TDSB) and a number of community-based immigrant service agencies. Since its inception the program has expanded to other cities in Ontario and also developed in French-language schools. Initial evaluation suggests that the program has been very successful in providing increased support to newcomer children and youth, in helping their parents understand and interact with the school as an institution and in building productive partnerships amongst various agencies involved in newcomer settlement.

## Public defence of refugee rights

Another and vital area of public policy efforts with respect to newcomer inclusion must be the defence of basic refugee rights, which have become particularly vulnerable in the post-911 climate as interpreted by both politicians and the media. The vulnerability of newcomers in this context is of course focused on particular groups, such as Muslim women (Forcese 2002). But we are witness as well to an increasing general fragility of refugee rights, as the fundamental legal and human rights of refugees become secondarized or even displaced through the pretext of concerns for security. Examination of the evidence suggests that the growing legislative and administrative restriction of refugee rights in Canada is motivated very little by actual security threats arising within the refugee community but very much by a pre-911 agenda that favours increased mobility for skilled immigrants and restricted asylum rights for refugees (Adelman 2002).

Policy efforts to defend the basic human and legal rights of refugees in Canada must be based in broad public education and advocacy. Such programs offer an opportunity for new voices to speak out in support of newcomer inclusion and for members from our immigrant and refugee communities to take up an active role of leadership.

## Student loans and exclusion of newcomers

The *Canada Student Loans Act* is the primary vehicle that is used by Canadians to finance their post-secondary education, and loans are available to Canadian citizens and landed immigrants. However, there are currently a few intended and unintended forms of exclusion for newcomers. Convention refugees who are waiting for landing and are caught up in the identity issue are not eligible for student loans (Brouwer 2000). As well, landed immigrants are not allowed access to student loans until they have completed one year of residency in any given province, although we know that the first year of engagement in training and upgrading is often determinant for newcomers in terms of future attachment to the occupational sector of their previous training, education and experience (Goldberg 2000). Furthermore non-degree and non-diploma courses at universities and community colleges, courses that could aid newcomers in the establishment of equivalencies leading to licensing and/or employment in their previous field, are not eligible for student loans.

As a response to the situation of Convention refugee youth, The Maytree Foundation has established a scholarship program to provide access to post-secondary education. The program aims to give high-performing young men and women, who would not otherwise have access, an opportunity to participate in a community college or university program of their choice. It also seeks to facilitate the landing process for participating students and their families, and to promote social responsibility through volunteer service.

Other policy reforms in this area offer the potential of simple and practical steps to combat the intentional or unintentional forms of exclusion that currently exist and therefore to promote incremental progress to-wards social inclusion.

## Towards an integrated settlement policy

Perhaps the most important application of the social inclusion framework to newcomer settlement would be a redefinition of the basic notion of settlement. The current crisis of settlement policy in Canada is directly related to the lack of a long-term, multi-dimensional and pan-Canadian vision of the settlement process. The settlement journey for newcomers is one that lasts a lifetime and extends into the second generation, and our public policy response must accept this basic reality as a point of depar-ture. The elaboration of a new vision of settlement therefore involves the identification of mutual obligations and benefits for both newcomers and the host society with respect to all the social, economic and political institutions of Canadian society.

One essential component of such a visioning process must be the clarification of our notions of public accountability with respect to newcomer settlement. All levels and departments of government must be held accountable for the results of newcomer settlement, not only with respect to the provision of adequate resources for newcomer settlement, but also in terms of the necessity for broad public policy discussion on the nature and goals of the newcomer settlement journey and its impact on our social, cultural and political institutions. Indicators are required not just for measuring the effectiveness of service provision but also for evaluating the capacity of our labour markets and public institutions to combat exclusion and promote inclusion for newcomers. Immigrants and refugees, and their associations and their allies, must be more vocal and more organized in demanding such accountability.

Another essential component of an integrated settlement policy must be the restoration of adequate resources for settlement services. Another still is the protection of the autonomy of the community-based agencies in the front lines of settlement service delivery, which play an essential role in program innovation and in advocacy for newcomer rights. Another again is the development of mechanisms to directly include the voices of leaders from the immigrant and refugee communities in the definition and monitoring of our settlement policies.

The clarification and elaboration of a integrated, pan-Canadian and multi-faceted settlement policy therefore represents an essential element for testing and elaborating the relevance of the social inclusion perspective, both conceptually and practically, to the challenges of newcomer settlement in Canada.

## Conclusion

In this chapter we have attempted to document the process of growing exclusion for Canada's newcomers and to argue that the social inclusion framework provides a valuable perspective for re-examining our policies on newcomer settlement. The questions that are posed by the tension between newcomer inclusion and exclusion are fundamental. Will we fulfill our promises to utilize immigrant skills, welcome refugees and build a truly multicultural and anti-racist society? Or will we instead be pressured by international and domestic forces into consolidating various forms of newcomer exclusion and reproducing a hierarchy of rights based on ethno-racial and immigration status?

The visioning of true social inclusion for Canada's newcomers must be profound. True inclusion would mean not only a radical reform of our policies of newcomer settlement, but also the development of economic, political, social and cultural mechanisms and practices that include immigrants and refugees as full participants. Such a vision must begin with an anti-exclusion, anti-discrimination and anti-racist framework and progress towards new concepts and deeper notions of the value of diversity and the potential for new forms of citizen participation and engagement.

The ultimate test of the social inclusion framework, however, rests in its usefulness in framing practical policy alternatives to the growing reality of exclusion for Canada's newcomers. Such policies should be defined in concrete terms appropriate for incremental implementation and must as well win public acceptance. In this chapter we have suggested the points of departure for a number of such policies promoting social inclusion for Canada's newcomers; we invite our readers to critique these and to suggest others.

## Notes

1.  We want to express our deep gratitude to the reviewers of the first draft of this chapter for their insightful and constructive comments. We also want to give special acknowledgement to Mwarigha M.S., for his assistance with the conceptual framework; to Anthony Richmond, for sharing his current work on the concepts of refugees, social exclusion and "global apartheid"; to Tim Rees for his critical and insightful comments; to Valerie Preston for her feedback on immigrant women; and to Naomi Alboim for her work in development on a Municipal Immigration Program. Finally we must express our deepest appreciation to the Laidlaw Foundation for the opportunity to participate in, and hopefully make some small contribution to, this vital contemporary policy debate.
2.  See the Appendix (below) for some brief background information on the historical origins of Canadian immigration policy and the status of refugees in Canada.

## Appendix

### Immigration in Canada

The development of Canada during the last several hundred years has been shaped by waves of immigration from all corners of the world, to such an extent that Canada is often described as "a nation of immigrants." Immigration is generally assumed to be beneficial to long-term economic growth. Historically in Canada both government and industry have generally supported relatively high levels of immigration, although the absolute levels have varied significantly and sometimes declined during periods of economic recession. Due to our aging workforce and declining birth rates, immigration is also considered to play an essential role in augmenting Canada's workforce and maintaining our tax base for social services. Canada has one of the highest proportions of immigrants to total resident population of any country in the world: approximately 17 percent compared to 10 percent for the U.S. and less for European countries.

The *Immigration Act* of 1953 listed countries by preference and was judged in this sense to be racially discriminatory. Pressures to eliminate this discriminatory aspect came both from domestic human rights advocates and international diplomacy. These pressures eventually led to the *Immigration Act* of 1976 in which racial criteria for immigration were formally eliminated and three broad classes of immigration were established: independent (point-selected), family reunification and refugees.

During the period of time since these changes were implemented the principal source countries for immigration to Canada have shifted from Europe (including Great Britain) and the United States to Africa, the Middle East, Latin America, the Caribbean and particularly Asia. However the source of this change must be located not only in the policy and regulatory changes but also in the changing preferences of potential immigrants. Rising economic prosperity in Europe in the past decades, in particular, has limited the number of potential immigrants from European countries.

Historically, the system since 1967 for selected immigrants has been based on points assigned on the basis of skills of the prospective immigrant and labour market needs. Attributes assessed have included age, education, occupational demand, skill level, arranged employment and province of intended destination within Canada. The mix of points has varied over time through administrative decisions and has recently been revised through legislation. Current policy favours a greater proportion of skilled immigrants ("the best and the brightest") and a lower proportion of family class immigrants than in the past.

Some immigrants are also chosen as business or entrepreneurial class immigrants based on their potential economic contributions through investment and resulting job creation. Immigration regulations also permit entry for a temporary period for students and others; and the Temporary Foreign Worker Program of the federal government provides assistance to Canadian employers in recruiting foreign workers to fill short-term labour market gaps (for example, as agricultural labours and in the high technology sector).

The government of Canada has been committed to a long-term goal of increasing immigration levels to approximately one percent of the population or 300,000 annually. Actual numbers have been less but greater than 200,000 annually. In 2002 Citizenship and Immigration Canada expects to receive 140,000 selected on qualifications or investment potential, 62,000 family class and 30,400 refugees.

## Refugees

The Canadian government is committed under its international obligations and as part of its immigration program to provide support for resettlement of refugees. Historically Canada has not only maintained an ongoing policy of refugee resettlement as an integral component of its immigration program, but also provided rapid responses to refugee situations around the world. Examples include the acceptance of large numbers of refugees from Hungary in the 1950s, from Vietnam in the 1970s, and more recently from Kosovo. As well the conditions of many of those who immigrated to Canada from Europe immediately after the Second World War, who were at the time described as "displaced persons," were similar to those of today's "refugees." As a result a large portion of Canada's immigrant population is made up of persons who came to our country as refugees.

While immigrants come to Canada by choice, refugees arrive here because they are fleeing human rights abuses in their home countries. They are hoping for a safe haven in Canada and a chance to live in freedom and security. Refugees that are selected abroad include both government-sponsored and privately assisted refugees; they arrive in Canada with an established legal status as permanent residents and receive some social support. Inland refugees or refugee claimants are those that make a claim to status as a Convention refugee, after arrival in Canada either as a legal visitor or without legal status. The determination of refugee claimants seeking status as Convention refugees is dealt with by a separate administrative body, the Refugee Division of the Immigration and Refugee Board (IRB).

During recent years the number of refugees admitted annually has varied between about 20,000 and 30,000; refugees represent approximately 12–13 percent of the total number of immigrants. Inland refugee claimants are about half the total number of refugees coming to Canada. In 2001, there were over 40,000 refugee claims made in Canada.

# Social Inclusion, Anti Racism and Democratic Citizenship

*Anver Saloojee*

## Introduction

The utility of the concept, social inclusion, will depend on the extent and degree to which it successfully deals with social exclusion and the extent to which it promotes social cohesion in a society that is fractured along numerous fault lines. John Veit-Wilson distinguishes between weak versions of the social exclusion discourse, which focus on changing the excluded and integrating them into society, and stronger versions of the discourse, which focus on power relations between the excluded and those doing the excluding (Veit-Wilson 1998: 45). The weak versions focus simply on integration of the excluded (via a state commitment to multiculturalism), while the stronger versions take a structural approach that focuses on historical processes that continually reproduce oppression, discrimination and exclusion. Strong approaches to the social inclusion discourse therefore are intimately concerned with rights, citizenship and restructured relations between racialized communities and the institutions of the dominant society. The focus is on valued recognition and valued participation by those excluded from full participation in society and the benefits of society.

Those who recognize the salience of social exclusion as an explanatory tool need to be cognizant of one possible unintended consequence of the analysis — the re-victimization and marginalization of the excluded. Individuals and groups who are excluded on the basis of race (or other socially constructed criteria) need to be included both in the discussions about their social conditions of existence and in the debate about the eradication of exclusion. The various manifestations of racism as important expressions of social exclusion need to be tabled before there can be a meaningful and constructive discussion of social inclusion. Thus for social inclusion to matter, for it to resonate, it must provide space for a discussion of oppression and discrimination. Social inclusion has to take its rightful place, not along a continuum (from exclusion to inclusion), but as emerging out of a thorough analysis of exclusion. It has to simultaneously transcend the limits of essentialism,[1] critique hierarchies of oppression and promote a transformative agenda that links together the various, often disparate, struggles against oppression, inequality and injustice. And the glue that would bind these social movements together is a kind of inclusion that would lead to the creation of a more just and equitable society. In this conceptualization, social inclusion can provide a coherent critique of the multiple forms of social injustices and the concomitant institutional policies and practices. The first section of this chapter explores the relationship between social exclusion and racial exclusion and identifies and locates racism as a form of social exclusion. The second section assesses state responses to racism in the form of multiculturalism and identifies the limits and shortcomings of multiculturalism as public policy, using the lens of social inclusion and the notion of democratic citizenship. The third section of the chapter argues that a discourse on social inclusion is more compelling than one on exclusion, precisely because it posits the radical alternative to racial exclusion and is a viable political and public policy response to the multiple manifestations of exclusion. This section also identifies both the public policy implications of a commitment to anti-racist social inclusion and the building blocks necessary to creating an inclusive society from an anti-racist perspective.

## Racism as Social Exclusion

In this section the following argument will be constructed: simply put, racism is a form of social exclusion and racial discrimination in all its forms and manifestations is the process by which that exclusion occurs.[2] In order fully unpack this argument, it is necessary to first analyze how the term "social exclusion" is used in contemporary discourse and then link it to a broader discussion of racism, racial discrimination and racialized poverty.

Walker and Walker (1997) define social exclusion as "a comprehensive formulation, which refers to the dynamic process of being shut out, fully or partially, from any of the social, economic, political or cultural systems which determine the social integration of a person in a society. Social exclusion may therefore be seen as the denial (non-realization) of the civil, political and social rights of citizenship" (Walker and Walker 1997: 8). Gore (1995) notes that social exclusion has come to refer to the "process of social disintegration," a "rupture" in the relationship between the individual and society that resultes from structural changes in the economy and seriously impedes the mobility and integration into the labour market of younger workers and creates long-term unemployment for unskilled workers and immigrant workers. This in turn results in increased social problems and a tearing of the social fabric — increased homelessness, increased social tensions and periodic violence. Social exclusion as rupture is linked to Silver's solidarity paradigm — one of three paradigms she uses to link exclusion, citizenship and social intergration (Silver 1994: 62).

For many including Walker and Walker (1997) the opposite of exclusion is integration — into the labour market or more generally into a broader conception of citizenship with an interlocking set of reciprocal rights and obligations (Byrne 1999: 2; Gore 1995: 2). By 1989 the European Economic Community (later called the European Union, or EU) began to link social exclusion with inadequate realization of social rights. In 1990 the European Observatory on National Policies for Combating Social Exclusion was established to look at "the basic rights of citizenship to a basic standard of living and to participation in major social and economic opportunities in society" (Room, cited in Gore 1995: 2). Room notes that while poverty is focused on "distributional issues," notions of social exclusion "focus primarily on relational issues, in other words inadequate social participation, lack of social integration and lack of power" (cited in Gore 1995: 5). The link between social exclusion and citizenship then hinges for example, on the degree to which individuals from racialized and marginalized communities encounter structural and systemic barriers and are denied or restricted from participating in society. Duffy similarly notes that social exclusion refers to "the inability to participate effectively in economic social, political and cultural life, and, in some characterizations, alienation and distance from the mainstream society" (Duffy, cited in Barry, 1998: 2).

This concept of social exclusion is highly compelling because it speaks the language of oppression and enables the marginalized and the victimized to give voice and expression to the way in which they experience globalization, the way in which they experience market forces and the way in which they experience liberal democratic society. The concept of social exclusion resonates with many, including those who (i) are denied access to the valued goods and services in society because of their race, gender, religion, disability, etc; ii) lack adequate resources to be effective, contributing members of society; and (iii) are not recognized as full and equal participants in society. The roots of exclusion are deep, historical and indeed continually reproduced in both old and new ways in contemporary society (Freiler 2001c: 13). David Byrne argues that in the post-industrial developed world, "exclusion is a crucial contemporary form of exploitation, and... indeed there is nothing new about it" (Byrne 1999: 57). For him the battle against exclusion is a "battle against exploitation" (Byrne 1999: 57). This is reductionism for it asserts the primacy of class without looking at forms of oppression and the related forms of exclusions and marginalization. The struggle against class exploitation is not coterminous with the struggles against racial oppression and racial discrimination. What is required is a subtle, more nuanced approach that understands the specificity of racism as a form of social exclusion and does not subsume it under the guise of exploitation.

Without undertaking an analysis of the "political economy of exclusion," the attraction of the current discourse is that it focuses attention on social exclusion as failure to integrate into the labour market. But the contemporary discourse on social exclusion is too narrowly focused on poverty and integration into the paid labour market, and it potentially obscures a bigger debate about exploitation and the extent to which racism creates a dual labour market that leads to the super-exploitation of workers of colour. Within the European arena this could include a more systematic analysis of the super exploitation of "guest workers" and the concomitant denial of certain rights. In the North American arena this could include an analysis of the way in which formal accreditation processes restrict access to certain trades and professions for newcomers to Canada. It could also include an analysis of the way the delays associated with seeking asylum in Canada create an underground economy in which asylum seekers end up working at low paid, marginalized and insecure jobs. Broadening out the analysis of social exclusion to include the discourse on racism and conversely broadening out the concept of social inclusion to embrace an anti-racism discourse, both then require an analysis of race and racism in contemporary society.

Race is usually associated with somatic differences (such as skin colour) that distinguish the various groups which comprise the human species.[3] The concept of race is a social construct that has no empirical grounding and no scientific merit (Cox 1948; Banton 1977; Anderson and Freideres 1981; Dreidger 1989). Racism is both an ideology and a set of practices. As an ideology racism seeks to both legitimate the inequality faced by racialized groups and proclaim the superiority of the racial group that that constitutes the status quo.[4] Racism also consists of a set of mechanisms to ensure socio-political domination over a racial group (or groups). And racism involves discriminatory practices that work to constantly exclude, marginalize and disadvantage the subordinate racialized groups and reproduce the power, privilege and domination of the super-ordinate racialized group (Fleras and Elliott 1992: 335; Saloojee 1996: 2). Here it is also important to identify another term that is used in this chapter —"racialization," which refers to the process of attributing meaning to somatic differences.[5] The process of attaching meaning or significa-tion leads to policies and practices of exclusion and inclusion, and "collec-tive identities are produced and social inequalities are structured" (Kalbach and Kalbach 2000: 29).

The United Nations has provided an exceptionally well-thought-out, all encompassing definition of racial discrimination:

> In this Convention, the term "racial discrimination" shall mean any distinction, exclusion, restriction or preference based on race, colour, descent, or national or ethnic origin which has the purpose or effect of nullifying or impairing the recognition, en-joyment or exercise, on an equal footing, of human rights and fundamental freedoms in the political, economic, social, cultural or any other field of public life. (United Nations, International Convention on the Elimination of all Forms of Racial Discrimi-nation 1965, Article 1).

From this vantage point racial discrimination is undoubtedly a form of social exclusion, albeit one that has race as a social construct at the heart of exclusion. Its roots and manifestations however are different when compared to other forms of exclusion. Racism is unequal access to rights, it is unequal assess to the valued goods and services in society, it is about unequal access to the labour market and it extends to all fields of public life. It is about incomplete citizenship, undervalued rights, undervalued recognition and undervalued participation. The study of structured racial inequality, discrimination, rights and privileges hinges on a recognition that in Canadian society, women, racialized individuals and communities, persons with disabilities and First Nations people who enter the labour market, enter the educational system and seek goods and services (among other things) will face a structure of opportunities that are mediated by their race, gender, disability, etc. Precisely because of the existence of discrimination and barriers all people in Canadian society do not start from the same spot and do not compete on an equal footing with each other.

The study of racial inequality and racial discrimination is a study of racialization — how human differences are structured, imbued with meaning, continually reproduced, and used to deny people access to the valued goods and services in society. Structured racial exclusion is the process by which individuals from the dominant white racialized group in society are better positioned (than are individuals from subordinate racialized and marginalized minority groups) to secure a greater share of society's valued goods, services, rewards and privileges and to use these benefits to reinforce their control over rights opportunities and privileges in society. Through this process racial inequality and unequal access to the valued goods and services in society are structured and continually reproduced.

Racial inequality and discrimination are both the product and the confirmation of power imbalances in society; as well, they are a function of structural constraints that are rooted in the fabric of society. These structural constraints operate in such a way as to disadvantage members of racialized minority communities as they access the labour market and as they seek to advance within organizations. Race, ethnic and gender differences and inequalities persist in spite of the widely held assumption that the operation of market forces is blind to these differences between and among humans. The market has been unable to equitably distribute resources, goods and services in a society where inequality and discrimination are structurally embedded. Equality in society as well as in the workplace has proved to be very difficult to achieve.

Racial discrimination is manifested at the individual, institutional, structural and systemic levels. It can result from ill will or evil motive; it can be blatant and result from deliberate differential treatment or denial of access, or it can result from apparently neutral policies and practices that, regardless of intent, have adverse impacts on racialized individuals and communities. This latter concept of systemic discrimination has been repeatedly tested in human rights cases in Canada.

Justice Bertha Wilson while on the Supreme Court of Canada wrote:

> I would say then that the discrimination may be described as a distinction, whether intentional or not but based on grounds relating to personal characteristics of the individual or group, which has the effect of imposing burdens, obligations, or disadvantages on such individual or group not imposed upon others, or which withholds or limits access to organizations, benefits, and advantages available to other members of society. (Cited by Agocs et al. 1992:118)

She went on to clarify:

> In determining whether there is discrimination on grounds relating to the personal characteristics of the individual or group, it is important to look not only at the impugned legislation which has created a distinction that violates the right to equality but also to the larger social, political and legal context. McIntyre J. emphasized in Andrews:
>
> *For as has been said, a bad law will not be saved merely because it operates equally upon those to whom it has application. Nor will a law necessarily be bad because it makes distinctions.*
>
> Accordingly, it is only by examining the larger context that a court can determine whether differential treatment results in inequality or whether, contrariwise, it would be identical treatment which would in the particular context result in inequality or foster disadvantage. A finding that there is discrimination will, I think, in most but perhaps not all cases necessarily entail a search for disadvantage that exists apart from and independent of the particular legal distinction being challenged. (Cited by Agocs et al. 1992: 118)

Given the multidimensionality of racism and the multiple manifestation of racial discrimination, providing precise measures of and explicitly quantifying racism has proved problematic (Henry et al. 1995: 49). The indicators of racism and the measures of racism are important as they have significant policy and practice implications. These measures are also complicated by the importance many researchers have rightly attached to the intersection of race, gender, class, disability etc. Over the years there has developed an extensive body of research that has documented the extent and pervasiveness of racial discrimination in Canadian society. This research seeks to measure racism through a variety of mechanisms, including a study of attitudinal polls, analyzing human rights commission reports, assessing the relationship between race and economic variables (rates of employment, rates of unemployment, distribution across occupational categories, distribution across income categories, etc) and the intersection of race and poverty and race and educational attainment. The challenge of measuring racial discrimination is that it is extremely difficult to measure intentionality; thus the earlier distinctions between intention and effects are critical. Measures of racial discrimination invariably focus on the effects of the discriminatory actions not on the intentions of the perpetrators. While this chapter is not about detailing the research on the multiple forms of racism as exclusion, it nonetheless very briefly summarizes recent research that looks at racism and labour participation and racism and poverty. The measures of racism as it is manifested in labour force participation include measuring:

- rates of employment;
- rates of unemployment;
- income differentials; and
- employment segregation.

One of the most pervasive myths is that since members of racialized groups are found in the workforce there is no widespread discrimination to their entry into the labour force. Once they enter the labour force, the argument goes, they encounter the "glass ceiling" an invisible barrier that prohibits their upward mobility within the workplace\organizational hierarchy. Members of racialized groups, it is argued only progress up to a certain point, beyond which advancement and progress are difficult, and since they encounter a "glass ceiling," they can see the upper echelons of the hierarchy but cannot detect the barriers that prevent their attaining those positions. The assumptions embedded in the "glass ceiling theory" are that (i) members of racialized groups do gain entry to the active labour force, they are hired, they do have a foot in the door; (ii) once hired there is movement up the hierarchy to a certain point; and (iii) their retention rates are not a significant human resources problem.

Contrary to these assumptions, the prevalence of prejudice and discrimination in society at large guarantees that many members of racialized minority groups encounter the "steel door" before the glass ceiling. It is the gatekeepers of the steel doors who bar or facilitate entry to employment. Members of racialized minority groups first encounter prejudice and discrimination in the pre-employment stage and then once in, face other forms of discrimination at the workplace itself. Thus it is important to separate the two levels of discrimination and disadvantage that they face — the first level is in access to employment opportunities and the second level is within organizations after they have secured employment. At the first level, access to employment, disadvantage is manifested in a number of areas — e.g., differential unemployment and labour force participation rates compared to white, able-bodied males and occupational ghettoization. For those who do secure employment the indices of disadvantage include income levels, occupational clustering and ghettoization, upward mobility and promotion rates, distribution across the organizational employment hierarchy, rates of retention (staff turnover rates) and experiences of harassment.

While members of racialized minority groups experience disadvantage and barriers in seeking employment as well as after securing employment, it is important to recognize that these disadvantages are the result of both direct intentional discrimination and systemic discrimination. When the so called gatekeepers exercise power to reinforce their prejudices and stereotypical views to the disadvantage of designated group members, then discrimination has occurred. When people are denied access to employment or employment opportunities, when they work in a poisoned work environment, when their advancement within the organization is hindered because of their status as members of racialized groups, then it is clear they are excluded and disadvantaged, and that discrimination has occurred. (For details on racial discrimination and labour market participation, see Ontario Human Rights Commission 1983; Henry and Ginzberg 1985; Billingingsley and Musynzski 1985; Canadian Civil Liberties, *Toronto Star*, January 21, 1991; Hou and Balakrishnan 1996; Frank 1997; Li 1998; The Canadian Race Relations Foundation 2000; Galabuzi 2001.) Recent reports suggest that members of racialized minority groups experience lower rates of employment – 66 percent compared to 75 percent for non-racialized minorities (CRRF 2000: 18; Galabuzi 2000). Concomitantly they experience higher rates of unemployment — based on the 1996 Census data, men in racialized groups had a 13.2 percent unemployment rate compared to 9.9 percent for men in general, while women in racialized groups had an unemployment rate of 15.3 percent compared to 9.4 percent for other women (CRRF 2000: 19). There is also strong evidence of a labour market that is split into two primary segments. One is well paying, has a wide distribution of occupations, relatively high rates of unionization and reasonably good working conditions and high rates of employment. The other is characterized by less favourable rates of pay, types of work and working conditions, little job security and low rates of unionization and higher rates of unemployment. This split intersects with race to create a split labour market that is highly stratified by race and by gender. This is a situation where workers from racialized groups are overrepresented in low-end jobs and under represented in highly paid employment (see Ontario Human Rights Commission 1983; Henry and Ginzberg 1985; Billingingsley and Musynzski 1985; Canadian Civil Liberties, *Toronto Star*, January 21, 1991; Hou and Balakrishnan 1996; Frank 1997; Li 1998; The Canadian Race Relations Foundation 2000; Ornstein 2000; Galabuzi 2001; Canadian Council on Social Development 2002).

The split labour market along with other factors translates into significant income disparities between racialized group members and other Canadians. In 1998 racialized Canadians earned an average of $14,507 compared to $20,517 for non-racialized Canadians. This was tantamount to a 28 percent gap in median income before taxes and a 25 percent gap in median income after taxes. Andrew Jackson made an important distinction between racialized Canadians born in Canada and those who were foreign born. Analyzing Statistics Canada data from 1995, Jackson found that members of racialized groups who were immigrants and who were fully employed for over a year were earning $32,000 per year compared to $38,000 for their Canadian counterparts (Jackson 2001: 7). More recently Jeffrey Reitz assessed 1996 Census data and concluded that immigrant workers in Canada lost $15 billion in earning because of a "brain waste" — the discounting and undervaluing of the education, professional training and experience of immigrants prior to coming to Canada. Underutilizing the skills of skilled immigrants cost them $2.4 billion in lost wages, while undervaluing their skills (by paying them less than their Canadian-born counterparts cost immigrant workers $12.6 billion. White immigrants reported less pay inequities than immigrants of colour (Gorrie 2002: A23).

Just over ten years ago the Ontario Ministry of Citizenship released its report on the need for employment equity in Ontario. In assessing the data at that point the Ministry concluded that entrants to the labour force from racialized groups faced a number of barriers to employment, including:

- blatantly overt discriminatory hiring policies;
- job requirements that have nothing to do with what is needed to perform the job;
- an unfair assessment of qualifications and work experience from abroad;
- invisible barriers such as biases, stereotyping and discrimination based on a person's colour, rather than an assessment of a person based on their actual skills or performance;
- the vicious cycle of lower expectations leading to lower achievement; and
- a hostile\poisoned work environment caused by racial jokes, abusive slurs and on occasion physical abuse (Office of the Employment Equity Commissioner, Ministry of Citizenship 1991: 9).

The barriers which create unequal access to the labour market, the glass ceiling which significantly inhibits promotion to higher skilled better paying jobs and the reality of a split labour market over-determined by race all contribute to another significant phenomenon — the racialization of poverty. The data is very stark[6]:

- The 1996 Census revealed an overall poverty rate in Canada of 21 percent (pre-tax LICO measure). For members of racialized groups (70 percent of whom were foreign born) the poverty rate was 38 percent. For those who immigrated to Canada prior to 1986 the rate was less than 20 percent, for the post 1986 to 1990 group the rate was 35 percent and for those who arrived between 1991 and 1996 the poverty rate was 52 percent.
- Family poverty rates demonstrate a similar pattern — 19 percent for racialized groups and 10.4 percent for non racialized group.
- Poverty among children from racialized groups was 45 percent compared to 26 percent for all children living in Canada.
- In Canada's urban centres as a whole racialized group members account for 21 percent of the population and 33 percent of the urban poor. The Canadian Council on Social Development found that in Vancouver, Markham, Richmond Hill, Toronto and Mississauga over 50 percent of the poor are racialized group members.
- The Ornstein Report, *Ethno-Racial Inequality in Toronto*, found that "African, Black and Caribbean ethno-racial groups" experience much more poverty and family incomes significantly below the Toronto average. The percentages of families with incomes below the LICO is 47.6 percent, 48.7 percent and 40.5 percent respectively. For groups from Africa the situation is much more devastating. The figures for Ethiopians, Ghanaians, Somalis and "other African nations" are 69.7 percent, 87.3 percent 62.7 percent and 52.2 percent. Ornstein also found that 28.7 percent of Indian families and over 50 percent of the Pakistani, Bangladeshi, Sri Lankan and Tamil families were below the poverty line. For Central American and South Americans the figures were 51.6 percent and 40.2 percent respectively (Ornstein 2000: 112–15).
- Approximately 40 percent of foreign-born members of racialized groups who had less than a high school education were among the poorest 20 percent of Canadians.
- Twenty percent of foreign-born members of racialized groups with a university education were also found in that group of the poorest 20 percent of Canadians (for more details, see Galabuzi 2000; Ornstein 2000; Jackson 2001).
- The Canadian Council on Social Development found that despite the economic recovery of the 1990s poverty among recent immigrants as a group (75 percent of whom are members of racialized minorities), was 27 percent in 1998 compared to 13 percent among the rest of the Canadian population. "Unfortunately, the situation of recent immigrants compared to other Canadians has worsened considerably" the report concluded (Carey 2002: A1).

Just being in the labour force and seeking employment therefore is not enough for members of racialized groups. Often they encounter prejudice and discrimination that deny them employment opportunities or deny them access to skilled and more highly valued employment. The results of these attitudes and structural barriers are that they face the prospect of higher unemployment rates, occupational ghettoization, lower earning power, higher rates of impoverishment and if they repeatedly encounter discriminatory barriers they eventually give up seeking employment entirely. Thus the intersection of race and poverty requires a systematic discussion of "racialized poverty." The intersection of labour market exclusion and race requires a systematic discussion of racial exclusion that exacerbates the general effects of exclusion. Labour market inclusion therefore is not the only answer to poverty eradication; nor is it the only answer to labour market exclusion that results from racial discrimination.

Clearly, exclusion in general and racial exclusion in particular results in economic, social, political and cultural disadvantage. Those who are included have access to valued goods and services in society while those who are excluded do not. In turn, those who are disadvantaged, marginalized and "othered" in society do not have access to valued goods and services and are consequently excluded. There is therefore a mutually reinforcing relationship between exclusion and disadvantage, and it is necessary to both unpack that relationship and to address each of its multiple manifestations in order to break what I call the "vicious cycle of exclusion and disadvantage." The answer to this lies with political struggle that embraces an inclusionary solidarity movement.

## Social Inclusion and Democratic Citizenship: Understanding the Limits of Multiculturalism

Identity formation and social cohesion of racialized and immigrant communities is a complex response to many factors. Their respective citizenship claims are intimately linked to making equality claims and to ensuring their rights and freedoms enshrined in the Charter are not eroded. In a country like Canada, these citizenship claims are in no small measure mediated by the histories of immigrants in the sending countries, by the state in the host country and its multicultural practices, and also by the reality of discrimination and exclusion. Discrimination undermines citizenship and erodes a person's ability to develop their talents and capacities. This dual mediation is reflected in the two phases of multiculturalism in Canada. Through an official policy of multiculturalism, the state in Canada has attempted to deal with racial discrimination and significantly determine the nature of state/minority relations within a liberal tradition that promotes equality and encourages group social cohesion and social inclusion.

In the narrow sense, citizenship is exclusionary. It is about who is a citizen of a nation state and what bundle of rights that citizen can exercise. It is about what that citizen is entitled to as a member of the nation state. In the realm of formal equality the laws, the constitutions, the human rights codes proclaim the equality of all citizens. In this realm, it is just that citizens should be equally entitled to certain rights typically associated with a democracy — the right to vote, to freedom of association, freedom of religion, etc.

Social inclusion forces the discourse beyond the realm of formal equality and into the realm of substantive equality, which is characterized by challenges to discrimination, exclusion and inequality. Social inclusion begins from the premise that it is democratic citizenship that is at risk when a society fails to develop the talents and capacities of all its members. The move to social inclusion is eroded when the rights of minorities are not respected and accommodated and minorities feel "othered." For social inclusion there is no contradiction between democratic citizenship and differentiated citizenship (where people can hold dual and even multiple loyalties). Democratic citizenship is about valued participation, valued recognition and belonging. At a minimum, it is characterized by:

- all the political rights associated with formal equality;
- a right to equality and a right to be free from discrimination;
- an intimate relationship between the individual and the community;
- reciprocal relationship of rights and obligations;
- barrier free access, a sense of belonging and not being "othered" and marginalized;
- a commitment on the part of the state to ensure that all members of society have equal access to developing their talents and capacities; and
- providing all members of society with the resources to exercise democratic citizenship.

It was the Abella (1987) report that advanced the notion that equality does not mean sameness and that equality means that we have to treat differences differently. This is the necessary minimum precondition for achieving social inclusion. The Supreme Court of Canada has noted that minority rights do not erode democratic citizenship, rather "the accommodation of differences is the essence of true equality."

Accommodating differences and eliminating barriers to equality of opportunity are the hallmarks of social inclusion. The latter, however, ought not to be confused with social cohesion for multiple forms of exclusion can exist in a socially cohesive society. Nonetheless, important questions persist: cohesion around what vision and inclusion to what? Are we talking about assimilation? Is this a new way of managing state-minority relations? Is this "Anglo conformity" or even "multiculturalism" in a new guise? As Kymlicka and Norman point out there have been major disputes both about the legitimacy of assimilation as a way of eliminating differences and about multiculturalism as the official recognition of differences (Kymlicka and Norman 1994: 14–16).

In Canada, the first phase of multiculturalism was a response to the recommendations of the 1970 final report of the Royal Commission on Bilingualism and Biculturalism. Prime Minister Pierre Elliot Trudeau called this phase "multicultural in a bilingual framework" (Trudeau October 8, 1971). In this phase, the state encouraged ethnic groups to preserve their distinct ethnic cultures by funding a range of initiatives to preserve their language and culture. In this phase multiculturalism was not seen in strictly political terms; it was a reflexive response to the growing ethnic diversity of Canadian cities. In the second phase multiculturalism was accorded a protected place in the Canadian Constitution and as such it began to inform the discourse on national identity in a new way.

In the first phase, the Canadian state through its multicultural policies encouraged group social cohesion (preservation of culture and language). Retention of cultural, linguistic and religious differences in a multicultural society is important in celebrating differences. However this iteration of the discourse quickly reached its limit. It was becoming readily apparent to many marginalized communities in Canada that while they were developing internal social cohesion they were, at a broader level, consigned to the margins and excluded from the centres of decision-making. Minority culture was not seen as part of the mainstream culture. Further, there was appearing on the political horizon a backlash against celebrating difference. The dominant discourse was being framed around issues of national unity and whether unity could be forged through promoting differences. It was not being framed around the challenges of social inclusion.

The recognition of the absence of social inclusion, coupled with the reality of exclusion and discrimination, prompted among these marginalized communities a reflexive or what Castells (1997) calls a "defensive" assertion of identity. The assertion of an identity against discrimination and exclusion in turn creates a politics of inclusion and social cohesion that is no longer rooted simply in the desire to hold on to that which is unique. Rather the politics of inclusion cuts across intergroup and intra-group identity and builds a movement of solidarity capable of challenging the dominant discourse. This is similar to Giddens' notion of "dialogic democracy" based on a mutual respect, a shared understanding of the effects of exclusion and marginalization and the emergence of solidarity: "Dialogic democracy ... concerns furthering of cultural cosmopolitanism and is a prime building block of that connection of autonomy and solidarity... dialogic democracy encourages the democratization of democracy within the sphere of the liberal-democratic polity" (Giddens 1994: 112). The growth of the multicultural society, therefore, is producing the conditions for the emergence of a new sense of social inclusion, what David Held calls a "cosmopolitan democracy" that recognizes differences, respects differences and argues for substantive equality and not just formal equality (Held 1995: 226–31). The old policy of multiculturalism was simply incapable of responding to a set of issues, which were now intensely political. In Canada, ethnoracial communities were shifting their focus from "song and dance" to an assessment of their rightful place in a democratic society that espoused the ideals of equality. In the highest law of the land, the constitution gave constitutional recognition to the value of multiculturalism. By 1987 the Parliamentary Standing Committee on Multiculturalism stated that the old policy was "floundering" and needed "clear direction" (Government of Canada Standing Committee on Multiculturalism 1987).

The core issues that preoccupied racialized communities now included issues of power, access, equity, participation, removal of discriminatory barriers, institutional accommodation and anti-racism. The clear direction that the Parliamentary Standing Committee on Multiculturalism called for came in the form of the *Multiculturalism Act* of 1988. With the passage of the legislation, multiculturalism came to occupy a position of considerable significance in the debate on Canada's national identity. This position of importance was first openly acknowledged in the Canadian constitution, where in the *Charter of Rights and Freedoms*, multiculturalism is constitutionally entrenched. According to section 27 of the Charter, "This Charter shall be interpreted in a manner consistent with the preservation and enhancement of the multicultural heritage of Canadians." The continued politicization of multiculturalism with the passage of the *Multiculturalism Act* elevated multiculturalism from a celebration of diversity to the heart of Canada's nation building project. The federal government sought to delicately balance a number of critical issues, namely, diversity and social cohesion, minority rights and majority rights, cultural identity and citizenship and cultural pluralism, inclusion and equality. The government developed a public policy on multiculturalism that committed it to three primary activities: first, recognizing and promoting the understanding that multiculturalism is a fundamental characteristic of Canadian society; second, eliminating barriers to full and equitable participation faced by members of minority communities in all spheres of Canadian society; and third, ensuring that all individuals receive equal treatment and equal protection of the law, while respecting and valuing their diversity.

Advocates within minority communities argue that minority rights are a natural extension of and perfectly consistent with liberal democratic rights. On the other hand critics argue that the promotion of minority rights detracts from building "common citizenship" and goes a considerable distance in eroding what Kymlicka and Norman call "democratic citizenship" (Kymlicka and Norman 2000: 10). Bibby, a critic of multiculturalism, argues that the policy has not led to increased tolerance; rather it has led to increased fragmentation, hyphenation and insularity.

Multiculturalism, he notes, has resulted in the production of "individual mosaic fragments" (Bibby 1990:14–15). For Glazer, the politicization of minority rights elevates ethnicity as a defining variable in public life and is inherently divisive (Glazer 1983: 227–28). Kymlicka and Norman summarize the arguments of the critics as follows:

> A more moderate (and more plausible) version states that while minority rights may not lead to civil war, they will erode the ability of citizens to fulfil their responsibilities as democratic citizens — e.g., by weakening citizens' ability to communicate, trust, and feel solidarity across group differences. As so, even if a particular minority rights policy is not itself unjust, examined in isolation, the trend towards increased salience of ethnicity will erode the norms and practices of responsible citizenship, and so reduce the overall functioning of the state. (2000: 10)

They go on to suggest that the argument about whether multiculturalism, which promotes a heightened "salience of ethnicity," is fundamentally divisive because it detracts from democratic citizenship and erodes social cohesion has to be assessed in specific contexts and cannot be assessed in the abstract. For them, these arguments turn on four ideas: citizenship status, citizenship identity, citizenship activity and citizenship cohesion (Klymicka and Norman 2000: 31).

What the critics of multiculturalism, anti-racism and employment equity policies fail to appreciate is the significant power and privilege enjoyed by the majority and denied others because of their race, disability or gender. Weinfeld concludes that "the ideals behind the rhetoric of multiculturalism have not been attained.... Canadian native people and other non-whites continue to be victimized, a fact reflected in economic inequality or in patterns of social exclusion, abuse, and degradation" (Weinfeld 1981: 69). It is the pervasiveness of prejudice directed at disadvantaged groups and the widespread existence of discrimination that have contributed to the fragmentation, hyphenation and insularity in the urban environment.

The two iterations of multiculturalism in Canada also point to the failure of state sponsored actions to deal with social inclusion. Day is more critical: "I would suggest that integration within multiculturalism in a bilingual framework is best seen as a creative reproduction of the colonial method of strategic simulation of assimilation to the Other, and not as an overcoming or break with this past" (2000: 197). The modern nation state, Day notes, "*simulated its unity and dissimulated its multiplicity*" The postmodern multicultural Canadian state however "*dissimulates its unity and simulates a multiplicity*" (2000: 205).

The multicultural society is now the site where ethno-racial communities are contesting the ideas of identity, citizenship and cohesion and inclusion. They are struggling to have their identities recognized alongside the dominant culture. Charles Taylor argues that the refusal to recognize minority rights can be seen as a "form of repression" and he points to the importance of the "links between recognition and identity" (1992: 50). The struggle for recognition is inherently a political struggle against the dominant discourse. It is the state and the dominant discourse that are in the position of conferring "recognition" and thereby affirming both their legitimacy and their positions of pre-eminence. The current policy of multiculturalism is one where "the state does not recognize the value or equality of "communities" rather it merely recognizes their *"existence"'* (Day 2000: 198).

Multiculturalism, even in its second iteration as recognition, has not lead to "valued recognition," "valued participation" and increased equality for minority groups. It has not overturned the pre-eminent position of the English and the French in Canadian society. Rather it preserves national and linguistic duality and the "Other Ethnic Groups [are] arranged in a complex ever changing hierarchy" (Day 2000:198). It has not promoted social inclusion and thus what is required is a more proactive policy that accommodates the needs of minority communities and creates conditions under which they can develop their talents and capacities and in which they can become valued and respected and contributing members of society. Such a proactive policy can only enhance their attachment to a common identity. Rather than being corrosive it can be binding. Kymlicka and Norman, however, are less definitive:

> In sum, whether we are concerned with citizenship status, virtue or cohesion, the relationship between minority rights and citizenship is more complicated than it might initially appear. We see legitimate worries about the potential impact on citizenship, but also countervailing arguments showing that some minority rights can actually enhance citizenship. (2000: 40)

Has decades of state commitment to multiculturalism enhanced citizenship and led to social inclusion in Canada's most multicultural and multiracial city? In 1999 the City of Toronto released a report that suggested that identity formation and social cohesion in the city were being eroded by the exclusion and marginalization experienced by many immigrant groups: "If the situation [of under representation in decision-making] is not addressed, as well as the incidents of hate activity and discriminatory practices and prejudicial attitudes that unfortunately continue to plague our city, it can only lead to a growing sense of frustration" (City of Toronto 1998). Discrimination, prejudice, exclusion and marginalization in an ostensibly multicultural, multiracial city forms the context in which the search for identity and social cohesion is experienced. Representation and participation in public institutions and civic life is critical to the development of social cohesion, but they constitute only one important indicator of social inclusion.

Unlike multiculturalism, which stagnates at incomplete and highly contested integration, social inclusion is precisely about the democratization of democracy. By developing a new way of approaching old problems, by positing a radically different conception of citizenship and community, by arguing for new measures of accountability, by providing the impetus for the emergences of new modes of evaluation of public policies, by arguing for increased representation and participation by marginalized groups and above all by encouraging the development of skills, talents and capacities of all, social inclusion will democratize democracy. The growth of the multicultural, multiracial nation therefore is producing the conditions for the emergence of a new sense of social inclusion that recognizes differences, respects differences and that argues for substantive equality and not just formal equality.

## Public Policy Approaches That Make Social Inclusion Real

The structural processes of racial exclusion engendered among racialized communities the struggle for legitimacy and "place claiming." This is the dawn of a new type of politics. The struggle for example, by racialized communities for the redistribution of power and resources takes a non-class specific dimension. And herein lies the political value of social inclusion. It posits the radical alternative to exclusion and is a viable political response to exclusion. The value of social inclusion is that it is fully capable of meeting the greatest challenges posed by diversity — to build on the traditions of equality espoused in liberalism and to move to the incorporation of the ideals of anti-racism and anti-discrimination as core ideals exemplifying national values. Social inclusion is capable of this because it is about respect for differences and it is about the removal of barriers to effective and equitable participation in all spheres of public life. And it is about more than this, it is about engaging in inclusive practices, it is about continuous evaluations of institutions, laws, policies and practices to ensure that they promote social inclusion. Thus, it is about evaluation for the purpose of public accountability.

The politics of social inclusion is about an inclusive democracy that places issues of social justice at the heart of the urban question. Democracy is the locus of citizenship and it is essential to recognize that the very definition of the public sphere and citizenship in the urban environment is contested by racialized minority groups. There is no single public sphere, no single acceptable notion of citizenship and no single notion of social cohesion. There are instead multiple spheres and spaces in which historically marginalized groups develop their own sense of cohesion to contest oppression, discrimination and exclusion — where they posit a different understanding of space, citizenship and social cohesion. In positing this different and alternate understanding, they are challenging the dominant discourse and accentuating the politics of difference that puts issues of inequality and social justice at the heart of a reclaimed social inclusion. When historically marginalized groups contest notions of rights and conceptions of citizenship they are simultaneously seeking an alternative. The alternative is about inclusion as valued participants in a society that is committed to the eradication of discrimination and disadvantage in all its forms and manifestations.

Benick and Saloojee (1996) defined an inclusive learning environment as one that "fosters the full personal, academic and professional development of all students. It is one that is free of harassment and discrimination... it is about respecting students and valuing them as partners" (1996: 2). Despite its narrow focus this definition comes close to Freiler's notion of social inclusion as a process that encourages the development of talents, skills and capacities necessary for children and youth to participate in the social and economic mainstream of community life (2001c: 8–10). What makes a discourse on social inclusion more compelling than one on exclusion are the following:

- Social inclusion is the political response to racial exclusion. Most analyses of racism for example, focus on the removal of systemic barriers to effective participation and focus on equality of opportunity. Social inclusion is about more that the removal of barriers — it is about a comprehensive vision that includes all. It is about valued recognition and valued participation in the struggle for an inclusive society.
- Social inclusion is proactive. It is about anti-discrimination. It is not about the passive protection of rights it is about the active intervention to promote rights. It confers responsibility on the state to adopt and enforce policies that will ensure social inclusion of all members of society (not just formal citizens, or consumers or taxpayers or clients). It also demands that the agencies of the state be proactive in advancing an anti-racist, inclusive vision of society.
- Social inclusion promotes solidarity. Individuals, organizations and communities from diverse backgrounds can come together on the basis of common purpose and engage in an inclusionary politics, directed at the creation of inclusive communities, cities and society.
- Social inclusion, by virtue of the fact that it is both process and outcome, can hold governments and institutions accountable for their policies. The yardstick by which to measure good government therefore becomes the extent to which it advances the well-being of the most vulnerable and the most marginalized in society.
- Social inclusion is about advocacy and transformation. It is about the political struggle and the political will to remove barriers to full and equitable participation in society by all, and in particular by members

of racialized communities. Furthermore, the vision of social inclusion is a positive vision that binds its proponents and adherents to action.

• Social inclusion is embracing. It posits a notion of democratic citizenship as opposed to formal citizenship. Democratic citizens possess rights and entitlements by virtue of their being a part of the polity, not by virtue of their formal status (as immigrants, refugees, or citizens).

Social inclusion is about social cohesion *plus*, it is about citizenship *plus*, it is about the removal of barriers *plus*, it is anti-essentialist *plus*, it is about rights and responsibilities *plus*, it is about accommodation of differences *plus*, it is about democracy *plus*, and it is about a new way of thinking about the problems of injustice, inequalities and exclusion *plus*. It is the combination of the various pluses that make the discourse on social inclusion so incredibly exciting. Within this context a commitment to anti-racist social inclusion has a number of public policy implications.

First, there has to be a renewed commitment at the federal, provincial and municipal levels to employment equity. An employment creation strategy in the absence of a proactive policy to bring down barriers to employment and advancement for members of racialized minority communities is insufficient. An economic strategy that promotes economic growth and increased employment is a necessary but insufficient condition to promote inclusion. Strategies directed at labour market integration have to be accompanied by strategies to bring down barriers to labour market participation and advancement by members of racialized minority communities.

Second, the reach and scope of the employment equity policies has to extend beyond the public and para-public sectors and deep into the private sector. Concomitant with this reach there has to be greater enforcement of equity legislation and greater accountability by public and private organizations for their policies and practices. There are many important strategies that organizations can pursue to both eliminate barriers to effective participation by members of racialized communities and create inclusive anti-discrimination organizations.

Third, federal and provincial governments need to strengthen human rights commissions. These commissions play vital investigative and mediation functions. However given their limited resources they do not vigorously pursue their public education functions. Human rights commissions need to be more proactive in promoting human rights and not simply be passive recipients of complaints which they then investigate.

Fourth, the federal and provincial governments need to urgently develop a national strategy in concert with universities, colleges and professional accreditation bodies to deal with the issue of foreign credentials, foreign training and foreign experience. Studies are now commenting on the "brain waste" to Canada as a result of the significant underutilization of the skills and experience of foreign trained and educated professionals. Further the systemic barriers associated with vetting the education, training and experience of foreign trained professional (the vast majority of whom are from racialized minority communities) affects their employability, their earning capacity and their upward mobility.

Fifth, municipal governments, as democratically elected governments, as employers, as service providers and as the most readily accessible level of government, have very important roles to play, including:

- making the representation of elected officials and the participations by diverse communities more inclusive and representative;
- pursuing an employment equity policy, a contract compliance policy and an inclusive purchasing policy;
- identifying and bringing down barriers faced by members of racialized communities seeking to access municipal services. Municipal governments can promote inclusive policies by enhancing communication with racialized minority communities, providing racially and culturally sensitive programs, addressing the funding imbalances between mainstream organizations and organizations representing the interests of racialized minority communities and engaging in meaningful consultation with members and organizations from racialized minority communities on the range of issues affecting their lives — not just on issues of equity and racism; and
- directly confronting the challenges associated with racialized poverty, and becoming a champion of the poor and the racialized poor. Municipal governments need to vociferously argue with the federal government and with provincial governments to drastically strengthen Canada's social safety net, increase social expenditure in education, childcare, and health care and increase the availability of affordable and accessible housing. As the Campaign 2000 to the United Nations special session on children noted, "Racialized families are over represented in poor neighbourhoods where the quality of living conditions and access to social programs including childcare, health, education and recreation are compromised." The report concluded: "The erosion of Canada's social safety net has had a particularly negative impact on those families that have historically experienced exclusion and disadvantage in society" (Campaign 2000 2002: 9).

Sixth, all levels of government need to promote and strengthen community organizations representing the interests of diverse communities. Promoting and strengthening organizations in civil society results in stronger political participation and a greater sense of belonging. Community involvement and engagement is an essential component of building inclusive communities and societies. These organizations become the eyes and ears of inclusion, and they can monitor initiatives designed to eradicate racism and promote inclusion. These organizations need to be well funded and given a place of legitimacy in the policy process.

Seventh, all levels of government need to be proactive in promoting democratic citizenship, which as was noted above, is about valued participation, valued recognition and belonging. This entails providing all members of society with the resources to exercise democratic citizenship; actively promoting all the political rights associated with formal equality; promoting equality and freedom from discrimination; promoting barrier-free access to employment and services and committing resources to ensure that all members of society have equal access to developing their talents and capacities. The latter requires governments to invest in social infrastructure particularly in public education. Strengthening the bonds of civic engagement and democratic citizenship requires that society invest in children. It is through our publicly funded education system that we can collectively develop the talents and capacities off all. It is through the vehicle of public education that we can promote the virtue of respect and the appreciation of differences. A publicly funded education system that is strong, affordable and accessible is not only essential to developing the talents and capacities of all, it is an essential prerequisite for creating inclusive communities and cities.

Implementing these policy initiatives is one of the most important ways in which social inclusion can become real. Their implementation is essential to the realization of an inclusive society. From an anti-racist perspective then, an inclusive society is one that at a minimum:

- develops the talents and capacities of all its members;
- strives to close social distances and promote physical proximity;
- eradicates all forms of poverty including racialized poverty;
- promotes democratic citizenship;
- promotes inclusive participation in all walks of public life by members of racialized communities;
- strengthens organizations in civil society that represent the interests of historically disadvantaged communities and meaningfully engages them in the public policy process;
- is proactive about promoting equality rights and ensuring that members of racialized communities are not disadvantaged because of their race;
- consciously eschews a hierarchy of oppression and rights;
- actively combats individual and systemic racial discrimination;
- actively promotes and accommodates ethno-racial diversity;
- eradicates the racially split labour market;
- eliminates barriers to labour market participation by members of racialized communities;
- eliminates the glass ceiling that negatively impacts on the employment mobility of members of racialized communities;

- actively promotes and achieves equitable hiring practices and "equal pay for work of equal value";
- ensures that members of racialized communities are equitably represented in the decisionmaking centres in the social, economic, political and all other walks of public life; and
- values the participation of and provides valued recognition to members of racialized communities.

The commitment to creating an inclusive society is essentially a political commitment to individual, institutional, organizational, legal and systemic change. It must begin with recognition of the multiple forms of racial discrimination and it must be a political commitment to the eradication of racial discrimination. It has to be cognizant of the need for full participation (in decisionmaking and in mobilization) by members and groups from racialized communities — participation that is equitable, recognized and valued. Progress towards anti-racist social inclusion can only be nourished by political will and the political mobilization of the broadest possible coalition of counter hegemonic forces.

## Conclusion

The intersection of an anti-oppression discourse with social inclusion as process and outcome is an incredibly powerful impetus to social change and political solidarity. It presents a radical alternative to the dominant discourse that is steeped in liberal notions of formal equality and its concomitant commitment to multiculturalism. In the context of accommodating differences and promoting heterogeneous social cohesion there is space for the state to intervene to ensure equality of opportunity. Social inclusion involves a societal commitment to equality of opportunity that ensures that all members of society are provided with the opportunity to develop their talents and capacities and secure the valued goods and services free from discrimination. In the urban environment this requires a fundamental movement from tolerating diverse cultures to recognizing and respecting them. Social inclusion is fully capable of both recognizing the politics of difference and transcending its narrow confines precisely because it embraces an inclusive vision that suggests common purpose and shared community can be achieved through inter-group solidarity. Coalition politics comprising groups representing the interests of the historically disadvantaged is now producing the conditions for the vision of social inclusion to be embraced more readily. There has never been a better time to embrace the concept of social inclusion than now. September 11, 2001, has demonstrated to us the fragility of a nation built on tolerance. Canada will be a much stronger country if we embrace social inclusion as a transformative tool and as a normative ideal.

# Notes

1. Essentialism refers to the way in which the complex identities of groups of people are reduced to one primary characteristic and individual differences are either ignored or denied — for example, the signifier, the primary characteristic that defines individual members of racialized communities is the colour of their skin (see as well notes 3–5).
2. The roots of exclusion are deep, historical and continually reproduced in both old and new ways in contemporary society — see Freiler (2001c), who has identified multiple and varied sources of exclusion.
3. There is considerable debate about the analytical status of the concept "race." Does the use of the term even as a social construct reinforce the very notion it seeks to debunk — namely that humans are divided into a number of "races," each of which can be characterized by certain physical features and cultural practices? Is it necessary then to jettison the concept entirely and speak of racialization as the process of signification that attaches meanings to somatic differences?
4. It is important to distinguish between racism on the one hand and bias and prejudice on the other. Bias refers to an opinion, a preference arrived at subjectively and without reasonable scientific proof; it can be explicit or implicit, intentional or unintentional. Racial prejudice involves "racializing" groups of people and prejudging them based on a set of biases and stereotypes that are inaccurate and unscientific. It is attitudinal and can lead to racial discrimination.
5. The phrase "members of racialized minority communities" refers to individuals who because of the colour of their skin encounter barriers and discrimination resulting in social inequality and unequal access to valued goods and services.
6. As of the beginning of June 2002, data from the 2001 Census have not been made public and consequently have not been incorporated into this chapter.

# Dangers of a New Dogma: Inclusion or Else...!

*Uzma Shakir*[1]

People stare at me in disbelief when I say that I have problems with social inclusion. How could anyone possibly deny either the discourse or the opportunity to be included in something as desirable as society? The very potency, and dare I say orthodoxy, of this policy lingo is also one of the reasons that I am weary if not down right sceptical about it. This chapter is an attempt to explore my unease with the concept — or dogma, as I will argue it has indeed become — of "social inclusion."

## The History of Exclusion and Inclusive Discourse

It is worth noting at the outset that the term social exclusion pre-dates the concept of social inclusion. However, both these concepts have a history and a location in terms of time, geography and indeed material conditions in which they emerged. Discourse of "social exclusion" dates to the 1970s and '80s in Europe at a time when rapid changes in society on many fronts were causing considerable economic, political and social tensions across various European nations. To be more precise, social exclusion has its roots in the public discourse within France and was a response to several factors: the erosion of the welfare state through the retreat of the government; recognition that increasingly large numbers of people were slipping through the social welfare net; slow economic growth and "stagflation"; globalization and European integration leading to the intensive restructuring of European economies; greater numbers of immigrants and refugees coming from developing countries (many from former colonies); and the commensurate growth in racial and social tensions. In this historical and material context, the discourse of exclusion came about as a way of understanding and addressing issues of economic deprivation and of seeking social and political solutions to them. The discourse was soon adopted by the European Union (EU) as a broad and convenient label for describing and developing policy solutions to address the internal inequities among member countries.

Soon, the term found its way into the British, and particularly the Scottish, lexicon of public policy to the point where the British government created a Social Exclusion Unit in 1997. This occurred as the neo-conservative agenda of Thatcherite Britain was being replaced by the "New" Labour Party, which sought to mend the economic and racial rifts and tensions in the society whose governance it had inherited (Guildford 2000; Viswanathan et al. 2003). A few years later — it's difficult to identify just when — the term entered the Canadian consciousness, but in truly Canadian fashion, under the "kinder" and "gentler" reverse-labelling of social "inclusion." It occurred at a time in Canadian history when globalization was leading to several dramatic changes, including economic restructuring from full-time and relatively stable employment to contractual and often temporary work arrangements; the emergence of what is called "structural unemployment"(Guildford 2000: 7); free trade with the United States and Mexico; the shift to an increasingly knowledge-based economy; a declining birthrate leading to an aging and shrinking population; and the increasing need for immigration and the arrival of unprecedented numbers of immigrants from non-traditional (read non-European) countries.

Thus, conceptually both the terms "exclusion" and "inclusion" have a distinct history of emergence at a time when racial, social and economic changes in Western society were all seen to pose unmistakable threats. In other words, both social exclusion and inclusion, similar to "multiculturalism in its various guises clearly signals a crisis in the definition of "nation" (and) self-conscious(ly)" (Bennett 1998) offers an exit and entry point (either "exclusion from" or "inclusion into") to a pre-given, although uncontested, entity that is implied but never questioned. However, this entity is not neutral. It has a history and materiality that gives rise to the need for the social exclusion/inclusion discourse to emerge in the first place. It has values attached to it — for example, it is good to be "within it" and, correspondingly, bad to be "outside it." To be included becomes, in fact, the desired objective or goal of good public policy, and if public policy has a moral and ethical basis (Kenny 2004), then the entity is also morally and ethically defined. Thus, while exclusion/inclusion discourse has a history grounded in particular material conditions of different societies, the proponents of the discourse offer the concepts as universally neutral solutions — an important contradiction.

## The "Canadian" Version of Social Inclusion

From here on I focus on the "Canadian version" of social inclusion discourse. In Canada, the concept has followed the logic of social accommodation, which views inclusion as a continuum on which exclusion is the problem and inclusion is the solution. In this formulation social inclusion/exclusion are oppositional terms on a desired (albeit familiarly linear) continuum (Freiler 2001c).

Therefore, the "solution" lies in moving the excluded towards the included and thereby resolving the "problem." In this, paradigm change becomes a matter of having good intentions and facilitating events that are motivated by these conscious intentions. The underlying belief, indeed hope, is that the entity into which the excluded are to be included is uncritically desirable and will remain relatively unchanged in the future. Thus, in this formulation of the concept there is more emphasis on moral self-righteousness rather than critical thinking.

As a consequence, several questions arise: how and why do people become "excluded" in the first place? Is exclusion a quantitative problem? When excluded you have "a lack of...," whereas if included you have "more of..." If a Tamil refugee, who used to be a medical doctor in Sri Lanka and left because his life was in danger, is now living in Toronto and is employed, but is driving a taxi back and forth to the airport rather than practising oncology, is he included in, or excluded from, Canadian society? There is also an assumption that social inclusion is something you do "for" people — since those who are excluded presumably cannot change their circumstances (otherwise they would not be excluded in the first place), others now must make them feel wanted and help them to participate. Since there is no structural analysis of marginality or exclusion and the concept is, once again, familiarly linear, social inclusion becomes a paternalistic policy option rather than one that challenges historical and existing power imbalances in our society in order to create real change.

Other proponents of the Canadian social inclusion paradigm swing between arguing for a sophisticated notion of social inclusion and one that is relatively simplistic. On the one hand, they identify structural/economic barriers, historical oppression, discrimination, political/legal/institutional/ civic barriers and personal choice as the primary sources of exclusion. On the other hand, they attempt to reconcile these complex problems by describing inclusion/exclusion as merely a notion of proximity and distance, and thus the role of public policy is to close the gap and "grow a bigger middle " (SPNO materials 2002).

Terms such as "mutual accommodation" are used in order to argue that social inclusion will flow from public policies that attempt to "reduce economic, social and cultural inequities within the population (e.g., economic disparities, racism, age or gender discrimination, etc.)" (Clutterbuck and Novick 2002: 3), without explaining *why* these inequities exist in the first place, or how the root causes of inequality might be eliminated. Therefore, these proponents fail to investigate a crucial question: whether inclusion ought to be a goal of public policy or whether material conditions of contemporary exclusion of some groups in society may in fact be a product of existing public policy, all of which would at least appropriately place the spotlight on public policy as a contested space. To Canadian proponents, building social inclusion becomes a matter of "sustain(ing) productive communities of social and cultural diversity living in states of harmony" (Clutterbuck and Novick 2003: 4). The process of building this utopia is predicated on anticipating negative impacts on social cohesion by "marginal" subgroups and thus, issuing a thinly veiled warning that seeks to position "harmony" as the desired outcome. The un-stated assumption upon which this vision is built is that disenfranchised minorities pose a threat to society and also that a lack of harmony is detrimental. But is it actually detrimental? And if so, to whom? Will the desire for productive communities, co-existing in harmony, do anything to address the real social and economic conditions that have historically marginalized some groups in Canadian society and that the next generation will grow-up in? Is the fear of "chaos," the subconscious fear underlying the desire for harmony, actually a deep seated nostalgia for the political status quo and thus unquestioned perpetuation of cultural hegemony? We are left with the real possibility that social inclusion may be little more than the most politically correct retelling yet of the "Barbarians at the Gate" story (Ramos, Personal conversation, 2004).

Clearly, the term social inclusion remains deeply problematic. The un-stated assumption is that if those with privilege and those without would both just give a little, or if public policy could create a new middle made up of "shared values/principles and common commitments" (Clutterbuck and Novick 2003: 3), society could move towards a mutually beneficial space. This implies either that "someone" outside the lived reality of privilege and marginality in society exists and could benevolently create this middle or that those within could deliberately move in order to create it.

Just who is this benevolent but neutral outsider? As for the insiders, if the excluded could "move," why didn't they? Might there be an element of movement as well as self-control in marginalization? If so, why move to the middle unless everyone shares the same ideas about where they want to be? Yet surely the whole point of "diversity" is accepting the lack of a universal point of reference? That is, unless we pre-determine a norm. But isn't the only way to pre-determine a norm amidst diversity is to have the power to suppress both difference and dissent? How does this logic lead towards a state of "inclusion"? At best, this thought process is paternalistic and hegemonic, while at worst, it blames the victims for their exclusion.

Another question that remains unanswered in Canadian discourse is who is defining inclusion? Who is to include whom? The discourse of social inclusion in Canada is flawed because it never acknowledges its liberal pluralist roots where an "additive" model of representation is assumed to promote greater egalitarianism. Include more into your world of privilege, create more institutional representation, and you solve the problem of exclusion. Thus, all types of minorities become "add-ons" to the whole (Bennett 1998: 4–5). What is never questioned, nor investigated, are either the challenges to the monolithic whole by diversity nor, "the specific cultures of (social) institutions themselves, and their historical roles in reproducing social inequalities variously marked as racial, ethnic, sexual or cultural differences" (ibid.: 5).

Furthermore, if we accept diversity as a given, then how might we be expected to construct shared aspirations and values? The concept of social inclusion is presented in such a way that only commonality is permitted with inclusion. Differences are seen as manifestations of exclusion (Li 2003). Once again, question arises: is "difference" itself the problem, or rather difference emanating from an existing power structure within society? Surely, difference *per se* is not problematic, even though it is always socially constructed, as it merely points to lack of uniformity and similarity. By contrast, "different from ..." is constructed by entrenched power structures to define and execute politics of marginalization because it uncritically positions itself to be the given "norm" from which access to levels and degrees of power and privilege flow (ibid.). South Asians are different from Chinese people culturally, linguistically and in various other ways. Nevertheless, both are judged in terms of their level of inclusion or exclusion from a "societal norm" in Canada that is understood as being universal. Surely, the "norm" in Canada cannot be universal. It has a history and is very much defined by cultural, linguistic and racial specificity. However, it remains in a relationship of dominant power *vis-à-vis* the other two. Thus, the "norm" is defining the degree of "difference from ..."

This is a nearly pure relationship of power. So to create an inclusionary space without unmasking this culturally, linguistically and racially dominant relationship is to risk perpetuating marginality in the guise of inclusion. Social inclusion discourse in Canada chooses not to address this issue, and so it remains at best an unwitting tool for reinforcing the status quo and at worst a deliberate policy that obfuscates important differences between the systemic and the inevitable, or even desirable, forms of exclusion. It is interesting that both the emergence of the exclusion/ inclusion discourse and the actual formulation of its theoretical principles within Canada tend to present particular histories and specific cultural norms as "universal" notions — an interesting manifestation of what Edward Said calls "cultural imperialism" (Said 1979).

The question I ask next is: can any social reality be neutral and a-historical? That is what social inclusion demands. By definition, society is a construct and as such it must have a history. Therefore, the lived realities of inclusion/exclusion of an individual or a group within a society must also have a history. Yet the Canadian discourse has tended to ignore the historical aspects of minoritizing and racializing diversity and thus the very construction of marginality in our society. According to this uncritical theorizing of social inclusion, immigrants, refugees and racialized communities became marginalized in Canada for no particular reason other than accidents of history, no more predestined nor deserved than winning the lottery or being struck dead by lightning. So inclusion is not about negotiating a new possibility with new relations of power and privilege but rather preserving the existing reality by spreading the net wider and making it seem more palatable.

In Canadian social inclusion discourse there is an insistence on a range of normative assumptions which inevitably lead to the creeping emergence of a "meta-definition" of social inclusion. It uses various feel-good terms like "our society," "our common aspirations," "common life" and "common wealth" (Clutterbuck and Novick 2003). For example, one proponent says of social inclusion that it is, "The capacity and willingness of our society to keep all groups within reach of what we expect as a society" (Freiler 2001a). This usage indicates the presumption of a monolithic, integrative and uncontested entity called "society." But how can "our/we/common" normative values be adopted with neither an acknowledgement of the differential and minoritizing experiences of some Canadians, nor a proper negotiation/dialogue among diverse and unequal interests, individuals and groups? In other words, to suppose a monolithic solidarity in a meta-definition that governs the social inclusion discourse in Canada is to create an illusion of solidarity that has no basis in lived reality and that, in fact, creates discursive "harmony" by deliberately masking the material conditions of inequality (Yan 2001).

Several factors need to be kept in mind. First, there is no such thing at the level of society as a shared identity amounting to "one true self." Significant similarities always coexist alongside deep and significant differences. Also, power structures define the level of exclusion for some and inclusion for others. Therefore, it becomes logical to assume that social inclusion must be, at the very least, a dialectical concept.

Given the above, one is forced to ask what if "privilege" (or inclusion) is the inevitable outcome of "marginalization" (or exclusion) rather than a matter of proximity and distance. Is social inclusion even possible? One proponent of inclusion describes various European strategies for addressing social exclusion and concludes: "partnership, innovation and leadership are the key ingredients in developing effective policies to combat social exclusion and promote social inclusion" (Guildford 2000: 4). Oh really? And how should we go about building partnerships between and among structurally fragmented and, more importantly, unequal groups and institutions? "Fitting in" with a white, anglophone/francophone, Christian, European vision/uncontested norm of society is unlikely to result in real social inclusion for the Innu — or newcomer Somali Muslims for that matter — whether via innovation, enlightened leadership, magic or any other means we might think up.

Of late, some Canadian commentators have begun to question the discourse of inclusion by pointing out its limitation in dealing with issues of differential power relations and its inability to give meaning to demographic plurality (Viswanathan et al. 2003). Yet others have decided to insert the term exclusion into the Canadian discourse (see Galabuzi 2004). They describe the nature of marginalization in Canada and seek to unearth the conditions of exclusion in order to create inclusion. Galabuzi states: "In industrialized societies, social exclusion is a by-product of a form of unbridled accumulation whose processes commodify social relations and intensify inequality along racial and gender lines" (2004: 236). He goes on to provide evidence of how in societies like Canada's four principal forms of exclusion take place: from civil society (non-status etc.); from access to social goods (income security, housing, language services, etc.); from social production (ghettoizing cultural events, lack of mainstreaming, etc.); and economic exclusion from social consumption (lack of credential recognition, racism in hiring practices, etc.). He concludes that: "social exclusion speaks of both the process of becoming and the outcome of being socially excluded" (2004: 249) and argues that, for instance, health research has been unable to adopt a social inclusion lens because it is unable to reconcile its social determinants of health with the realities of exclusion.

Labonte (2004), in fact, questions whether "social inclusion/exclusion help or hinder our development of actions that will shrink the preventable differences in health, well-being and quality of life that still demarcate and segregate our communities and nations" (254–55). He argues that a society that does not manifest some form of social conflict is suppressed, and that "we need to retain a healthy scepticism of concepts that direct us towards a wishful desire for social harmony... [because they] blunt the sharp edges of mobilized criticism that has always been one of the necessary fuels for social reform" (255). He also points out that exclusion, be it racial or social or economic or gender based, is created by unequal structures in society which in turn are designed so that somebody can benefit from someone else's exclusion, be it women "as a source of cheap and surplus wage labour, and of free reproductive labour " or "contemporary racism," which is interconnected with the history of contemporary capitalism (257). In other words, the promise of inclusion is in fact the very same as the contradiction of exclusion! That is, while inclusion offers the possibility of entering into the Promised Land, the Promised Land can only be sustained by excluding some. Exclusion of some is, therefore, not simply an unforeseen by-product of a society's flaws but rather a necessary pre-condition for the inclusion of others.

Even in its most critical form, social inclusion and exclusion can only become a strategic means of continuing negotiation between isolated groups. Each individual, group and community has diverse interests and identities. Therefore, social inclusion is a selective process. Some interests and identities can be included while others must be excluded. Both inclusion and exclusion are part of the continuous and parallel living experiences of most people in contemporary society. In an ethnically, culturally, racially and linguistically diverse and heterogeneous society like Canada, any static notion of inclusion will inevitably be hegemonic and oppressive. To be meaningful, social inclusion can only be strategic and focused on some possible points of common interest (Yan 2001).

## Contextualizing Social Inclusion

Finally, the meaning of social inclusion has to be contextualized. For example, in the Greater Toronto Area, which I call home, demographic realities make the "excluded" the majority of residents. How, in Toronto then, does social inclusion relate to and account for the "social entity" in which this contradiction will be resolved? Is it a matter of "including" the excluded majority within the minority's social norms? If not, then is it possible (or desirable) to reconcile the demographic diversity of social and structural preferences with the existing "social entity" within which inclusion is being constructed? If so, what does this new entity look like? Should not social inclusion be "a matter of 'becoming' as well of 'being'"(Hall 1990), thereby making it belong to our future as well as the past? "Inclusion" discourse in Canada has not even begun to explore how the diversity of Canadian population could contest, re-imagine and thus re-design the Canada they may want to live in. This suggests that bringing the present and future into a relationship with the past will preclude any possibility of a linear progression from exclusion to inclusion.

As a social activist, I have had innumerable opportunities to debate the issue of social inclusion in public, policy and academic forums. I have been repeatedly struck by the lack of emphasis on history and race and gender — and their connections to structural inequities in our society — as relevant issues in the genesis of the social inclusion discourse in Canada. Living in the Greater Toronto Area, where the immigrant/non-Canadian/ racialized population is now above 50 percent of the population and where there is unmistakable evidence of poverty and marginality along race, gender, class and immigration status lines (Galabuzi 2000), particularly among women of colour (Khosla 2003), this silence in the discourse is dangerous. One exception is Saloojee (2003), who identifies racism as a form of social exclusion and posits social inclusion as not only a critique of multiculturalism but also the mechanism for building democratic citizenship. To him the goal of social inclusion ought to be democratic citizenship, that is, not only having political rights normally seen as markers of equality in society but, perhaps more importantly, "a relationship with one's community, and the resources necessary to exercise one's citizenship" (Saloojee (2003: 16). Saloojee clearly states that for inclusion to matter it must "provide space for a discussion of oppression and discrimination... (and) promote a transformative agenda that links the often disparate struggles against oppression, inequality and injustice" (19).

In spite of dissenting voices, in its popular formulation in Canada, social inclusion appears to be one of a list of concepts, along with multiculturalism, social cohesion, integration, etc., "invented" by liberal pluralism to deal with the challenges posed by communities of difference to the notion of "nation" (Bennett 1998). The minority demand to be "different" disrupts the linear progression of national history and cultural totality and raises the spectre of the construction of a nation that is not based on shared time, or territorial memories. If we do not recognize this possibility then we risk merely brainstorming strategies for inclusion/ integration that measure the degree to which minorities "converge to the average performance of native-born Canadians and within their normative and behavioural standards... the discourse nominally endorses cultural diversity, but specific cultural differences, especially those deemed to be far removed from the Canadian standard, are viewed as obstacles to integration" (Li 2003: 3).

So where might we now go from here? It is clear that both social inclusion and exclusion as discourses for social change have severe limitations and inherent dangers. Yet it will not do to simply reject social inclusion and thereby permit the deep social, economic and political fissures that are increasingly appearing along the fault lines of race, ethnicity, faith, language, gender etc. to persist, absent an alternative analytical and policy framework.

However, a new conceptual framework would need to remain cognizant of several key factors. It is important to remember that the nation or the state to which we are laying claims through the discourse of inclusion is not just a territorial, or a political entity but also an "imagined community" (Parekh 1998). In a changing demographic context as is Canada, we need to be willing to continuously re-imagine, re-evaluate and re-negotiate our understanding and our collective notion of the nation. Another key factor to keep in mind as we build the necessary alternative framework is that in an uneven and differentiated social polity, even "equality must be... applied in a discriminating but not discriminatory manner" (Parekh 1998). In other words, we need to balance equity, difference and structural change in such a society by acknowledging the "right of contestation, the legitimacy of dissent and the entitlement to be different" (Li 2003: 12) as well as the need for constant negotiations. We should also recognize that our collective heritage is not commonality but our shared experiences of complex, but differing lived realities in Canada of inter-sections of history, culture, race, class, gender, language and relations of unequal power. Finally, we have no other choice than to accept that given the diversity amongst us and differential relations of power and privilege between us, universal human rights discourse may yet remain the only just arbiter of social rights, since those rights are "not the privilege of citizens but the entitlement of all individuals" (Parekh 1998). The challenge for all those who care about these matters is to acknowledge when we may be complicit in perpetuating the problem.

The problem with social inclusion discourse in Canada is that it has integration of the margin into the centre as its desirable end. But that is the centre's dream! The aim at the margin may not be to integrate but to contest and de-centre and perhaps recreate a new social reality. One such example of contestation in the Canadian milieu is the challenge of the Alternative Planning Group (APG) to social planning in Toronto. It is interesting to note that those in Canada who are actually "talking" social inclusion are the least critical and structurally relevant proponents of inclusion; however, others who are actually producing innovative and critical research or action are in fact creating the genesis of an inclusionary framework without naming it as such. For example, Nuala Kenny (2004) has produced an insightful analysis of how aging and, therefore related services, are designed in our society and makes a compelling argument as to how policy can be used to create a more equitable and accessible society. Similarly, Professor Nadia Caidi explores the issue of what constitutes information in immigrant communities, thus giving some indication as to how to generate "relevant" information content and sources of dissemination (Caidi and Allard 2005).

APG is a distinctive partnership in the City of Toronto amongst the Chinese Canadian National Council Toronto Chapter (CCNCTO), Council of Agencies Serving South Asians (CASSA), Hispanic Development Council (HDC) and the African Canadian Social Development Council (ACSDC). These organizations have been working closely for several years for the specific purpose of creating and implementing collaborative strategies for inter-community planning and development, integrative research and organizing joint community events while simultaneously posing a challenge to planning as a discipline and as a civic and social activity. This specific motivation is an interesting example of "constructing" inclusion that is both critical and structurally relevant. The principles of engagement (internally/externally) underlying the development of THE APG structures are: flexibility; ability to be self-corrective; ability to evolve organically and situationally; collective decision-making by consensus; equity of decision-making power internally; adherence to collective decisions; negotiating differences internally; advancement of independent and collective principles; agreement not to represent each other but to act collectively; development of organic relations and structures; and individual and collective community-based planning (exercising inclusion and exclusion simultaneously).

APG activities entail joint committee representations; joint presentations; joint submissions; organizing major community activities: dialoguing with funders and with key policymakers at all levels of government on mutually identified priorities; monthly meetings; joint board strategic planning meetings; key media events; implementation of social planning activities individually and collectively; research on specific topics; and articulating an "Alternative Policy Development Framework" for the City.

Using the principle of "engagement through negotiations," the *raison d'être* of the APG is to construct a City that is equitable. Given the reality of a city like Toronto, the group assumes, monolithic social planning, whether done by the state or community, to be, by definition, "partial" and "fragmented." It is their belief that to be truly democratic in a pluralistic setting requires holistic but diverse, decentralized but equitable social planning based on principles of equity and shared vision through negotiation (Tang et al. 2003). This philosophy is reflected in the work of the partners with their respective communities; in the relations between the partners and in the negotiation of the partnership with other key stakeholders.

Thus, membership of the APG collective, of which I am a founding member, is based on:

> conscious identification of commonality of interest and ability to negotiate difference from an equitable position. This is achieved by recognizing that the partnership needs to build equity of power relations (not capacities or experience) internally. The underlying learning of the partnership is that working together enhances individual and collective capacity but more importantly it engages diversity of population in decision-making and ultimately defining social goals and objectives regarding social policy and urban development. (Tang et al. 2003: 1).

This in turn builds the "common good."

From an alternative planning perspective, the action necessitated by the shifting demographic trend and growing needs of "racialized communities" means recognizing emerging stakeholders and their ability to negotiate and create requisite structural changes in society to accommodate their emerging and competing demands. The "public" is no longer homogenous or indeed, monolithic (Tang et al. ibid).

Hence, according to the APG, *planning* that is alternative, innovative, diverse and equitable can be a tool for channelling new currents of ideas in the field while legitimizing and recognizing marginalized knowledge. It is by documenting and practising the latter (i.e., marginalized knowledge) that the Alternative Planning Group feels that its contribution to the city's processes is highly beneficial and practical. The APG, therefore, is both an end and a process that offers a unique and necessary perspective on *engaging and negotiating diversity through equity*.

This shows that inclusion is being constructed in our existing milieu through critical, deliberative contestation albeit in discreet research or isolated practice. However, claiming to be inclusionary is not the same as creating and living inclusion! Inclusion is an enactment, a process that marginalized groups, communities and individuals need to traverse — and power structures need to be susceptible to — rather than an end itself. Possessing and exercising the right and, more importantly, the ability to contest, to re-structure relations of power and ultimately re-imagine Canada is social inclusion!

## Note

1.  I would like to acknowledge the support, deliberative and thoughtful edits/ additions and intellectual inspiration of Alina Chatterjee, Arif Raza and James Appleyard, without whom I could never have been able to finish this chapter. I would also like to thank the sheer persistence of Ted Richmond and Anver Saloojee to encourage me and provide me with the right opportunity to write words where my mouth often is.

# Urban Aboriginal Peoples: A Challenge to the National Character

*National Association of Friendship Centres (NAFC)*

There is one aspect of Canadian society, one aspect of our history, that casts a shadow over all that we have achieved. The continuing gap in life conditions between Aboriginal and other Canadians is intolerable. It offends our values and we cannot remain on our current path. With our partners, we will tackle head-on the particular problems faced by the increasing number of urban Aboriginals and Métis. We will not allow ourselves to be caught up in jurisdictional wrangling, passing the buck and bypassing their needs. (Hon. Paul Martin, Hansard, February 4, 2004)

## Introduction

### Who we are

The Friendship Centre Movement (FCM) originated fiftey years ago in response to the needs of Aboriginal peoples who were migrating to urban areas in search of a better life — a migration rooted in the unjust and culturally destructive historical policies and practices of the Government of Canada.

Today, the FCM has in place a national service infrastructure and networking capacity that is unmatched by any other Aboriginal organization. There are 117 Friendship Centres at the local community level, situated in every region of Canada. Friendship Centres are represented at the provincial level by seven provincial/territorial associations (PTAs), and at the national level by the National Association of Friendship Centres (NAFC).

The FCM was built on, and still relies heavily on, volunteerism and grassroots support. Friendship Centres are, and have always been, accountable to our communities in a way that is matched by few other Aboriginal or non-Aboriginal entities. Each entity within the movement is incorporated separately, autonomous, not-for-profit and governed by an elected, volunteer board of directors. Friendship Centres have become permanent and irreplaceable institutions in the lives of urban Aboriginal peoples and moreover, have become a significant social and economic presence within the wider non-Aboriginal communities in which we are located.

## What we do

The FCM deliver a broad range of health, justice, youth, education, sports, cultural, employment, language, housing and economic development programs and services in off-reserve and urban settings to a client base of approximately 757,000 Aboriginal peoples through the delivery of approximately nine hundred individual programs. While Friendship Centres are located off-reserve, our programs and services are available to all Aboriginal people, regardless of *Indian Act* status or place of residence, as well as non-Aboriginal people.

In addition to our role as the primary providers of programs and services targeted to Aboriginal peoples living in the urban environment, Friendship Centres play a critical role in community and economic development. We provide employment, create spin-off services in our communities, and some develop and operate for-profit businesses. Friendship Centres continue to be a training ground for local, regional and national leaders, with creative expertise in many fields of interest. Friendship Centres have provided the training, experience and physical space for many of the other urban Aboriginal institutions and organizations, from housing to health services to daycare.

Throughout our history, the FCM has continually demonstrated measurable results, through our programs and services, delivered in a transparent, accountable and efficient manner. We have always pursued a "people-first" approach to community and economic development initiatives, as opposed to participating in programs for the sake of accepting funding. Programs have developed from expressed community needs rather than government or corporate agendas. Our response has been delivered in a culturally appropriate manner and, above all, through a process that is accountable to our constituency. For fifty years, the FCM has been at the forefront of urban Aboriginal community development and tireless in our efforts to restore the dignity of Aboriginal peoples.

Investing in healthy communities, securing safe and affordable housing, contributing to life-long learning and creating opportunity are positive steps in the right direction. Moreover, we need to dig deep into the "fiscal toolkit" to ensure that we have the right tools for ensuring the maximum benefit of these investments and to critically examine our fiscal toolkit. This may entail expanding our fiscal toolkit if we are seriously committed to alleviating the "shameful" conditions faced by urban Aboriginal peoples.

## Investing in healthy communities

We have been at the forefront of public health for more than three decades. The evidence linking health status and the social determinants of health is substantive. There is growing recognition of the need for all sectors to adapt program and policy changes that address the social determinants of health: food isecurity, early learning, housing and human capital (Friendly

2000; Romanow Commission 2002; Canadian Association of Food Banks 2003; Shoush 2003). A number of cities have followed the lead of the City of Toronto in adopting the Strengthening the Social Determinants of Health, The Toronto Charter for a Healthy Canada.

A recent study released by Statistics Canada noted that "Aboriginal people who live off-reserve in cities and towns are generally in poorer health than the non-Aboriginal population" (Tjepkema 2002). The national study examined four health status measures: self-perceived health, chronic conditions, long-term activity restriction and depression. It showed that even when socio-economic factors such as education, work status and household income were taken into account, "the off-reserve Aboriginal population was still 1.5 times more likely than the non-Aboriginal population to report fair or poor health" (ibid. 2002). The study also showed that some illnesses were clearly linked to low income.

The 2001 *Aboriginal Peoples Survey* found that a large percentage (45 percent) of Aboriginal adults have been diagnosed with chronic conditions. Arthritis or rheumatism, high blood pressure and asthma were the most commonly reported conditions. Diabetes continues to be a serious health concern for the Aboriginal population. Among First Nation people living off-reserve, 8.2 percent of adults have been diagnosed with diabetes, compared to 2.9 percent of the Canadian population (age standardized to reflect the age structure of the Aboriginal population). The prevalence of diabetes continues to rise (Statistics Canada 2003).

In addition to the Naylor, Kirby and Romanow Reports, the health status of urban Aboriginal peoples has been more fully detailed elsewhere.[1] Public health is more than health care, which usually focuses on diagnoses and treatment for individual patients. Instead, public health focuses on communities and populations for the prevention of disease, promotion of health and protection of the public. It is also more than the programs that are often associated with public health services (Canadian Public Health Association 2003).

The Government of Canada must exercise leadership in the area of public health for urban Aboriginal peoples.[2] A renewed vision of an Aboriginal health system strives to ensure equitable access to quality health services, seamless service from community to hospital and greater focus on preventing illness and promoting good health (Jackman 2002).

## Securing safe and affordable housing

The Universal Declaration of Human Rights, Article 25(1), and the International Covenant on Economic, Social and Cultural Rights provide for the right to housing. In Canada, the recognition and implementation of a right to housing has not been recognized.

An affordable housing strategy would urge the federal government, as part of the New Deal for Communities, to expand and improve the delivery of the FPT (federal/provincial/territorial) Affordable Housing Program, expand the Residential Rehabilitation Assistance Program (RRAP) and urge provincial governments to revise the shelter component of welfare and institute income support related to housing costs, such as rent supplements or shelter allowances (Toronto City Summit Alliance 2003; McKnight 2004).

Hundreds of thousands of Aboriginal people live in towns and cities across Canada. The majority (61.3 percent) of the 396,100 Aboriginal households in 2001 were located in urban areas of more than 2,500 people (CMHC 2004). While this demographic reality is often cited, it is rarely reflected in policy decisions.

According to CMHC, approximately 25 percent of non-reserve Aboriginal households are in core housing need. In other words, one in four Aboriginal households in Canada's cities and towns live in homes that are unaffordable, overcrowded and/or are in need of major repairs. Affordability is the dominant reason for Aboriginal households falling into core housing need.

Recent analysis of housing need among non-reserve Aboriginal renter households by the National Aboriginal Housing Association found that 37 percent spend more than 30 percent of their income for rent. Even more striking, 15 percent of Aboriginal renter households off-reserve experience a severe rent burden, paying greater than 50 percent of household income for shelter. It is not difficult to imagine the constraints placed upon a family that is forced to spend more than half of their household income only to pay the rent, leaving little for other necessities.

Friendship Centres serve numerous Aboriginal peoples living in large urban centres where housing problems persist. Shocking disparities exist between the housing conditions of Aboriginal and non-Aboriginal peoples living in census metropolitan areas. In Saskatoon, for example, the percentage of Aboriginal peoples living in crowded conditions is nearly one in five, more than three times the percentage of non-Aboriginal peoples living in crowded conditions (Statistics Canada 2003).

On a national level, 17 percent of the non-reserve Aboriginal population live in crowded conditions, compared to 7 percent of all Canadians. Aboriginal children are particularly affected by these conditions — while 13 percent of Canadian children live in crowded conditions, 25 percent of Aboriginal children living off-reserve live in crowded conditions (Statistics Canada 2003). Health experts maintain that crowded conditions can lead to a host of difficulties, including increased risk for injuries, mental health problems, family tensions and violence (Health Canada 1999).

Data show that "owner" households experience much lower levels of core housing need than "renter" households. CMHC reports that in 2001 only half of non-reserve Aboriginal households owned their home, well below the 67.4 percent of non-Aboriginal households that are owners. There are many benefits to owning one's home — profits from house price inflation over time and declining house costs as the mortgage is paid off, for example, can lead to improved financial well-being and personal security. Studies have shown that homeowners are more likely than tenants to participate in mainstream political activities because homeowners have a stake in the social and economic benefits of property ownership (Darden and Kamel 2001). Federal, provincial and municipal policies are less likely to favour tenants and more likely to favour homeowners — tenants are penalized by the property tax treatment of apartments as "commercial property," which makes rent increasingly more expensive (Skaburskis 1996).

As of yet, there has been limited information on a proposed National Affordable Housing Strategy;[3] however, we continue to urge the inclusion of the urban Aboriginal community in any existing and proposed policy and program development activity which is anticipated to include a five-year commitment. A sense of optimism emerged from the National Aboriginal Roundtable where the Prime Minister committed to a National Strategy to deal with housing issues off-reserve (Hon. Paul Martin, National Aboriginal Peoples Summit, April 19, 2004).

## Contributing to life-long learning

Both the House Sub-Committee on Youth at Risk and the Senate Committee on Aboriginal Peoples have produced reports focused on urban Aboriginal children and youth. While painting a disturbing portrait of the lives urban Aboriginal children and youth, both reports provide timely and sound recommendations.

## Early childhood development

There can be no doubt that the quality of life of urban Aboriginal children is shameful. In many urban areas, Aboriginal peoples make up a large and rising proportion of residents of low-income neighbou rhoods (Statistics Canada 2004b). More and more Aboriginal children face life in Canada's racialized ghettos (OECD 2004).

The good news is that increasing numbers of Aboriginal children are attending early child development programs designed for them. According to the Public Health Agency of Canada, approximately 3,900 Aboriginal children are currently enrolled in Aboriginal Head Start projects (urban and Northern component). However, the demand for early child development programs will increase as 315,000 Aboriginal children will require these services over the next decade. If current funding levels are maintained, less than 20 percent of these children will have access to these valued programs (Government of Canada 2004).

We focus on what works, what doesn't work and what needs improvement, working to achieve better coordination, integration and increased efficiency. A great deal of collaboration, consultation and frankness with our community partners will be required to address these and other important policy matters.

The Government of Canada has made a commitment to the development of a new national system of early learning and childcare, to engage Aboriginal leaders and build on the successful Aboriginal Head Start (AHS) program (Federal-Provincial-Territorial Meeting of Ministers Responsible for Social Services Ottawa, Ontario — November 2, 2004). The NAFC supports the integration of the Fetal Alcohol Spectrum Disorder (FASD) Program, Community Action Program for Children (CAPC) and the Canada Prenatal Nutrition Program (CPNP) into an expanded national system. The House Standing Committee on Youth at Risk recommends the expansion of AHS, CAPC and CPNP.

On urban Aboriginal children, Dr. Fraser Mustard (2002) advises:

> If I were to give you some summary recommendations, they would be as follows. First, expand and integrate resources available for "early childhood development and parenting centres" in Aboriginal communities and for Aboriginal children in urban centres. That's rule number one.

We are concerned that the development of the national system will result in the creation of a regulated childcare program to the exclusion of early learning programs. The expertise in the design and delivery of these programs found in Friendship Centres is well known by stakeholders in the community (see Stone 2003).[4] Based upon this extensive experience, and other expert advice such as that of Dr. Mustard, we believe a national system that integrates both childcare and early learning and ensures universality is a positive step forward. All Friendship Centres should have the opportunity to participate in such a system.

The implementation of the principles of a new national system of early learning and childcare — namely, quality, universally inclusive, accessible and developmental — will no doubt be a source of anxiety for policymakers. The legal community will be examining whether such principles are justiciable. No doubt, the failure to announce a commitment to enshrine these principles in legislation was not an oversight (Dryden 2004).

## Program for Aboriginal peoples aged six to twelve

We support the ongoing work of Friendship Centres in securing funding for programming aimed at children six to twelve years of age. In response, it has been recommended that a program be developed for these children. Such a program should provide culturally oriented guidance and development services (House Sub-Committee on Youth at Risk 2003).

The 2001 Aboriginal Peoples Survey demonstrated a correlation between participation in extra-curricular activities and school achievement. Parents of Aboriginal children aged six to fourteen were asked to rate how well their children did in school based on their knowledge of the child's school work. In off-reserve areas, these parents reported that 45 percent of children who participated in sports four times or more a week were doing very well in school, compared with only 36 percent who never, or rarely, participated in sports. About one-half (51 percent) of Aboriginal children living off-reserve, who participated in art or music activities four times or more a week, were doing very well in school, compared with only 37 percent who never, or rarely, participated (Statistics Canada 2004a).

Not only do children who participate in organized extra-curricular activities do better in school, a recent Canadian study revealed that children who participate are more likely to possess greater self-esteem and to enjoy better social interactions with their friends (Statistics Canada 2001).

Opportunities to participate in organized extra-curricular activities should not be denied to children due to their socio-economic situation. Friendship Centre programs such as Li'l Beavers can provide valuable opportunities for extracurricular activities such as art, music, sports and cultural activities. The Senate Committee on Aboriginal Peoples calls for the reinstatement of this program.

## Elementary and high school

In 2001, almost half (48 percent) of the off-reserve Aboriginal population age 20–24 had incomplete high school as their highest level of schooling. This is compared to one in four Canadian youth of the same age (Statistics Canada 2003).

"Being bored with school" topped the reasons given by young off-reserve Aboriginal people (15–19) for leaving elementary or high school prior to completion (similar results have been reported for all Canadian youth). However nearly one in five (19 percent) young Aboriginal men (15–19) who had left school said they did so because they wanted to work. One in four (25 percent) young Aboriginal women (15–19) who had left school reported that they did so because of pregnancy or the need to care for children (Statistics Canada 2003).

Friendship Centre programs such as the Urban Multipurpose Aboriginal Youth Centres (UMAYC) are working to promote education among young people. A report commissioned by the Ontario Federation of Indian Friendship Centres found that teenage pregnancy lowers the probability of completing school and may be accompanied by high rates of unemployment, low levels of income, reliance on social assistance, having more pregnancies over a shorter period of time and absent fathers. Recommendations of the report highlight youth programs (such as community-based education programs, employment and training opportunities, workshops on cultural teachings and awareness campaigns) such as those found in many Friendship Centres across Canada.

## Post-secondary education

Aboriginal people are more likely than others to return to school later in life. According to the 2001 Census, a higher percentage of the off-reserve Aboriginal population aged 20 to 64 was attending school full-time than in the non-Aboriginal population. The only age group where a higher percentage of non-Aboriginal people were attending school full-time was among those aged 20 to 24 years. For example, 10 percent of the off-reserve Aboriginal population aged 30 to 34 was attending school full-time compared to only 5 percent of the Canadian population in this same age group (Statistics Canada 2001).

This means that many Aboriginal people are pursuing post-secondary education as mature students. The challenges facing older adults who return to school are different than those facing young adults. For example, a large number of Aboriginal people who are attending school are also raising children.

The 2001 Aboriginal Peoples Survey found that among the off-reserve Aboriginal population, family responsibilities and finances topped the list of reasons for not finishing post-secondary studies. Men were most likely to report financial reasons (24 percent) while the reason most frequently cited by women was family responsibilities (34 percent).

A higher education is a means by which Aboriginal peoples can begin to reverse the trend of their historic social and economic exclusion from influential centres of decision-making. Programs and services which facilitate the pursuit of post-secondary education for Aboriginal peoples who wish to return to school as mature students are critical to increasing the number of Aboriginal peoples with higher levels of formal education.

An analysis on education and income in Saskatchewan (Table 1) conducted by Dr. Eric Howe (2003) details the enormous impact that education can have for Aboriginal peoples. An Aboriginal dropout lives an economically marginalized life in which the male earns only a little more than a third of a million dollars, and the female earns less than $90,000. That is over an entire lifetime! If however they persist through university or technical school, they receive up to fourteen times more!

One program that has facilitated the achievement of post-secondary qualifications for many First Nations and Inuit students has been the Post-Secondary Student Support Program (PSSSP) of Indian and Northern Affairs Canada. For example, a 2001 study of Aboriginal single mothers found that:

> One of the strengths of Aboriginal single mothers is their willingness to upgrade their education by attending school as mature adults. It appears that existing programs and policies have been particularly effective in helping Aboriginal single mothers

Table 1     Aboriginal Education and Income in Saskatchewan

|  | Male Lifetime Earnings | Female Lifetime Earnings |
|---|---|---|
| An Aboriginal person drops out of school prior to receiving a high school diploma, and does not subsequently obtain a high school equivalency | $344,781 | $89,502 |
| An Aboriginal person obtains a high school diploma either by graduation or by subsequently completing high school equivalency, with no further formal education | $861,636 | $294,350 |
| An Aboriginal person attends a program at a non-university post secondary institution (a technical school), with no further formal education | $1,191,146 | $646,904 |
| An Aboriginal person attends a program at a university | $1,386,434 | $1,249,246 |

Source: Howe 2003.

pursue post-secondary (university and non-university) education at various age levels. (Hull 2001)

The PSSSP program budget must be increased and status-based restrictions must be eliminated. In other words, the program should be expanded to include other Aboriginal people (Senate Committee on Aboriginal Peoples 2003).

## Creating opportunity
There has been considerable attention and focus on the emerging skills and labour shortages throughout every jurisdiction in Canada. The demographic and geographic realities are putting many jurisdictions in competition with one another for scarce skilled and capable workers. The western provinces have invested heavily in understanding the policy challenges as the problems are more acute there. There is an abundance of evidence and reports addressing the employment and training needs of Aboriginal peoples (Mendelson 2004).

## Aboriginal human capital development
It is also clear that the circumstances of urban and off-reserve Aboriginal peoples are different and unique. The federal investment is through the

Aboriginal Human Resource Development Strategy (AHRDS). A renewed AHRDS must recognize and take these realities into account. The evidence in support of a significant increase in funding levels for the urban component of the AHRDS cannot be seriously challenged (Conference Board of Canada 2003).

On October 11, 2002, the Federal Court of Canada delivered its reasons in *Misquadis v. Canada* (*Misquadis*) and found that Human Resources Skills Development Canada (HRSDC) had violated section 15 of the Canadian Charter of Rights and Freedoms by refusing to enter into Aboriginal Human Resources Development Agreements (AHRDAs) with urban Aboriginal organizations mandated by the respondents' communities.

The Court found that the AHRDAs draw distinctions between First Nation band communities and First Nation non-band communities. While First Nation band communities have community control in developing and implementing training programs, First Nation non-band communities were denied these same benefits under the AHRDAs urban component. The courts ordered HRSDC to eliminate the discriminatory effect by providing community control over labour training programs to the applicants' communities.

One of the more important findings in Misquadis is the recognition of urban Aboriginal communities as organized, self-determined and distinct. Ordering HRSDC to negotiate AHRDAs with representative organizations mandated by the respondents' communities meaningfully vindicates the respondents' right to have the communities they have built accorded equal worth with more traditional Aboriginal communities. No longer will political authority for non-band First Nation peoples be vested exclusively in First Nation band communities. In response, HRSDC has chosen to extend the under-inclusive program rather than eliminate the AHRDAs outright.

By examining social, economic and demographic realities of urban Aboriginal communities, it becomes apparent that the priorities and needs of urban Aboriginal communities differ from reserve communities. Different needs and priorities require that the locus of control for the delivery and design of employment and training programs be found within the community that is being served. In other words, one may question the appropriateness of reserve-designed and delivered programs to address the needs and circumstances of off-reserve/urban Aboriginal communities.

According to Statistics Canada (2003), the majority (55 percent) of the North American Aboriginal people live off-reserve. A large proportion (29 percent) of those people do not have registered Indian status. Do North American Aboriginal people living in urban areas have access to AHRDAs programs and services on par with those living on reserves? Are diverse urban Aboriginal communities being adequately served under the current AHRDAs structure? Will these questions be addressed under renewed AHRDAs?

# The "Fiscal Toolkit'

## Canada Social Transfer

The Government of Canada announced the creation of a Canada Social Transfer (CST) in its 2003 Federal Budget in support of post-secondary education, social assistance and social services, including early childhood development.

> Although this Subcommittee has not explored the institutional mechanisms which could be put in place to ensure that funds be put aside for culturally relevant programs to urban Aboriginal people, both in discretionary program funding by federal government departments and in federally transferred funds to provincial/territorial governments, we wish to flag the importance of examining this issue further. (House Sub-Committee on Youth At-Risk June 2003)

A number of recent reports have documented the challenges faced by all levels of governments in efforts to ensure social, political and economic justice for all Canadians, particularly, the western provinces, which have an increasing proportion of Aboriginal peoples.

The Government of Canada has taken the position that provinces are responsible for providing services and supports for Aboriginal peoples within their legislative sphere, while provinces maintain the federal government is wholly responsible for all Aboriginal peoples. Municipal governments have expressed their desire to work with Aboriginal governments and institutions given the financial means. As a fourth option, Aboriginal service delivery providers, not unlike Friendship Centres, are a viable mechanism worthy of closer scrutiny.

To date, there has been limited public discourse on the CST in proportion to the number of issues that may be impacted. No longer are Canadians willing to allow large fiscal resources to be channelled to provincial coffers without a legitimate expectation of results. We have moved beyond entrusting governments with public funds while "cowering in the darkness," hopeful of positive change. There is an increased public expectation to know that we are getting the best return on investment.

The opportunity exists to set forth and clearly articulate principles that would guide the development of the CST. There has been convincing evidence suggesting that better targeting for social services, social welfare and education needs will have positive consequences while maintaining rigorous accountability (Singer 2003; Freiler et al. 2004). With priorities such as universal childcare coverage, homelessness, urban poverty and employment and training issues identified by numerous sectors of society, action is required.

A number of options and actions have been proposed over the course of the year, including dedicated cash and tax point transfers, itemized expenditures and "colour coding" funds to match spending priorities (*Toronto Star* 2004).[5]

## Reshaping Federalism

In reaching consensus on redesigned funding mechanisms, the Government of Canada is left with the difficult task of enforcing proposed national standards, accountability provisions and measured outcomes. However, fiscal federalism is a reality. In handing the "carrot" to the provinces in the form of increased cash and tax room, the acceptance of the "stick" may include the legislative authority to ensure compliance with a well-defined set of terms and conditions and national standards. In the wake of massive cuts to federal transfers to the provinces throughout the 1990s, the provinces have reason to be wary if not hostile to such overtures. With a federal government embracing "asymmetrical federalism" as a principle, the application of national standards (Stillborn 1997) and conditions for social programs become more remote. Given the necessity of a level playing field across all federal, provincial and Aboriginal jurisdictions, looking at these challenges will require not only seeing "the glass half empty" but possibly "the glass half full."

The provinces have long held the belief that the federal government collects far greater revenues than necessary to discharge its constitutional responsibilities. As a consequence, the provinces are left without sufficient revenues to meet an increasing number of funding pressures: rising health and education costs and an aging population. The notion of "fiscal imbalance" has been a rallying cry against the federal government. The federal position has been not to acknowledge not only the notion of "fiscal imbalance," but the very term "fiscal imbalance" itself. If one were to take the view that no "fiscal imbalance" exists then the provinces would be in an uncomfortable position of raising revenues through its own taxing authority. There is little precedent to indicate that raising taxes has led to electoral success.

More to the point, the federal and provincial governments have the necessary tools available to influence positive policy solutions. However, any substantive discussion must include Aboriginal governments, policymakers and community stakeholders.

## Conclusion

We provide countless urban Aboriginal children and their families residing in rural, remote and urban communities throughout Canada with the necessary, culturally appropriate and compassionate means to more fully participate in Canada's social, political and economic livelihood. Our approach to community development has garnered considerable support

(Blondin-Andrew 1993; House Committee on Finance 1996). Our expertise in program delivery and design has enabled us to be at the forefront of shaping public policy that aims to strengthen urban Aboriginal peoples and their communities. We have the benefit of a highly skilled and able workforce necessary to influence legislative action and change.

We recognize that we have a shared responsibility to our communities.

The Honourable Paul Martin has made much of his commitment to urban Aboriginal peoples and we look forward to working together to honour that commitment. [6]

## Notes

1. A number of public policy institutes have undertaken examination of urban Aboriginal issues with reference to health within the broader context, including Canada West Foundation, Conference Board of Canada, Campaign 2000, Canadian Policy Research Networks (CPRN) and the Caledon Institute on Social Policy. While the academic community has brought forth its own offerings, Policy Research Institute (PRI) released its publication, *Not Strangers in These Parts, Urban Aboriginal Peoples* and the University of Western Ontario released its publication, *Aboriginal Conditions: Research as a Foundation for Public Policy.*

2. "We could prevent up to 60 or 70 percent of all cancers, up to 90 percent of all heart disease, up to 60 percent of all strokes, up to 90 percent of all cases of chronic lung disease, up to 90 percent of all diabetes — all the things that are filling up our hospitals and our doctor's offices and our graveyards. I am deeply concerned that the entire focus of the general public, the current government and the health care system as a whole is to pull drowning people out of the river. I implore you to ensure we devote adequate time and resources to making sure people don't fall into the river in the first place" (Dr. Andrew Larder, Medical Health Officer, East Kootenay Region).

3. Martin was in Montreal to meet with social housing lobby group FREPRU. He told the group that he is putting together a five-year plan to deal with the country's housing crisis (Hon. Paul Martin, CBC Online News, February 24, 2004).

4. Hon. Ethel Blondin Andrew, Secretary of State for Children and Youth, Subcommittee on Children and Youth at Risk, February 19, 2003, made this most telling anecdote, "I must tell you that from my experience over the last... well, I had a previous profession or occupation, and even then, the friendship centres have always been one of the most excellent service delivery centres for different kinds of projects. They're very community-oriented. They reach out to everyone, and the door is always open, and they really are progressive in the way they take new projects, work with them, and integrate them into the community."

5. "But in establishing the Canada Social Transfer, we were hoping this bill and the budget generally would be more detailed with respect to that transfer. So this amendment is an attempt to break it down so that accountability and transparency would apply for each program under the CST. So it follows the

logic that was applied in moving from the CHST to the CHT in order to better track funding, to ensure accountability, and to avoid funds for health being used in other areas. We would recommend that the same logic be applied with respect to the CST. That would require some specificity in breaking down the CST into the components, as outlined later on in the bill. So the recommendation is that we list those aspects of the Canada Social Transfer, in order to ensure accountability and tracking for those areas in the same way we now expect will be the case in the area of health" Wasylycia-Leis 2003: 1540.

6.    The Hon. Paul Martin, May 3, 2003, states, "Does the federal government have jurisdiction when Aboriginals move to larger cities? Well let me tell you something. I don't know who has jurisdiction but I know that we have a massive moral responsibility to help the people who have moved and we have a massive moral responsibility to help [them stay]."

# References

Abbey, J.L.S. 1999. "Inclusion, justice and poverty reduction: Seminar notes and impressions." *Capacity International, Germany*. Villa Borsig Workshop Series, Inclusion, Justice and Poverty Reduction. <www.inwent.org> (accessed July 2005).

Abella, R.S. 1984. *Equality in employment: A Royal Commission report*. Royal Commission on equality in employment. Ottawa: Supply and Services, Government of Canada.

_____. 1987. *Employment equity: Implications for industrial relations*. Kingston: Industrial Relations Centre, Queen's University.

Adelman, H. 2002. "Refugees and border security post-September 11." *Refuge* 20(4), August.

Agocs, C., C. Burr and F. Somerset. 1992. *Employment equity*. Toronto: Prentice Hall Canada.

Alboim, N., and the Maytree Foundation. 2002. *Fulfilling the promise: Integrating immigrant skills into the Canadian economy*. Ottawa: Caledon Institute of Social Policy.

Alur, M. 2000. "Inclusion for children with disabilities in India." In *International scan of issues: Children with disabilities and their families*. A discussion document for the Sixth International Congress on the Inclusion of Children with Disabilities in the Community. Toronto: Roeher Institute.

Anderson, A., and J. Freideres. 1981. *Ethnicity in Canada: Theoretical perspectives*. Toronto: Butterworths.

Andrew, C. 2001. "What has space got to do with social inclusion?" Presentation to Laidlaw Foundation/Canadian Council on Social Development Conference, Social inclusion: A new way of thinking? Ottawa, 8–9 November.

*Andrews v. Law Society of British Columbia* (1989), 1 S.C.R. 143 at 171.

Anisef, P. 2000. "Navigating the life course: Themes and issues school-to-work transitions in the 1990s." In P. Anisef, P. Axelrod, E. Baichman-Anisef, C. James and A. Turritin (eds.), *Opportunity and uncertainty: The life course experiences of the class of '73*. Toronto: University of Toronto Press.

Anthias, F. 1997. "Anti-racism, multiculturalism and struggles for a multicultural democracy." In M. Roche and R. van Berkel (eds.).

Antle, B., and C. Frazee. 1999. *Creating a life of your own: Experiences of transition to independence among people with physical disabilities*. Gage Transition to Independent Living. Toronto: West Park Hospital.

Arnup, K. 1997. "In the family way: Lesbian mothers in Canada." In M. Luxton (ed.), *Feminism and families: Critical policies and changing practices*. Halifax: Fernwood.

Asch, A., and G. Geller. 1996. "Feminism, bioethics, and genetics." In S. Wolf (ed.), *Feminism and bioethics: Beyond reproduction*. New York and Oxford: Oxford University Press.

Atkinson, A.B. January 1998. "Social exclusion, poverty and unemployment." In A.B. Atkinson and J. Hills (eds.), *Exclusion, employment and opportunity*, CASE report 4. London: Centre for Analysis of Social Exclusion, London School of Economics.

Baker, M. 1995. *Canadian family policies: Cross-national comparisons.* Toronto: University of Toronto Press.

Baker-Collins, S. 2000. "Poverty: Concepts measures and policy responses." Unpublished paper. Toronto: Faculty of Social Work, University of Toronto.

Bakker, I. 1994. *The strategic silence: Gender and economic policy.* Ottawa: Zed Books and North-South Institute.

_____. 1996. *Rethinking restructuring.* Toronto: University of Toronto Press.

Bancroft, W., and S.C. Vernon. 1995. *The struggle for self-sufficiency: Participants in the self-sufficiency project talk about work, welfare and their futures.* Vancouver: Social Demonstration and Research Corporation.

Banton, M. 1977. *The Idea of Race.* London: Tavistock Publications.

Barata, P. February 2000. "Social exclusion: A review of the literature" Unpublished paper. Toronto: Laidlaw Foundation.

Barnes, C. 1991. *Disabled people in Britain and discrimination.* London: Hurst.

Barry, M. 1998. "Social exclusion and social work: An introduction." In M. Barry and C. Hallett (eds.), *Social exclusion and social work.* Dorset: Russell House.

Bauder, H., and E. Cameron. 2002. *Cultural barriers to labour market integration: Immigrants from South Asia and the former Yugoslavia.* Vancouver: Research on Immigration and Integration in the Metropolis (RIIM).

Beach, J., and J. Bertrand. 2000. *More than the sum of the parts: An early childhood development system for Canada.* Occasional paper no. 12. Toronto: Child-care Resource and Research Unit, University of Toronto.

Beach, J., J. Bertrand and G. Cleveland. 1998. *Our child-care workforce: From recognition to remuneration — More than a labour of love.* Ottawa: Child-care Human Resources Steering Committee.

Beauvais, C., and J. Jenson. 2001. *Two policy paradigms: Family responsibility and investing in children.* Ottawa: Canadian Policy Research Networks Inc.

Benhabib, S. 1986. *Critique, norm, and utopia: A study of the foundations of critical theory.* New York: Columbia University Press.

_____. 1987. "The generalized and concrete other." In S. Benhabib and D. Cornell (eds.), *Feminism as critique.* Minneapolis: University of Minnesota Press.

Benick, G., and A. Saloojee. 1996. "Introduction." In G. Benick and A. Saloojee (eds.), *Creating inclusive post-secondary learning environment.* Toronto.

Bennett, D. ed. 1998. *Multicultural states: Re-thinking difference and identity.* London: Routledge.

Berghman, J. 1995. "Social exclusion in Europe: Policy context and analytical framework." In G. Room (ed.), *Beyond the threshold: The measurement and analysis of social exclusion.* Bristol: Policy Press.

Bernhard, J.K., M.L. Levebvre, G. Chud and R. Lange. 1995. *Paths to equity: Cultural, linguistic and racial diversity in Canadian early childhood education.* Toronto: York Lanes Press.

Bezanson, K. January 2002. Unpublished PhD thesis. Toronto: Women's Studies, Graduate Program, York University.

*Bhinder* v. *Canadian National Railways* (1981), 2 C.H.R.R.D.\546 at D\S 9991.

Bibby, R. 1990. *Mosaic madness: The poverty and potential of Canadian life.* Toronto: Stoddard.

Billingsley, B., and L. Musynzski. 1985. *No discrimination here.* Toronto: Urban Alliance on Race Relations.

Blondin-Andrew. E. 1993. *House of Commons Debates (Hansard).* Ottawa: Government of Canada. 10 March.

_____. 2003. Statement. Secretary of State of Children and Youth, Subcommittee on Children and Youth at Risk. Ottawa: Government of Canada. 19 February.

Bloom, M., and M. Grant. 2001. *Brain gain: The economic benefits of recognizing learning and learning credentials in Canada.* Ottawa: Conference Board of Canada.

Bonacich, E. 1972. "A theory of ethnic antagonism: The split labour market." *American Sociological Review* 37: 547–59.

Bourgignon, F. 1999. "Absolute poverty, relative deprivation and social exclusion." *Capacity International, Germany.* Villa Borsig Workshop Series, Inclusion, Justice and Poverty Reduction. <www.inwent.org> (accessed July 2005).

Boushey, H., and B. Gundersen. 2001. *When work just isn't enough: Measuring hardships faced by families after moving from welfare to work.* Washington, DC: Economic Policy Institute.

Boyd, M. 1992. "Gender, visible minority and immigrant earnings inequality: Reassessing and employment equity premise." In V. Satzewich (ed.), *Deconstructing a nation: Immigration, multiculturalism and racism in the 1990s Canada.* Toronto: Garamond Press.

Boyd, S. 1989. "Child custody, ideologies and employment." *Canadian Journal of Women and the Law* 3: 111–33.

Bradshaw, J. 2000. "Wider aspects of poverty and social exclusion." In *Indicators of progress: A discussion of approaches to monitor the Government's strategy to tackle poverty and social exclusion*, CASE report 13. London: Centre for Analysis of Social Exclusion, London School of Economics.

Brandolini, A., and G. D'Allessio. 2000. "Measuring well-being in the functioning space." Paper prepared for the International Association for Research in Income and Wealth, Cracow, Poland, 27 August to 2 September. <www.iariw.org/papers/2000/brandolini.pdf> (accessed July 2005).

Brock, T., D. Butler and D. Long. 1993. *Unpaid work experience for welfare recipients: Findings and lessons from MDRC research.* MDRC Working Papers, New York: Manpower Demonstration Research Corporation.

Brodie, J. ed. 1996. *Women and Canadian public policy.* Toronto: Harcourt Brace.

Brooks-Gunn, J., and G.J. Duncan. 1997. "The effects of poverty on children." *The Future of Children* 7(2). Los Altos, CA: David and Lucielle Packard Foundation.

Brouwer, A. 1998. *Refugees in legal limbo.* Ottawa: Caledon Institute of Social Policy.

_____. 1999. *Immigrants need not apply.* Ottawa: Caledon Institute of Social Policy.

_____. 2000. *Student Loans for Convention Refugees in Limbo.* Toronto: The Maytree Foundation. <www.maytree.com> (accessed July 2005).

Bunch, G., and A. Valeo. 2000. "Educational inclusion of children with disabilities." In *International scan of issues: Children with disabilities and their families.* A discussion document for the Sixth International Congress on the Inclusion of Children with Disabilities in the Community. Toronto: The Roeher Institute.

Burchanel, M., D. Bryant, R. Clifford and E. Peisner-Feinberg. 2000. "Children's social and cognitive development and child-care quality: Testing for differential associations related to poverty, gender or ethnicity." *Applied Developmental Science* 4 (3): 149–65.

Byrne, D.S. 1999. "Social exclusion." *Issues in Society*. Buckingham, UK, Philadelphia: Open University Press.

Caidi, N., and D. Allard. 2005. (in press). "Social inclusion of newcomers to Canada: An information problem?" *Library and Information Science Research*, 27(3).

Campaign 2000. 2000. *Child poverty in Canada: Report card 2000*. Toronto.

_____. 2002. *Putting promises into action: A report on the decade of child and family poverty in Canada*. Toronto: Campaign 2000.

Canada Mortgage and Housing Corporation. 2004. "2001 Census housing series issue six: Aboriginal households." *Socio-Economic Series* 04-036. Ottawa: Canada Mortgage and Housing Corporation. <www.cmhc.ca> (accessed July 2005).

Canadian Association for Community Living. 1999. *Intellectual disability and the Supreme Court: The implications of the Charter for people who have a disability*. Toronto.

Canadian Association of Food Banks. October 2003. *Hunger count, 2003*. Toronto.

Canadian Council for Refugees. 1998. *Best settlement practices: Settlement services for refugees and immigrants in Canada*. Montreal: Canadian Council for Refugees.

Canadian Council of Christians and Jews. 1993. *Attitudes towards race and ethnic relations*. Toronto.

Canadian Council on Social Development (CCSD). 1999. *The progress of Canada's children into the millennium, 1999–2000*. Ottawa.

_____. 2001. Disability information sheet. Ottawa.

_____. 2002. *A Community Growing Apart: Income Gaps and Changing Needs in the City of Toronto in the 1990s*. Final report prepared for the United Way of Greater Toronto. By Andrew Jackson, Sylvain Schetagne and Peter Smith. #607. January.

Canadian Public Health Association. July 2003. Submission to the Naylor Commission. Ottawa: Government of Canada.

Canadian Race Relation Foundation. 2000. *Unequal access: A Canadian profile of racial differences in education, employment and income*. Ottawa.

Canadian Task Force on Mental Health Issues Affecting Immigrants and Refugees. 1988. *Review of the literature on migrant mental health*. Ottawa: Health and Welfare Canada.

Cannan, C. 1997. "The struggle against social exclusion: Urban social development in France." *IDS Bulletin* 28(2): 77–85.

Card, D., and P.K. Robbins. 1996. *Do financial incentives encourage welfare recipients to work? Initial 18-month findings from the Self-Sufficiency Project*. Vancouver: Social Research Demonstration Corporation.

Carey, E. 2002. "Jobs tougher to find for recent immigrants." *Toronto Star*. 26 February.

Castells, M. 1978. *City, class and power*. London: Macmillan.

_____. 1979. *The urban question: A Marxist approach*. Cambridge: MIT Press.

_____. 1996 *The rise of the network society*. Oxford: Blackwell.

_____. 1997. *The power of identity*. Oxford: Blackwell.

Caulfield, T, M. Burgess and B. Williams-Jones. 2001. "Providing genetic testing through the private sector: A view from Canada." *Isuma: Canadian Journal of Policy Research* 2(3), Autumn: 65–71.

Centre for Applied Social Research. 2002. "School settlement workers serving the needs of Canadian newcomers." *CASRNews* 4(1) (Spring). Toronto: Faculty of Social Work, University of Toronto.

Chambers, R. 1983. *Rural development: Putting the last first*. New York: Longman Scientific and Technical.

Chambon, A., and T. Richmond. 2001. "L'évaluation des services d'établissement pour les personnes immigrantes et réfugiées: Enjeux conceptuels et méthodologiques." *Cahiers de recherche sociologiques: L'évaluation sociale un enjeu politique* 35, Spring . Montreal: Département de sociologie, UQAM.

Chandler, W. April 1992. "The value of household work in Canada, 1992." *Canadian Economic Observer*, Statistics Canada, Catalogue no. 11-010. Ottawa: Government of Canada.

Chandoke, N. 1995. *State and civil society: Explorations in political theory*. New Delhi: Sage.

_____. 1999. *Beyond secularism: The rights of religious minorities*. New Delhi: Oxford University Press.

Chard, J., J. Badets and L. Howatson-Lee. 2000. "Immigrant women." *Women in Canada, 2000: A gender-based statistical report*. Ottawa: Statistics Canada.

Chief Administrator's Office. 2001. *In common cause: Cities dialogue on immigrant and refugee issues in Canada*. Toronto: City of Toronto.

Child-care Resource and Research Unit. 2000. *Early childhood care and education in Canada: Provinces and territories 1998*. Toronto: Centre for Urban and Community Studies, University of Toronto.

Chow, O., C. Freiler and K. McQuaig. May 6, 1999. "A national agenda for ALL families: Re-framing the debate about tax fairness." Presentation to the Finance Sub-Committee Studying the Fairness of the Tax and Transfer System for Families with Children. Toronto: Child Poverty Action Group and the Child-care Education Foundation.

Christie, N. 2000. *Engendering the state family, work, and welfare in Canada*. Toronto: University of Toronto Press.

City of Toronto. 1998. "Diversity our strength, access and equity our goal." Toronto: Task Force on Community Access and Equity, City of Toronto. <http://www.city.toronto.on.ca/accessandequity/exec_sum.htm> (accessed July 2005).

Cleveland, G., and M. Krashinsky. 1998. *The benefits and cost of good child-care: The economic rationale for public investment in young children*. Toronto: Child-care Resource and Research Unit, University of Toronto.

_____, eds. 2001. *Our children's future: Child-care policy in Canada*. Toronto: University of Toronto Press.

Clutterbuck, P., and M. Novick. June 2002. *Building inclusive communities: A social infrastructure strategy for Canadian municipalities*. Prepared for the Federation of Canadian Municipalities and the Laidlaw Foundation, FCM Social Infrastructure Committee's Policy Forum. Hamilton: Ontario.

_____. April 2003. *Building inclusive communities: Cross-Canada perspectives and strategies*. Prepared for the Federation of Canadian Municipalities and the Laidlaw Foundation. Toronto. <http://www.inclusivecities.ca/pdf/inclusive.pdf> (accessed 3 December 2004).

*C.N.R.* v. *Canada (Human Rights Commission)* (1987), 1 S.C.R.1114.

Code, L. 1987. *Epistemic responsibility*. Hanover, NH: University Press of New England.

_____. 1989. "Experience, knowledge and responsibility." In M. Griffiths and M. Whitford (eds.), *Feminist perspectives in philosophy*. London: Macmillan.

Cohen, M. 1997. "What women should know about economic fundamentalism." *Atlantis: A Women's Studies Journal* 21(2), Spring/Summer.

Cole, A. 2001. *Genetic discrimination: Looking back to the future?* Occasional paper. Toronto: Roeher Institute.

Commission of European Communities. 2000. *Building an inclusive Europe*. Brussels.

Commissioner of Community and Neighbourhood Services. 2001. *Immigration and settlement policy framework*. Toronto: City of Toronto.

Community Social Planning Council of Toronto. April 2001. *Preserving our civic legacy*. Toronto: Community Consultation on Social Development.

Conference Board of Canada. August 2003. *Insights on Western Canada*. Ottawa.

Courchene, T. 2001. *A state of minds: Toward a human capital future for Canadians*. Montreal: Institute for Research on Public Policy.

Couton, P. 2002. "Highly skilled immigrants: Recent trends and issues." *Isuma* 3(2), Fall. <www.isuma.net/v03n02/couton/couton_e.shtml> (accessed July 2005).

Covell, K., and R.B. Howe. 2001. *The challenge of children's rights for Canadians*. Waterloo: Wilfred Laurier University Press.

Cox, O. 1948. *Caste, class and race*. New York: Doubleday.

Cumming, P.A., E.L.D. Lee and D.G. Oreopoulos. 1989. *Access! Task force on access to professions and trades in Ontario*. Ontario: Ministry of Citizenship.

Dahlberg, G., P. Moss and A. Pence. 1999. *Beyond quality in early childhood education and care: Postmodern perspectives*. London: Falmer.

Darden, J.T., and S.M. Kamel. 2001. "Differences in homeownership rates between Aboriginal peoples and white Canadians in the Toronto Census metropolitan area: Does race matter?" *Native Studies Review* 14(1): 55–81.

Das Gupta, M. 1999. "Social exclusion and poverty: Preliminary thoughts from the World Development Report 2001." *Capacity International, Germany*. Villa Borsig Workshop Series, Inclusion, Justice and Poverty Reduction. <www.inwent.org> (accessed July 2005).

Day, R. 2000. *Multiculturalism and the History of Canadian Diversity*. Toronto: University of Toronto Press.

de Haan, A. 1998a. "Social exclusion: An alternative concept for the study of deprivation?" In A. de Haan and S. Maxwell (eds.), *Poverty and social exclusion in North and South*. Institute for Development Studies Bulletin 29(1): 10–19.

_____. 1998b. "Social exclusion in policy and research: Operationalizing the concept." In J.B. Figueiredo and A. de Haan (eds.), *Social exclusion: An ILO perspective*. Geneva: International Labour Organization.

DeVoretz, D.J. ed. 1995. *Diminishing returns: The economics of Canada's recent immigration policy*. Toronto: C.D. Howe Institute.

Dick, B. 1999. UNICEF Working Paper on Children's Rights. New York: United Nations Children's Fund. 29 November.

Doherty, G. 1993. *Quality child-care: Contextual factors*. Ottawa: Canadian Childcare Federation.

_____. 1997. *Zero to six: The basis for school readiness*. Ottawa: Human Resources Development Canada.

_____. 2001. *Targeting early childhood education and care: Myths and realities*. Occasional paper no.15. Toronto: Child-care Resource and Research Unit, Centre for Urban and Community Studies, University of Toronto.

Doherty, G., and M. Friendly. 2002. *Making the best of the You bet I care! Data sets: Final report on a research forum*. Toronto: Child-care Resource and Research Unit, University of Toronto.

Doherty, G., D. Lero., H. Goleman., A. LaGrange and J. Tougas. 2000a. *You bet I care! A Canada-wide study on wages, working conditions and practices in child-care centers*. Guelph: Centre for Families, Work and Well-being, University of Guelph.

_____. 2000b. *You bet I care! Quality in regulated family child-care across Canada*. Guelph: Centre for Families, Work and Well-being, University of Guelph.

Doherty, G., and B. Stuart. 1997. "The association between child-care quality, ratio and staff training: A Canada-wide study." *Canadian Journal of Research in Early Childhood Education* 6 (2): 127–38. Montreal: Concordia University.

Dreidger, L. 1989. *The ethnic factor: Identity in diversity*. Toronto: McGraw-Hill Ryerson.

Dryden, K. (Minister of Social Development, Liberal). October 13, 2004. "Moving Canada forward: The Paul Martin plan for getting things done." *House of Commons Debates (Hansard)*. Ottawa: Government of Canada.

Duffy, K. 1995. *Social exclusion and human dignity in Europe*. Strasbourg: Council of Europe.

Dunphy, C. 2000. "Innu tell tales to save children." *Toronto Star*, 11 December: A6.

*Eaton v. Brant (County) Board of Education*. (1995) O.R. (3d), Ontario Court Of Appeal. 22.

*Eaton v. Brant Country Board of Education* (1997), 1 S.C.R. 143 at 171.

*Eaton v. Brant County Board of Education*. (1997) S.C.R, Supreme Court of Canada. 1: 241.

Ebersold, S. 1998. *Exclusion and disability*. Paris: Centre for Educational Research and Innovation, Organisation for Economic Co-operation and Development. <www.oecd.org/dataoecd/20/17/1856907.pdf> (accessed July 2005).

Economic Council of Canada. 1991. *Economic and social impacts of immigration*. Ottawa: Supply and Services Canada, Government of Canada.

Eichler, M. 1988. *Families in Canada today: Recent changes and their policy consequences*. Toronto: Gage.

Elton, D., J. Sieppert, J. Azmicr and R. Roach. 1997. *Where are they now? Assessing the impact of welfare reform on former recipients*. Calgary: Canada West Foundation.

Employment and Immigration Canada. 1989. *Immigration to Canada: Issues for discussion*. Ottawa: Government of Canada.

Endean, Rebecca. 2001. "Opportunity for all: Monitoring the Government's strategy to tackle poverty and social exclusion." In *Indicators of Progress: A discussion of approaches to monitor the Government's strategy to tackle poverty and social exclusion*, CASE report 13. London: Centre for Analysis of Social Exclusion, London School of Economics.

Endicott, O. Unpublished paper. "Key trends in case law pertaining to supports for persons with disabilities."

Environics Research Group. 1998. *Child-care issues and the child-care workforce: A survey of Canadian public opinion*. Toronto.

European Commission Network on Child-Care. 1996. *Quality targets in services for young children. Proposals for a ten year action plan.* London: Thomas Coram Research Unit, University of London.

European Foundation for the Improvement of Living and Working Conditions. 1995. *Public welfare services and social exclusion: The development of consumer oriented initiatives in the European Union.* Dublin.

Evans, B.M., and J. Shields. 2002. "The third sector: Neo-liberal restructuring, governance, and the remaking of state-civil society relationships." In C. Dunn (ed.), *The handbook of Canadian public administration.* Toronto: Oxford University Press.

Evans, M. 1998. "Behind the rhetoric: The institutional basis of social exclusion and poverty." In A. de Haan and S. Maxwell (eds.), *Poverty and social exclusion in North and South.* Institute for Development Studies Bulletin 29(1): 42–49.

Evans, P., S. Bronheim, J. Bynner, S. Klasen, P. Magrab and S. Ransom. 2000. *Social exclusion and children — Creating identity capital: Some conceptual issues and practical solutions.* Geneva: Organisation for Economic Co-operation and Development.

Federation of Canadian Municipalities. 2004. *Moving forward: Refining the FCM recommendations for a national affordable housing strategy.* Canada: FCM.

Figueiredo, J.B., and A. de Haan, eds. 1998. *Social exclusion: An ILO perspective.* Geneva: International Labour Organization.

Finnie, R. 1997. *The earnings mobility of Canadians, 1982–1992.* Working paper W-97-3Ea. Ottawa: Human Resources Development Canada, Applied Research Branch.

_____. 2000. *The dynamics of poverty in Canada: What we know, what we can do.* Toronto: C.D. Howe Institute.

Fleras, A., and L.J. Elliott. 1992. *Multiculturalism in Canada: The challenge of diversity.* Toronto: Oxford.

_____. 1999. *Unequal relations: An introduction to race, ethnic, and Aboriginal dynamics in Canada.* Scarborough: Prentice Hall Allyn Bacon Canada.

Folbre, N. 1994. *Who pays for the kids? Gender and the structures of constraint.* New York: Routledge.

Forcese, L. 2002. "To be a Canadian Muslim after 9-11." *INSCAN* 15(3), Winter 2002.

Frank, J. 1997. "Indicators of social inequality in Canada: Women, Aboriginal people and visible minorities." In A. Frizzell and J. Pammett (eds.), *Social inequality in Canada.* Ottawa: Carleton University Press.

Fraser, N. 1996. "Rethinking the public sphere: A contribution to the critique of actually existing democracies." In C. Calhoun (ed.), *Habermas and the public sphere.* Cambridge: MIT Press.

Freiler, C. 2000. *Social inclusion as a focus of well being for children and families.* Toronto: Laidlaw Foundation.

_____. 2001a. "From experiences of exclusion to a vision of inclusion: What needs to change?" Presentation to Laidlaw Foundation/CCSD Conference, *Social inclusion: A new way of thinking?* Ottawa: Laidlaw Foundation and Canadian Council on Social Development. 8-9 November.

_____. 2001b. *Toward a vision of social inclusion for all children.* Toronto: Laidlaw Foundation.

_____. 2001c. *What needs to change? Social inclusion as a focus of well-being for children, families and communities.* Toronto: Advisory Committee of the Children's Agenda Programme, Laidlaw Foundation. May.

Freiler, C., L. Rothman and P. Barata. May 2004. *Pathways to progress: Structural solutions to address child poverty.* Campaign 2000 Discussion papers. Toronto.

Friedlander, D., and G. Burtless. 1995. *Five years after: The long-term effects of welfare-to-work programs.* New York: Russell Sage Foundation.

Friendly, M. 1995. *Putting the pieces together: Child-care policy in Canada.* Don Mills, ON: Addison Wesley Ltd.

_____. 2000. "A national child-care program: Now is the time." *Pediatrics and Child Health* 5(5), June/July.

_____. 2001. "Canary in a coal mine: Child-care and Canadian federalism in the 1990s." In G. Clevland and M. Krashinsky (eds.), *Child-care in Canada in the 21st century: Preparing the policy map.* Toronto: University of Toronto Press.

Friendly, M., G. Cleveland, S. Colley., D. Lero and R. Shillington. (in press). "Early childhood education and care: An agenda for national data." Toronto: Child-Care Resource and Research Unit, Centre for Urban and Community Studies, University of Toronto.

Friendly, M., and L. Rothman. 2000. *Early childhood development services: How much will they cost?* Briefing note. Toronto: Child-Care Resource and Research Unit, Centre for Urban and Community Studies, University of Toronto.

Martha Friendly and Laurel Rothman (for Campaign 2000). 2000. <wwww.childcarecanada.org/pubs/pdf>. (accessed July 2005).

Galabuzi, G. 2000. *Canada's creeping economic apartheid.* Ottawa: Canadian Race Relations Foundation.

_____. 2001. *Canada's creeping economic apartheid: The economic segregation and social marginalization of racialized groups.* Toronto: CJS Foundation for Research and Education.

_____. 2004. "Social exclusion." In D. Raphael (ed.), *Social determinants of health: Canadian perspectives.* Toronto: Canadian Scholars' Press.

Gallagher, J., R. Rooney and S. Campbell. 1999. "Child-care licensing regulations and child-care quality in four states." *Early Childhood Research Quarterly* 14(3): 313–33.

Gavigan, S. 1997. "Feminism, familial ideology and family law: A perilous ménage à trois." In M. Luxton (ed.), *Feminism and families: Critical policies and changing practices.* Halifax: Fernwood.

Geronimo, J. 2000. *A search for models: From collaboration to co-optation. Partnership experiences in settlement and human services for newcomers.* Toronto: The GTA Consortium on the Coordination of Settlement Services. <www.settlement.org> (accessed July 2005).

Giddens, A. 1994. *Beyond left and right.* Cambridge: Polity Press.

Glazer, Nathan. 1983. Ethnic Dilemmas: 1964–1982. Cambridge, MA: Harvard University Press.

Goelman, H., and A. Pence. 1987. "Effects of child-care, family, and individual characteristics on children's language development: The Victoria Day Care Project." In D. Phillips (ed.), *Quality in child-care: What does the research tell us?* Washington, DC: National Association for the Education on Young Children.

Goelman, H., G. Doherty, D. Lero, A. LaGrange and J. Tougas. 2000. *You Bet I Care! Caring and Learning Environments: Quality in Child Care Centers across Canada.* Guelph, ON: Center for Families, Work and Well-Being, University of Guelph. CCCNS No L-010-Goe/FCC.

Goldberg, M. 2000. *The facts are in! Newcomers' experiences in accessing regulated professions in Ontario.* Ontario Ministry of Training, Colleges and Universities, Access to Professions and Trades Unit.

Golden, L., and D. Figart. 2000. "Doing something about long hours." *Challenge* 43(6).

Gore, C. 1995. "Introduction: Markets and citizenship." In G. Rodgers et al. (eds.), *Social exclusion: Rhetoric, reality, responses.* Geneva, Switzerland: International Labour Organization Publications.

Gorrie, P. 2002. "Discrimination costly." *Toronto Star,* 20 March: A23.

Government of Canada. November 2004. "Aboriginal lifelong learning: Background paper." Unpublished paper. Ottawa.

Government of Sweden. 2001. *Sweden's action plan against poverty and social exclusion.* Stockholm, Sweden.

Guildford, J. 2000. *Making the case for economic and social inclusion.* Ottawa: Population and Public Health Branch, Health Canada.

Gutman, A. ed. 1994. *Multiculturalism: Examining the politics of recognition.* Princeton, NJ: Princeton University Press.

Habermas, J. 1998. *The inclusion of the other: Studies in political theory.* Cambridge, MA: MIT Press.

Hall, S. 1990. "Cultural identity and diaspora." In J. Rutherford (ed.), *Identity: Community, culture, difference.* London: Lawrence and Wishart.

Hamilton, R., and M. Barrett. eds. 1986. *The politics of diversity: Feminism, Marxism and Canadian society.* London: Verso.

Hanberger, A. 2001. "Policy and program evaluation, civil society and democracy." *American Journal of Evaluation* 22(2): 211–28.

Hanvey, L. 2001. *Children and youth with special needs.* Ottawa: CCSD.

Harvey, C. 2002. "Introduction: Securing refugee protection in a cold climate." *Refuge* 20(4), August.

Harvey, D. 1976. *Social justice and the city.* London: Edwin Arnold.

_____. 1989. *The conditions of post-modernism.* Oxford: Blackwell.

_____. 1996. *Justice, nature and the geography of difference.* Oxford: Blackwell.

Harvey, E.B., and B. Siu. 2001. "Immigrants' socioeconomic situation compared, 1991–1996." *INSCAN* 15(2), Fall.

Hatfield, M. 2001. "The causes of persistent low income: A key barrier to social inclusion." Presentation to Laidlaw Foundation/Canadian Council on Social Development conference, Social inclusion: A new way of thinking? Ottawa, 8–9 November.

Health Canada. 1999. *A second diagnostic on the health of First Nations and Inuit people in Canada.* Ottawa: Government of Canada.

Held, D. 1995. *Democracy and the global order: From the modern state to cosmopolitan governance.* Cambridge: Polity Press.

Henry, F., et al. 1995. *The colour of democracy.* Toronto: Harcourt, Brace.

Henry, F., and E. Ginzberg. 1985. *Who gets the work? A test of racial discrimination in employment.* Toronto: Urban Alliance on Race Relations and Social Planning Council of Metropolitan Toronto.

Henry, F., and C. Tator. 2000. "The theory and practice of democratic racism in Canada." In M.A. Kalbach and W.E. Kalbach (eds.), *Perspectives on ethnicity in Canada.* Toronto: Harcourt Canada.

Hertzman, C. 1995. *Child development and long-term outcomes: A population health perspective and summary of successful interventions*. Toronto: Canadian Institute for Advanced Research.

Hill Collins, P. 1998. *Fighting words, Black women and the search for justice*. Minneapolis: University of Minnesota Press.

Holden, C. 2000. "Globalization, social exclusion and Labour's new work ethic." *Critical Social Policy* 19(4): 529–38.

Holder, B.S. 1998. "The role of immigrant serving organizations in the Canadian welfare state: A case study." Ph.D. Dissertation, Department of Adult Education, Counseling Psychology and Community Development, University of Toronto. CERIS Virtual Library <ceris.metropolis.net>.

Holston, J. 1995. "Spaces of insurgent citizenship." In *Planning Theory* Special Issue: 35–52.

Holtzberg, M., and B. Howard. 1996. *Portrait of spirit: One story at a time*. Oakville, ON: Disability Today Publishing Group.

Honneth, Axel. 1995. *The fragmented world of the social: Essays in social and political philosophy*. C.W. Wright (ed.). Albany, NY: State University of New York.

hooks, bell. 1984. *From margin to center*. Boston: South End Press.

Hou, F., and T.R. Balakrishnan. 1996. "The integration of visible minorities in contemporary Canadian society." *Canadian Journal of Sociology* 21(3): 307–26.

House Committee on Finance. December 1996. *1997, Budget and beyond*. Ottawa: Government of Canada.

House Sub-Committee on Youth At-Risk. 2003. *Building a brighter future for urban Aboriginal children*. Ottawa: Government of Canada. 12 June.

Howe, E. 2003. *Education and lifetime income for Aboriginal people in Saskatchewan*. Regina: University of Regina.

Hull, J. 2001. *Aboriginal single mothers in Canada, 1996: A statistical profile*. Ottawa: Department of Indian and Northern Affairs Canada, Government of Canada. 7 June.

Human Resources Development Canada (HRDC). 2000. "High risk factors behind poverty and exclusion." *Applied Research Bulletin* 6 (1), Winter/Spring.

_____. 2001. "Recent immigrants have experienced unusual economic difficulties." *Applied Research Bulletin* 7(1), Winter/Spring.

_____. 2002. *Knowledge matters: Skills and learning for Canadians - Canada's innovation strategy*. Ottawa: HRDC. <www.hrdc-drhc.gc.ca/sp-ps/sl-ca/doc/summary.shtml> (accessed July 2005).

Ignatieff, M. 2000. *The rights revolution*. New York: Anansi.

Irwin, S.H. 1992. *Integration of children with disabilities into daycare and after school programs*. Ottawa: Disabled Persons Unit, Health Canada.

Irwin, S., and D. Lero. 1997. *In our way: Child-care barriers to full workforce participation experienced by parents of children with special needs — and potential remedies*. Sydney, NS: Breton Books.

_____. 2001. "In the absence of policy: Moving towards inclusion of children with special needs in Canada's child-care centres." In S. Prentice (ed.), *Changing child-care: Five decades of child-care advocacy and policy in Canada*. Halifax: Fernwood.

Irwin, S., D. Lero and K. Brophy. 2000. *A matter of urgency: Including children with special needs in child-care in Canada*. Sydney, NS: Breton Books.

Jackman, M. October 2002. *The implications of section 7 of the Charter for Health Care*

*Spending in Canada.* Discussion paper no. 31. Ottawa: Romanow Commission.

Jackson, A. 2001. "Poverty and racism." *Perception* 24(4): 6–7.

Jackson, A., and K. Scott. 2000. *Labour markets and the social inclusion/exclusion of children.* Ottawa: CCSD.

James, C. 2000. "The experiences of first generation Canadians." In P. Anisef et al. (eds.), *Opportunity and uncertainty: The life course experiences of the Class of '73.* Toronto: University of Toronto Press.

James, C., D. Plaza and C. Jansen. 1999. "Issues of race in employment experiences of Caribbean women in Toronto." *Canadian Woman Studies/Cahiers de la femme* 19: 129–33.

Jenkins, J., and D. Keating. 1998. *Risk and resilience in six- and ten-year-old children.* Ottawa: Human Resources Development Canada, Applied Research Branch, Strategic Policy.

Jenkins, J.R., S.L. Odom and M.L. Speltz. 1989. "Effects of social integration on preschool children with handicaps." *Exceptional Children* 55: 420–28.

Jenson, Jane. 1998. *Mapping social cohesion: The state of Canadian research.* CPRN Study No. F|03. Ottawa: Canadian Policy Research Networks (CPRN). <www.cprn.org> (accessed July 2005).

_____. 2000. *Backgrounder: Thinking about marginalisation: What, who and why?* Ottawa: CPRN.

_____. 2001. *Time to strengthen Canada's commitment to diversity.* Ottawa: CPRN.

_____. 2002. *Citizenship: Its relationship to the Canadian diversity model.* Ottawa: CPRN.

Jenson, J., and M. Papillon. 2001. *The changing boundaries of citizenship: A review and a research agenda.* Ottawa: CPRN.

Johnson, K., D. S. Lero, and J. Rooney. 2001. *Work-Life Compendium 2001: 150 Canadian Statistics on Work, Family and Well-Being.* University of Guelph, Ontario: Centre for Families, Work and Well-Being and HRDC, Women's Bureau.

Johnson, M., H. Ladd and J. Ludwig. 2001. "The Benefits and Costs of Residential Mobility Programs For The Poor." Paper presented to conference. Opportunity, Deprivation and the Housing Nexus: Transatlantic Perspectives, Washington, DC, May.

Jordan, J. 1978. "Old stories: New lives." Keynote address to Child Welfare League of America. In *Moving towards home: Personal essays, 1989.*

Kaprielian-Churchill, I., and S. Churchill. 1994. *The pulse of the world: Refugees in our schools.* Toronto: OISE Press.

Kazemipur, A., and S. Halli. 1997. "Plight of immigrants: The spatial concentration of poverty in Canada." *Canadian Journal of Regional Sciences* Special Issue XX (1/2), Spring/Summer: 11–28.

_____. 2000. *The new poverty in Canada.* Toronto: Thompson Educational Publishing.

Kearney, R. 1998. *Poetics of imagining: Modern to post-modern.* New York: Fordham University Press.

Keating, D. 2001. "Health and human capital." Paper presented at *Canada in international perspective: The human capital paradigm.* Kingston, ON: Queen's University International Institute on Social Policy. 27–29 August.

Keating, D., and C. Hertzman.1999. *Developmental health and the wealth of nations.*

New York: The Guilford Press.

Keck, J. 1998. "Twenty-five years of women working at Inco." Paper presented at the Learned Society meetings. June.

Kenny, N. 2004. "What's fair? Ethical decision-making in an aging society." Research report F/44. Ottawa: Canadian Policy Research Networks Inc. and The Change Foundation. May.

Khosla, P. 2003. *If low-income women of colour counted in Toronto*. Toronto: Community Social Planning Council.

Kilbride, K.M, P. Anisef, E. Baichman-Anisef and R. Khattar. 2000. *Between two worlds: The experiences and concerns of immigrant youth in Ontario*. Toronto: CERIS and CIC-OASIS. <www.settlement.org> (accessed July 2005).

Klasen, S. 1997. "Poverty, inequality, and deprivation in South Africa: An Analysis of the 1993 SALDRU survey." *Social Indicator Research* 41: 51–94.

_____. 1998. *Social exclusion and children in OECD countries: Some conceptual issues*. Paper presented at OECD Experts Seminar. OECD, Centre for Educational Research and Innovation.

Knox, V., C. Miller and L.A. Gennetian. 2000. *Reforming welfare and rewarding work: A summary of the Final Report on the Minnesota Family Investment Program*. New York: Manpower Demonstration Research Corporation.

Kome, P. 1983. *The taking of Twenty-Eight: Women challenge the Constitution*. Toronto: Women's Press.

Kumin, J., and D. Chaikel. 2002. "Taking the agenda forward: The roundtable on separated children seeking asylum in Canada." *Refuge* 20(2) February. Toronto: Centre for Refugee Studies, York University.

Kymlicka, W. 1989. *Liberalism, community, and culture*. Oxford: Clarendon Press.

_____. 1995. *The rights of minority cultures*. Oxford: Oxford University Press.

Kymlicka, W., and W. Norman. 1994. "Return of the citizen: A survey of recent work on citizenship theory." *Ethics* 194, 2 (January): 352–81.

_____. 2000. "Citizenship in culturally diverse societies: Issues, contexts and concepts." In W. Kymlicka and W. Norman (eds.), *Citizenship in divided societies*. Oxford: Oxford University Press.

Labonte, R. 2004. "Social inclusion/exclusion and health: Dancing the dialectic." In D. Raphael (ed.), *Social determinants of health: Canadian perspectives*. Toronto: Canadian Scholars' Press.

Lamb, M. 1998. "Non-parental child-care: Context, quality, correlates and consequences." *Handbook of Child Psychology* 4: 73–133.

Law Commission of Canada. 2000. *Restoring dignity: Responding to child abuse in Canadian institutions*. Ottawa.

*Law v. Minister of Human Resources Development* (1999).

Lee, Y. 1999. "Social cohesion in Canada: The role of the immigrant service sector." *OCASI Newsletter* 73, Summer/Autumn.

Le Grand, J. "Social exclusion in Britain today." Unpublished speaking notes.

Leithwood, K., M. Fullan and P. Laing. 2002. "Towards the schools we need." *University of Toronto Bulletin*, April 22: 20. Toronto: University of Toronto.

Levitas, R. 1996. "The concept of social exclusion and the new Durkheimian hegemony." *Critical Social Policy* 16(1): 5–20.

_____. 1998. *The inclusive society? Social exclusion and New Labour*. London: Macmillan Press.

Li, P. 1998. "The market value and social value of race." In V. Satzewich (ed.),

*Racism and social inequality in Canada: Concepts, controversies and strategies of resistance.* Toronto: Thompson Educational Publishing.

_____. August 2003. *Deconstructing Canada's discourse of immigrant integration.* Working paper no. WP04-03. Prairie Centre for Excellence.

Lipton, M. 1998. "Selected notes on the concept of social exclusion." In J.B. Figueiredo and A. de Haan (eds.), *Social exclusion: An ILO perspective.* Geneva: International Labour Organization.

Little, M. 1998. *"No car, no radio, no liquor permit:" The moral regulation of single mothers in Ontario, 1920–1997.* Toronto: Oxford University Press.

Lloyd, G. 1984. *The man of reason: "Male" and "female" in Western philosophy.* Minneapolis: University of Minnesota Press.

Lo, L., V. Preston, S. Wang, K. Reil, E. Harvey, E. and B. Siu. 2000. *Immigrants' economic status in Toronto: Rethinking settlement and integration strategies.* Toronto: CERIS Working Paper. <ceris.metropolis.net>.

Loprest, P. 2001. *How are families that left welfare doing? A comparison of early and recent welfare leavers*, Series B, No. B-36. Washington, DC: The Urban Institute. April.

Lowe, G.S. 2001. *Final report on the National Learning Roundtable on Learning.* Ottawa: CPRN.

Lunman, K. 2000. "Timing of federal apology questioned." *Globe and Mail*, 11 December: A3.

Luxton, M. 1980. *More than a labour of love: Three generations of women's work in the home.* Toronto: Women's Press.

_____. 1983. "Conceptualizing 'women' in anthropology and sociology." In *Knowledge reconsidered: A feminist overview.* Ottawa: Canadian Research Institute for the Advancement of Women papers.

_____. 1997. "Feminism and families: The challenge of neo-conservatism." In M. Luxton (ed.), *Feminism and families, critical policies and changing practices.* Halifax: Fernwood.

_____. 2001. "Family coping strategies: Balancing paid employment and domestic labour." In B. Fox (ed.), *Family bonds and gender divisions: Readings in the Sociology of the family.* Toronto: Oxford University Press.

_____. 2001. "Feminism as a class act: Working-class feminism and the women's movement in Canada." *Labour/le Travail* 48, Fall.

Luxton, M., and J. Corman. 1991."Getting to work: The challenge of the women back into Stelco campaign." *Labour/le Travail* 28: 149–85.

_____. 2001. *Getting by in hard times: Gendered labour at home and on the job.* Toronto: University of Toronto Press.

Luxton, M., and H.J. Maroney. 1992. "Begetting babies, raising children: The politics of parenting." In J. Roberts and J. Vorst (eds.), *Socialism in crisis? Canadian perspectives.* Winnipeg/Halifax: Society for Socialist Studies, Fernwood.

Luxton, M., and L. Vosko. 1998. "Where women's efforts count: The 1996 Census campaign." *Studies in Political Economy* 56, Summer: 49–81.

Lyon, M., and P.M. Canning. 1997. "Auspice, location, provincial legislation and funding of day care in Atlantic Canada: Relationships with centre quality and implications for policy." *Canadian Journal of Research in Early Childhood Education* 6(2): 139–55.

MacDonald, R., ed. 1997. *Youth, the "underclass" and social exclusion.* London: Routledge.

MacIntyre, A. 1981. *After virtue.* London: Duckworth.

Mackeith, M. 1999. "The importance of friendship." *Parents for inclusion.* <http://www.parentsforinclusion.org/voices.htm> (accessed July 2005).

Mackelprang, R., and R. Salsgiver. 1999. *Disability: A diversity model approach in human service practice.* Pacific Grove, CA: Brooks/Cole Publishing.

Mahon, R., and S. Phillips. 2002. "Dual-earner families caught in a liberal welfare regime: The politics of child-care policy in Canada." In S. Michel and R. Mahon (eds.), *Child-care policy at the cross-roads: Gender and welfare state restructuring.* New York: Routledge.

Mansbridge, J. 2000. "What does a representative do? Descriptive representation in communicative settings of distrust, uncrystallized interests, and historically denigrated status." In W. Kymlicka and W. Norman (eds.), *Citizenship in divided societies.* Oxford: Oxford University Press.

Marcil-Gratton, N., and C. Le Bourdais. 1999. *Custody, access and child support: Findings from the National Longitudinal Survey of Children and Youth.* Ottawa: Department of Justice.

Maroney, H.J., and M. Luxton. 1997. "Gender at work: Canadian feminist political economy." In W. Clement (ed.), *Understanding Canada: Building on the new Canadian political economy.* Montreal and Kingston: McGill-Queen's University Press.

Marshall, T.H. 1965. *Class, citizenship and social development.* New York: Anchor.

McAndrew, M. 2001. *Immigration et diversité à l'école: Le débat Québécois dans une perspective comparative.* Montreal: Les Presses de l'Université de Montréal.

McCain, M., and F. Mustard. 1999. *The early years study: Reversing the real brain drain.* Toronto: Ontario Children's Secretariat.

McKnight, J. 2004. Federation of Canadian Municipalities. 16 February.

Mendelson, M. 2004. *Aboriginal people in Canada's labour market: Work and unemployment, today and tomorrow.* Ottawa: Caledon Institute of Social Policy.

Middleton, L. 1999. *Disabled children: Challenging social exclusion.* Oxford: Blackwell Science Limited.

Ministry of Citizenship. 1989. *A theoretical context for employment equity.* Toronto: Government of Ontario.

Minow, M. 1990. *Making all the difference: Inclusion, exclusion, and American law.* Ithaca: Cornell University Press.

Mitchell, A. November 1998. "Leaving welfare for work?" *Workfare Watch Bulletin #8.* Toronto: The Community Social Planning Council and the Ontario Social Safety Network. <www.welfarewatch.toronto.on.ca/wrkfrw/bul8.htm> (accessed July 2005).

_____. May 2001. "Mandatory drug and literacy testing." *Workfare Watch Bulletin #12.* Toronto: The Community Social Planning Council and the Ontario Social Safety Network. <www.welfarewatch.toronto.on.ca/wrkfrw/PDF/Bulletin%2012.pdf> (accessed July 2005).

Mittelstaedt, M. 1996. "Harris blames parents for hunger: Breakfast program for schools unveiled." *Globe and Mail,* 11 November: A1.

Mohamed, H. 2002. "Neither here nor there: The social cost of refugees in limbo." *INSCAN* 15(3), Winter.

Mojab, S. 1999. "De-skilling immigrant women." *Canadian Woman Studies/Cahiers de la femme* 19: 123–28.

Montgomery, C. 2002. "The 'Brown Paper Syndrome': Unaccompanied minors and questions of status." *Refuge* 20(2), February. Toronto: Centre for Refugee Studies, York University.

Monture-Angus, P. 1995. *Thunder in my soul: A Mohawk woman speaks.* Halifax: Fernwood.

Morris, P., and C. Michalopoulos. June 2000. *The Self-Sufficiency Project at 36 months: Effects on children of a program that increased parental employment and income.* Vancouver: Social Demonstration Research Corporation.

Morrissette, R., and X. Zhang. 2001. *Experiencing low-income for several years. Perspectives on labour and income.* Statistics Canada, Catalogue no. 75-001-XIE, 2(3): 25–35. Ottawa: Government of Canada.

Mosoff, J. 2001. "Is the human rights paradigm 'able' to include disability? Who's in? Who wins? What? Why?" *Queens Law Journal* 26.

Mustard, F. 2002. Sub-Committee on Children and Youth at Risk. Ottawa: Government of Canada. 13 March.

Mwarigha M.S. 2002. *Towards a framework for local responsibility: Taking action to end the current limbo in immigrant settlement — Toronto.* Toronto: Maytree Foundation.

Myles, J., G. Picot and W. Pyper. 2000. *Neighbourhood inequality in Canadian cities.* Paper presented at the Canadian Economics Association meetings and CERF conference, June.

National Council of Welfare. 1998–1999. *A new poverty line: Yes, no or maybe?* Ottawa: National Council of Welfare. Winter.

_____. 2000. *Poverty profile 1998.* Ottawa: National Council of Welfare.

_____. 2001. *Child poverty profile 1998.* Ottawa: Human Resources Development Canada.

Navarro, V. 2000. "Development and quality of life: A critique of Amartya Sen's development and freedom." *International Journal of Health Services* 40(3): 661–74.

Nedelsky, J. 1993. "Reconceiving rights as relationship." *Review of Constitutional Studies* 1(1): 21.

Norwegian Ministry of Children and Family Affairs. 1998. *Thematic review of early childhood education and care policy: Background report from Norway.* Paris: Organisation for Economic Co-operation and Development.

Novick, M. 1997. *Prospects for children: Life chances and civic society.* Discussion paper for the Children at Risk Symposium. Toronto: Laidlaw Foundation. Revised February 1999.

_____. 2001. "Social inclusion: The foundation of a national policy agenda." Presentation to Laidlaw/Canadian Council on Social Development conference, A new way of thinking? Towards a vision of social inclusion. Ottawa, 8–9 November.

Odom, S.L., C.A. Peck, M. Hanson, P.J. Beckman, A.P. Kaiser, J. Lieber, W.H. Brown, E.M. Horn and I.S. Schwartz. 1996. "Inclusion at the preschool level: An ecological systems analysis." *SRCD Social Policy Report* 1(2–3): 18–30.

Office of the Employment Equity Commissioner 1991. *Working towards equality.* Ministry of Citizenship. Toronto: Government of Ontario.

Offord, D. 1997. *Bridging development, prevention and policy.* Toronto: Canadian Institute for Advanced Research.

Oliver, M. 1996. "Defining impairment and disability: Issues at stake." In C. Barnes and G. Mercer (eds.), *Exploring the divide: Illness and disability*. Leeds, UK: Disability Press, University of Leeds.

Omidvar, R. 2002. "A sense of belonging: Immigration across the ages." *INSCAN* 15(4), Spring.

O'Neill, J. 1994. *The missing child in liberal theory: Towards a covenant theory of family, community, welfare and the civic state*. Toronto: University of Toronto Press, in association with the Laidlaw Foundation.

Ontario Council of Agencies Serving Immigrants (OCASI). 2000. *Immigrant settlement counseling: A training guide*. Toronto: OCASI.

Ontario Federation of Indian Friendship Centres. March 2002. *Tenuous connections: Urban Aboriginal youth sexual health and pregnancy*. Toronto.

Ontario Human Rights Commission. 1983. *The experience of visible minorities in the work world: The case of MBA graduates*. Toronto.

Ontario Ministry of Community and Social Services. 1998. *Survey of individuals who left social assistance*. Toronto.

Organisation for Economic Co-operation and Development, 1995. *Our children at risk*. London.

_____. 1997. *Societal cohesion and the globalising economy*. Paris.

_____. 2001. "Starting strong: Early childhood education and care." In *Thematic review of early childhood education and care*. Paris.

_____. October 2004. *Early childhood education and care policy: Canada country note*. Paris.

Ornstein, M. 2000. *Ethno-racial inequality in the City of Toronto: An analysis of the 1996 Census*. Toronto: Diversity Management and Community Engagement, Strategic and Corporate Policy Division, Chief Administrator's Office, City of Toronto. CERIS Virtual Library. <ceris.metropolis.net>.

Owen, T. 1999. *The view from Toronto: Settlement services in the late 1990's*. Toronto: CERIS Virtual Library. <ceris.metropolis.net>.

Parekh, B. 1998. *The report: Commission on the future of multi-ethnic Britain*. <http://www.runnymedetrust.org/projects/meb/reportIntroduction.html>. Accessed 4 November 2004.

Peck, J. 1998. "Help and hassle: Means, motive and method in local workfare strategies." Paper presented at Model USA: Social justice through growing employment? Berlin: Freie Universität.

_____. 2001. *Workfare states*. New York: Guilford Press.

Penashue, P. 2000. "Help us to help ourselves." *Globe and Mail*, 7 December: A19.

Pendakur, R. 2000. *Immigrants and the labour force: Policy, regulation and impact*. Montreal: McGill-Queen's University Press.

Penn, H. 1999. *How should we care for babies and toddlers? An analysis of practice in out-of-home care for children under three*. Occasional paper no.10. Toronto: Child-care Resource and Research Unit, Centre for Urban and Community Studies, University of Toronto.

Pentney, W. 1996. "Belonging: The promise of community — Continuity and change in equality law, 1995–96." *Canadian Human Rights Reporter* C6.

Phillips, A., 1999. *Which equalities matter?* Cambridge: Polity Press.

Phipps, Shelley, with Lori Curtis. 2000. "The social exclusion of children in North America." Paper presented at the Laidlaw Foundation Roundtable on Social Exclusion of Children, January.

Picchio, A. 1992. *Social reproduction: The political economy of the labour market.* Cambridge: Cambridge University Press.

Polakow, V., T. Halskov and J. Per Schultz. 2001. *Diminished rights: Danish lone mother families in international context.* Brisol, UK: Policy Press.

Prentice, Alison, P. Bourne, G. Cuthbert Brandt, B. Light, W. Mitchinson and N. Black. 1996. *Canadian women: A history.* Second edition. Toronto: Harcourt Brace.

Preston, V., and G. Man. 1999. "Employment experiences of Chinese immigrant women: An exploration of diversity." *Canadian Woman Studies/Cahiers de la femme* 19: 115–22.

Public Health Agency of Canada. 2004. *Aboriginal head start: Program overview.* Ottawa.

Qadeer, M. 2003. "Ethnic segregation in a multicultural city, Toronto, Canada." Toronto: ceris Working Paper No. 28 <www.ceris.metropolis.net> (accessed July 2005).

Quinn, J. 2002. "Food bank clients often well-educated immigrants." *Toronto Star,* 31 March: A12.

Raffo, C., and M. Reeves. 2000. "Youth transitions and social exclusion: Developments in social capital theory." *Journal of Youth Studies* 3(2): 147–66.

Raphael, D. 2000. "Health inequalities in Canada: Current discourses and implications for public health action." *Critical Public Health* 10: 193–216.

Rector, R. 1997. "Wisconsin's welfare miracle." *Policy Review,* March/April: 20-6.

Reform Party. 1995. *The taxpayers' budget: The Reform Party's plan to balance the federal budget and provide social and economic security for the twenty-first century.* 1 February.

Reitsma- Street, M. 1989–90. "More control than care: A critique of historical and contemporary laws for delinquency and neglect of children in Ontario." *Canadian Journal of Women and the Law* 3(2): 510–30.

_____. 1990. "Implementation of the Young Offenders Act five years later." *Canadian Social Work Review* 7 (2), Summer: 137–58.

Reitz, J.G. 1995. *A review of the literature on aspects of ethno racial access, utilization and delivery of social services.* Toronto: CERIS Virtual Library. <ceris.metropolis.net>.

_____. 1998. *Warmth of the welcome: The social causes of economic success for immigrants in different nations and cities.* Boulder, CO: Westview Press.

_____. 2001. "Immigrant skill utilization in the Canadian labour market: Implications of human capital research." *Journal of International Migration and Integration* 2(3), Summer.

Report of the Royal Commission on Aboriginal Peoples. 1996. *Looking forward, looking back.* Ottawa: Canada Communication Group Publishing.

Reynolds, E.B. 1995. "Subsidized employment programs: The Quebec experience." In A. Sayeed (ed.), *Workfare: Does it work? Is it fair?* Montreal: Institute for Research on Public Policy.

Riccio, J., D. Friedlander and S. Freedmam. 1994. GAIN: *Benefits, costs, and three-year impacts of a welfare-to-work program.* New York: Manpower Demonstration Research Corporation.

Richmond, A. 1994. *Global apartheid: Refugees, racism and the new world order.* Toronto: Oxford University Press.

_____. 2000. "Global apartheid: Migration, racism and the world system." In

M.A. Kalbach and W.E. Kalbach (eds.), *Perspectives on ethnicity in Canada.* Toronto: Harcourt Canada.

Richmond, T. 1996. *Effects of cutbacks on immigrant service agencies.* Toronto: City of Toronto Public Health Department. <ceris.metropolis.net>.

Richmond, T., D. Beyenne, C. Butcher and B. Joe. 1996. "Immigrant service agencies: A fundamental component of anti-racist social services." In C.E. James (ed.), *Perspectives on racism and the human services sector.* Toronto: University of Toronto Press.

Rioux, M. 1994. "Towards a concept of equality of well-being: Overcoming the social and legal construction of inequality." In M. Rioux and M. Bach (eds.), *Disability is not measles: New research paradigms in disability.* Toronto: Roeher Institute.

Roche, M., and R. Van Berkel, eds. 1997. "Introduction." In *European Citizenship and Social Exclusion,* xvii–xxxiv. Aldershot, UK: Ashgate.

Rodgers, G. 1995. "What is special about a 'social exclusion' approach?" In G. Rodgers et al. (eds.), *Social Exclusion: Rhetoric, reality responses.* Geneva, Switzerland: International Labour Organization.

Rodgers, G., C. Gore and J. Figueiredo, eds. 1995. *Social exclusion: Rhetoric, reality, responses.* Geneva, Switzerland: International Labour Organization Publications.

Roeher Institute. 1988. *Vulnerable: Sexual abuse and people with an intellectual disability.* Toronto.

_____. 1993. *On-target? Canada's employment-related programs for persons with disabilities.* Toronto.

_____. 1995. *Harm's way: The many faces of violence and abuse against persons with disabilities.* Toronto.

_____. 2000a. *International scan of issues: Children with disabilities and their families.* A discussion document for the Sixth International Congress on the Inclusion of Children With Disabilities in the Community. Toronto.

_____. 2000b. *Towards inclusion: National evaluation of deinstitutionalization initiatives.* Toronto.

_____. 2000c. *Labour force inclusion of parents caring for children with disabilities.* Toronto.

_____. 2001a. *Community inclusion initiative: Participatory action research final report 2000–2001.* Toronto.

_____. 2001b. *Developing an inclusive approach to monitoring child development and learning outcomes.* Toronto.

_____. 2001c. *Moving in unison into action.* Toronto.

_____. 2001d. *Toward an inclusive approach to monitoring investments and outcomes in child development and learning: Draft discussion document.* Toronto.

Romanow Commission. 2002. *Dialogue on Aboriginal health: Sharing our challenges and successes.* Ottawa: Government of Canada. 26 June.

Room, G. ed. 1995a. *Beyond the threshold: The measurement and analysis of social exclusion.* Bristol: Policy Press.

_____. 1995b. "Poverty and social exclusion: The European agenda for policy and research." In G. Room (ed.), *Beyond the threshold: The measurement and analysis of social exclusion.* Bristol: Policy Press.

Ross, D. *Child poverty in Canada: Recasting the issue.* Ottawa: Canadian Council on Social Development. <www.ccsd.ca/pubs/recastin.htm> (accessed July 2005).

Royson, J. 2000. "Something's really wrong when infidelity's normal." *Toronto Star*, 2 December: A5.

Rupert, J. 2000." Love versus the law: A father defends his actions." *Ottawa Citizen*.

Sadoway, G. 2002. "Introduction: Children at risk." *Refuge* 20(2), February. Toronto: Centre for Refugee Studies, York University.

Said, E. 1979. *Orientalism*. New York: Vintage Books.

Saloojee, A. 1996. *Issues in equity and human rights: A distance education workbook*. Toronto: Ryerson University.

_____. 2002. *Social inclusion, citizenship and diversity: Moving beyond the limits of multiculturalism*. Toronto: Laidlaw Foundation.

_____. 2003. *Social inclusion, anti-racism and democratic citizenship*. Working Paper Series. Toronto: Laidlaw Foundation.

Sandel, M. 1982. *Liberalism and the limits of justice*. Cambridge: Cambridge University Press.

Sandercock, L. 1998. *Towards cosmopolis*. Chichester, UK: John Wiley.

Saraceno, C. 2001. "Social exclusion: cultural roots and diversities of a popular concept." Conference on social exclusion and children, Columbia University, The Clearinghouse on International Developments in Child, Youth and Family Policies.

Sarlo, C. 1992. *Poverty in Canada*. Vancouver: Fraser Institute.

Satzcewich, V., ed. 1998. *Racism and social inequality in Canada: Concepts, controversies and strategies of resistance*. Toronto: Thompson Educational.

Saunders, P. 1981. *Social theory and the urban question*. London: Hutchinson.

Seccombe, W. 1974. "The housewife and her labour under capitalism." *New Left Review* 83: January/February.

_____. 1992. *A millennium of family change: Feudalism to capitalism in northwestern Europe*. London: Verso.

_____. 1993. *Weathering the storm: Working class families from the industrial revolution to the fertility decline*. London: Verso.

Sen, A. 1992. *Inequality re-examined*. New York: Russell Sage Foundation.

_____. 1999. *Development as freedom*. New York: Alfred A. Knopf.

_____. 1999. "Investing in early childhood: Its role in development." Speech to the Inter-American Development Bank, Washington.

_____. 2000. *Development as freedom*. New York: Anchor Books, Random House.

_____. 2001. *Development as freedom*. London: Oxford University Press.

Sen, G, A. Germain and L. Chen, eds. 1994. *Population policies reconsidered: Health, empowerment and rights*. Cambridge, MA: Harvard Center for Population and Development International Women's Health Coalition.

Senate Committee on Aboriginal Peoples. 2003. *Urban Aboriginal youth: An action plan for change*. 30 October.

Serageldin, I. 1999. "Poverty and inclusion: Reflections on a social agenda for the new millennium." *Capacity International, Germany*. Villa Borsig Workshop Series, Inclusion, Justice and Poverty Reduction. <www.inwent.org> (accessed July 2005).

Shakespeare, D.T., D.M. Priestley et al. 1999. *Life as a disabled child: A qualitative study of young people's experiences and perspectives*. Leeds: University of Leeds, Disability Research Unit.

Sheth, D.L. 1991. "An emerging perspective on human rights in India." In S.

Kothari and H. Sethi (eds.), *Re-thinking human rights*. New York: New Horizons Press.

Shields, J. 2002. "No safe haven: Markets, welfare and migrants." Paper presented to the Canadian Sociology and Anthropology Association, Congress of the Social Sciences and Humanities. Toronto. 1 June.

Shillington, E. Richard. 1998. *Social assistance and paid employment in Alberta, 1993–1996*. A report prepared for the Population Research Laboratory, Department of Sociology, University of Alberta.

Shonkoff, J., and D. Phillips. 2001. *From neurons to neighborhoods: The science of early childhood development*. Washington: National Academy Press.

Shoush, B. 2003. *Institute of Aboriginal peoples' health*. Ottawa: Canadian Institutes of Health Research (CIHR), Standing Senate Committee on Social Affairs, Science and Technology. May 28.

Siddiqui, H. 2002. "Don't turn Canada into Germany." *Toronto Star*, 27 June: A27.

Siemiatycki, M., and E. Isin. 1997. "Immigration, ethno-racial diversity and urban citizenship in Toronto." *Canadian Journal of Regional Sciences* Special Issue XX (1/2), Spring/Summer: 73–102.

Silver, H. 1994. "Social exclusion and social solidarity: Three paradigms." *International Labour Review* 133 (5/6): 531.

_____. 1998. "Policies to reinforce social cohesion in Europe." In J.B. Figueiredo and A. de Haan (eds.), *Social exclusion: An ILO perspective*. Geneva: International Labour Organization.

Simich, L. 2000. *Towards a greater Toronto charter: Implications for immigrant settlement*. Toronto: Maytree Foundation.

Singer, R. 2003. *The impact of poverty on the health of children and youth*. Campaign 2000 Discussion papers. Toronto. April.

Skaburskis, A. 1996. "Race and tenure in Toronto." *Urban Studies* 33(2): 223–52.

Smith, E., and A. Jackson. 2002. *Does a rising tide lift all boats? The labour market experiences and incomes of recent immigrants, 1995 to 1998*. Ottawa: Canadian Council on Social Development.

Social Exclusion Unit, Prime Minister's Office, United Kingdom. n.d. <www.cabinet-office.gov.uk/seu/index> (accessed July 2005).

Social Planning Network of Ontario (SPNO). n.d. <www.spno.ca>, <http://www.closingthedistance.ca/> (accessed July 2005). Social and Economic Inclusion Initiative, SPCO.

Sparkes, Jo. 1999. *Schools, education and social exclusion*. CASE Brief. London: Centre for Analysis of Social Exclusion, London School of Economics, 12 November.

Statistics Canada. 1994. *Initial data release from the 1992 general social survey on time use*. Ottawa.

_____. 1997. *Income distributions by size in Canada, 1996*. Catalogue no. 13-207-XPB. Ottawa: Ministry of Industry.

_____. 2000a. *Labour force historical review, 1999*. Catalogue no. 71F0004-XCB. Ottawa: Ministry of Industry.

_____. 2000b. *Labour force survey: Special tabulation*.

_____. 2000c. *Income in Canada, 1998*. Catalogue no. 75-202-XIE. Ottawa: Ministry of Industry.

_____. 2000d. "Workforce participation of mothers by age of youngest child." *Labour force historical review*. Catalogue no. 771F004-XCB. Ottawa.

_____. 2001. "National longitudinal survey of children and youth: Participation in activities, 1998/99." *The Daily*. 30 May.

_____. 2002. *Women in Canada: Work chapter updates.* Catalogue no. 89F0133-XIE. Ottawa.

_____. 2003. *Aboriginal peoples survey 2001 — Initial findings: Well-being of the non-reserve Aboriginal population.* Ottawa.

_____. 2004a. "A portrait of Aboriginal children living in non-reserve areas: Results from the 2001 Aboriginal peoples survey." *The Daily*. 9 July.

_____. 2004b. "Low-income in Census metropolitan areas." *The Daily*. 7 April.

Stiglitz, J. 1998. *World bank gender and development workshop.* 2 April.

Stillborn, Jack. 1997. *National standards and social programs: What the federal government can do.* Ottawa: Political and Social Affairs Devision, Parliament of Canada.

Stone, K. 2003. Acting Director. Statement. Ottawa: Division of Childhood and Adolescence, Department of Health, House Subcommittee on Children and Youth at Risk. 29 January.

Sullivan, P.M., M. Vernon and J. M. Scanlon. 1987. "Sexual abuse of deaf youth." *American Annals of the Deaf* 32(4): 256–62.

Swift, K. 1995. *Manufacturing "bad mothers": A critical perspective on child neglect.* Toronto: University of Toronto Press.

Tang, C., D. Ramos, F. Khayre and U. Shakir. June 2003. *Re-defining the urban planning agenda: A joint alternative community perspective.* Toronto.

Taylor, C. 1989. *Sources of the self: The making of the modern identity.* Cambridge: Harvard University Press.

_____. 1992. "The politics of recognition." In A. Gutman (ed.), *Multiculturalism: Examining the politics of recognition.* Princeton, NJ: Princeton University Press.

• Teague, P., and R. Wilson. 1995. "Towards an inclusive society." *Social exclusion, social inclusion* Report No. 2. Belfast: Democratic Dialogue.

Thomas, C. 1999. *Female forms: Experiencing and understanding disability.* Buckingham: Open University Press.

Tjepkema, M. 2002. "The health of the off-reserve Aboriginal population." *Supplement to health reports* 13.

Toronto City Summit Alliance. April 2003. *Enough talk: An action plan for the Toronto region.* Toronto.

*Toronto Star.* 1995. "Find your own sitters, working moms told." 18 September, A1.

_____. 2004. "Hard to dismantle a bad deal." 5 May.

Tougas, J. 2002. *Quebec's early childhood care and education: The first five years.* Occasional paper no. 17. Toronto: Child-care Resource and Research Unit, University of Toronto.

Townsend, P. 1979. *Poverty in the United Kingdom.* Harmondsworth: Penguin.

Trocme, N, B. MacLaurin, B. Fallon, J. Daciuk, D. Billingsley, M. Tourigny, M. Mayer, J. Wright, K. Barter, G. Burford, J. Hornick, R. Sullivan and B. McKenzie. 2001. *Canadian incidence study of reported child abuse and neglect: Final report.* Ottawa: Minister of Public Works and Government Services Canada.

Troper, H. 2000. *History of immigration since the Second World War: From Toronto "the good" to Toronto "the world in a city."* Toronto: CERIS Working Paper. <ceris.metropolis.net>.

Trudeau, P. 1971. Statement by the Prime Minister in the House of Commons.

1971. Ottawa: Government of Canada. 8 October.

Tully, J. 1995. *Strange multiplicity: Consitutionalism in an age of diversity.* Cambridge: Cambridge University Press.

Tyyska, V. 2001. *Long and winding road: Adolescents and youth in Canada today.* Toronto: Canadian Scholars' Press.

United Nations. 1965. *International Convention on the Elimination of all Forms of Racial Discrimination.* New York: United Nations.

United Nations Children's Fund. (UNICEF). 1998. "Indicators for global monitoring of child rights." Background paper. International meeting sponsored by UNICEF. Geneva, Switzerland: Division of Evaluation, Policy and Planning, UNICEF. 9–12 February.

———. 1999. *The State of the World's Children 1999.* New York.

———. 2000a. "A league table of child poverty in rich nations." *Innocenti Report Card 1.* Florence: Innocenti Research Centre, UNICEF. June.

———. 2000b. *First call for children World Declaration and Plan of Action from the World Summit for Children* and *Convention on the Rights of the Child.* New York: UNICEF. May.

———. 2000c. *Emerging issues for children in the twenty-first century.* Preparatory Committee for the Special Session of the General Assembly for Follow-up to the World Summit for Children in 2001, United Nations General Assembly, Economic and Social Council, United Nations Children's Fund, Executive Board, Annual session 2000, Item 4 of the Provisional agenda. A/ac.256/3-E/icef/2000/13, 22–26. May.

———. 2001. *The state of the world's children 2001.* New York: UNICEF.

United Nations Development Program. 1995. *Human Development Report 1995.* New York: Oxford University Press.

———. 1997. *Human Development Report 1997.* New York: Oxford University Press.

———. 2000. *Human Development Report 2000.* New York: Oxford University Press.

United Nations Fourth World Conference on Women. 1995. *Platform for action.* New York: United Nations.

Ursel, J. 1992. *Private lives, public policy: One hundred years of state intervention in the family.* Toronto: Women's Press.

Vanier Institute of the Family. 2000. *Profiling Canada's families II.* Ottawa: Vanier Institute.

Veit-Wilson, J. 1998. *Setting adequacy standards.* Bristol: Policy Press.

Vickers, J., P. Rankin and C. Appelle. 1993. *Politics as if women mattered: A political analysis of the National Action Committee on the Status of Women.* Toronto: University of Toronto Press.

Viswanathan, L., U. Shakir, C. Tang and D. Ramos. April 2003. *Social inclusion and the city: Considerations for social planning.* Toronto: Alternative Planning Group.

Vosko, L. 2000. *Temporary work: The gendered rise of a precarious employment relationship.* Toronto: University of Toronto Press.

Walker, A., and C. Walker, eds. 1997. *Britain divided: The growth of social exclusion in the 1980s and 1990s.* London: Child Poverty Action Group.

Walker, R. 1997. "Poverty and social exclusion in Europe." In A. Walker and C. Walker (eds.), *Britain divided: The growth of social exclusion in the 1980s and 1990s.* London: Child Poverty Action Group.

Waring, M. 1988. *If women counted: A new feminist economics*. San Francisco: Harper and Row.

Wasylycia-Leis, J. (Winnipeg North Centre, NDP). 2003. HCF, Evidence, (1540). 7 May.

Wayland, S. 1997. "Immigration, multiculturalism and national identity in Canada." *International Journal on Group Rights* 5: 33–58. Netherlands: Kluwer Academic Publishers.

Weedon, C. 1987. *Feminist practice and post-structuralist theory*. Oxford: Blackwell.

Weinfeld, M. 1981. "Canada." In R.G. Wirsing (ed.), *Protection of ethnic minorities*. New York: Pergamon Press.

Weir, L. 1996. "Recent developments in the government of pregnancy." *Economy and Society* 25(3): 372–92.

Wente, M. 2000. "Let's trash all high schools." *Globe and Mail*, 7 April: 15.

White, J. 1993. *Sisters and solidarity: Women and unions in Canada*. Toronto: Thompson Educational Publishing.

Whitebook, M., C. Howes and D. Phillips. 1990. *Who cares? Child-care teachers and the quality of care in America*. Final Report of the National Staffing Study. Oakland, CA: Child-Care Employee Project.

Winter, E. 2001. "National unity versus multiculturalism? Rethinking the logic of inclusion in Germany and Canada." *International Journal of Canadian Studies* 24, Fall/Autumn: 165–93.

Wolf, S. 1994. "Comment." In A. Gutman (ed.), *Multiculturalism: Examining the politics of recognition*. Princeton, NJ: Princeton University Press.

_____. 1995. "Beyond 'genetic discrimination': Toward the broader harm of geneticism." *Journal of Law, Medicine and Ethics* 23: 34–353.

Yan, M.C. 2001. Internal memo for the Alternative Planning Group discussions. Toronto: Chinese Canadian National Council Toronto Chapter.

Young, I. M. 1990. *Justice and the politics of difference*. Princeton: Princeton University Press.

_____. 2000. *Inclusion and democracy*. Oxford: Oxford University Press.

*Youth Bowling Council of Ontario v. McLeod*. (1990) C.H.R.R., Ontario Division Court of Appeal. 14: D/120.

Zaslow, M.J., K.A. Moore, D.R. Morrison, and M.J. Coiro. 1995. "The Family Support Act and children: Potential pathways of influence." *Children and Youth Services Review* 17(1/2). Washington, DC: Child Trends.

# Index